Kevin Nosh

Memoirs of a Carp Fisher
The Demon Eye

by Kevin Nash

Edited by Rosie Barham

ISBN:978-0-9574146-0-0

Printed by Butler, Tanner & Dennis

Dedication

In gratitude to all those who have influenced my life and touched my soul. Special thanks go to Hazel and Carol, and to the ones who give me much more than it ever will be possible for me to give them; my sons Lee and Joe, my fiancée Bev, and my dear friend Alan. For the future, who knows ... but hey, let's have a party!

Acknowledgements

To my mind, the nicest element of writing this book about a forgotten era has been the people that came back into my life after so long. There were some bizarre coincidences; at the exact time when I was writing about Bob Poore and Eric Aris, Bob's son Robert contacted me on my Facebook page, with a short note saying, 'Hi', and telling me that his Dad often reminisced about when he fished with me. I had been thinking about Bob, and had been trying to track him down in the hope that he might have the odd photo from the past, as most of mine are long gone. Both Bob and Eric had moved to different parts of England and I had no idea where they were. It has been so nice to revive our friendship, and I thank Bob and Eric for their help with recollections and the odd photo.

I think I should explain those last words. The biggest challenge was not the writing of this book, but rather, tracking down photos. In the 60s and 70s we took few photos, maybe just one of each specimen we caught. Photography was expensive in those days, and we carp anglers fished for ourselves with no desire for publicity, so at best we would have one photo to look back on. Then, as the demands for my writing increased, editors took my few photos and most were never returned. So I apologise if some areas of this book are a bit thin on the photo front and I trust it is a good enough read to compensate for that.

Bill Lovett features strongly, as we fished together in the late 70s and 80s and I had a phone number for him, but it wasn't current; the last time I'd seen Bill on a lake was at the Snake Pit in 1988. While writing this book, a new challenge came out of the blue and in the form of a very large water, home to uncaught carp, some of which are immense - this is my kind of fishing and so I couldn't resist it. While I was hidden away in a reed bed, I heard another angler moving through the reeds and I suppose I shouldn't have been surprised that it turned out to be Bill. He is a kindred spirit who also seeks out unfished lakes of mystery, but it was a coincidence nonetheless, that after all of these years we bumped into each other while I was writing about him. So a special thanks to Bill for climbing up into his loft and seeking out old magazines and photos, and for allowing me to reproduce some of his writing from a series of articles he had published in David Hall's Coarse Fishing Magazine in the 80s.

Another eerie coincidence was Stuart Barry, or 'Stuart the Pear', as he is affectionately known among old-school carpers. I haven't heard from him for donkey's years, but then Stuart also contacted me through Facebook and helped out with some photos, so thanks to Stuart.

One of the greatest ambassadors in carp fishing, and a nicer guy you will not meet, the one and only Julian Cundiff, also spent countless hours leaping through his immense collection of old carp mags, seeking out photos for me. So thanks, Julian.

Tim Paisley came down to fish the Church Lake for a week and somehow wires got crossed. Unbeknown to me, while Jules was spending countless hours rifling through old magazines looking for relevant photos, Tim was doing the same. So thanks for the efforts spent on my behalf Mr Paisley.

Thanks also to Oli Davies and Nick Maddix, who spent the day up in Peterborough at the offices of the Angling Times searching through their archives, and to the AT people who helped. Oli also helped out with the other photos.

Derek Stritton provided a rare picture of Fred Wilton, and was kind enough to write a piece on his recollections of our first meeting. Not only do I wish to thank him for going to the trouble, but also I have to say, his words were generous, to say the least!

My ex-wife Carol came up trumps with a picture of our Doberman, Khan. I was gutted that I couldn't find one remaining photo of this immense dog. It is with some pleasure that I can say, despite Carol and I not being able to hold on to our marriage, that we still remain great friends. So a special thanks to you also Carol, for your support, not only for putting up with my zillions of hours of absence while fishing, but for helping me to get Happy Hooker up and running. It still amuses me when I recall the day I made a conscious decision to change the name to Kevin Nash Tackle after your continuous protests about having to answer the phone "Happy Hooker!"

To Simon Lavin, Chris Ladds and Steve Briggs, thanks for the Harefield photos; and to Shirley Baker, the famous landlady of the Horse and Barge during its magical era of the 80s. Her status can only grow when you see one of the photos she was kind enough to send. To Shirley, a special thanks, not only for the photos, but also for the memories.

Fred Wilton reviewed my account of his achievements for accuracy, for which I thank him.

Chris Ball, that amazing historian of all things carp, had to deal with my frequent requests for archive material and did so tirelessly. Chris, a special thanks – you are a gentleman.

Kevin Clifford also helped me with material from his immense carp archive, for which I thank him.

To Matt Downing, Richard Ballard, Nigel Botherway, Lester Holcombe and my fiancée Bev Handley -my gratitude for reading draft chapters, your observations, and encouragement.

In the writing and rewrites I had help from several with much faster and nimbler fingers than me. Thank you to my two sons, Lee and Joe. Richard Ballard deserves a special mention – another one with nimble fingers - for taking the hefty workload of organising the photos off me. I am also immensely proud that my youngest son Joe contributed and managed the organisation of illustrations. Thanks also to Simon Cotts, and Jake Hughes for the rest of the illustrations.

Thanks to Jemima Musson for her invaluable advice, encouragement, and for laying out the book with her Angling Publications team.

Finally, I must single out two very special people. This book would never have been written without the immense and tireless efforts of Rosie Barham, who worked on the drafts with me and made sense of my grammar in her accomplished editing. While I cannot understate her efforts, or the importance of that task, it was Rosie's constant encouragement and friendship above all else that saw this book through to completion. Bless you Rosie, from the bottom of my heart.

My deepest gratitude and thanks to Alan Blair. It was while we were fishing and he was reading the first draft that we got into a heavy debate about the current state of carp fishing. I was stunned at his take on it and was lost for words, until out of the blue he had a run. It was after we returned the immense carp that it seemed fitting to ask him to write the foreword to this book. I confess that reading his foreword bought a tear to my eye, but as well as that it reinforced my absolute belief that this amazing young man will continue the success of Nash Tackle, and be a passionate ambassador for the cause well after I am gone.

Finally, for the many I haven't mentioned; the anglers and characters I have met along the way and to all who have supported me, and Nash Tackle, over the decades – my heartfelt gratitude.

Contents

Foreword by Alan Blair

K ev and I were first acquainted in the summer of 2007 when we met briefly while I was carrying out some work on his beautiful lakes in Essex. Not long after, I was back in Essex again but this time I was more suitably dressed and confined to his office where, after a gruelling three-hour interview, Kevin decided to appoint me as a member of staff.

I can say without any hesitation or doubt that the last five years of my life have been the most amazing ever. It would be easy to presume that my life has been so amazing simply due to working for a large global company like Nash Tackle, with all its perks, but there is one underlying reason why I have had such an epic journey, and that is because of the man himself, Mr Kevin Robert Nash.

I will now struggle to put into words what Kevin Nash is to me, and so many others, as I believe very few people really know him due to his shy and reserved manner. Kev is far more than the outstanding boss of a large and thriving fishing tackle business, who has mentored me through the ups and downs, trials and tribulations of my upbringing in the industry. He is far more than a mate who you share a pint with or a session on the bank; he is more than a father figure who you can rely on when things aren't going to plan, even in the darkest of times. He is Kevin Nash, a truly unique gentleman who has gone above and beyond to ensure that I, and so many others, have the brightest of futures. He is a man who deserves only the highest regard for what he has done to shape the way carp fishing is today, and he is a man who holds morals so highly in his life that he hasn't a spiteful or hurtful bone in his body.

Kev is an innovator, a thinker and a man who *must* understand why something is not working, use every ounce of his energy and enthusiasm to solve a problem, and then share it with others. He's a soldier who won't give up and fights to the bitter end whether for his family, friends, the pursuit of the largest of carp or ensuring that an item of tackle is designed and built to the highest of specifications. Nothing is ever too much for him, be it fishing, work or his personal life, and I have yet to meet someone with so much drive and determination, even after all these years in the game. He doesn't hold back his secrets and above all else he wants to see other people flourish and achieve. In fact, he gets more from life seeing others happy than selfishly worrying about his own little bubble, and that alone, is very rare in the world that we live in. I am extremely grateful to have met Kev, as are so many other people along his journey, and I know that I'll be saying this on behalf of so many people: Thank you, Mr Nash!

I think Kev was as shocked me when he suggested that I write this foreword; originally, there was never one planned. We were both part way through a two-day session on a new water we had been targeting over the last few months. We were yet to catch, but it had been a great opportunity for me to finish the final few chapters of Kev's first draft copy of this book.

As I turned the last page and absorbed the final few lines of text, I sat there with a sudden dazed feeling of jealousy, resentment, frustration and dare I say, sadness. In a bizarre twist of events my mood had changed. I had enjoyed reading such an epic masterpiece of one angler's journey through time; the story of Kevin as just a young boy with one rod, the world at his feet and so many waters and new challenges to explore. His fishing turned into passion that led on to obsession; the obsession turned into his life and he can now be hailed as one of the true pioneers of our sport. He assisted with the adding of pieces to the so-called puzzle that has shaped carp fishing into what it is today. So why was I now sitting on the bank, with a warm southerly blowing into my face, 100 acres of water, not another angler in sight, and feeling so negative?

As Kev and I entered into discussions on what I thought about the initial read of the book, I was open and honest and felt compelled to explain how I was truly feeling. Kevin had been a pioneer of our sport; he had been there, with a few others, from almost the start of the carp fishing revolution. These guys had seen a glimmer of hope that carp could be caught, then went out there and made it possible, made it happen. After understanding the behaviour of the carp, their habits and their 'world', they unlocked the key to catching them – watercraft, rigs, bait, and tactics – all the time trying to stay one step ahead. They opened the doors for the future and after years of hard work, they laid the blueprint for carp fishing as we know it today. Having just read Kev's account from this period I was left somewhat overwhelmed by it all. I wished that I had been part of this era of discovery and the development of what is such an important way of life for so many anglers today.

So, what was left for me today? What was left for us, the hundreds of thousands of carp anglers spread across Europe? HNV baits won't ever be invented again; I am never going to walk into a health food shop only to stumble across a mass of potential new flavours and additives; we're never going to meet up in numbers to sit and talk 'carp' all night, how can we possibly re-invent the hair rig, find untapped and un-fished waters and slowly put the pieces together in order to understand truly the essence of carp fishing?

I was saddened to think that carp fishing is not the sport now that it was back then. As we are all too fully aware, carp fishing can now be such an instant sport. Gone has the mystery, the unknown, the days of having to make your own tackle, roll your own bait and search the country for the chance of catching an unnamed big fish. We're now part of an industry that's driven by marketing, technologically advanced products, the latest wonder-baits and venues which, if they don't contain a 40, then they're deemed not worth fishing! So there you have it. There's my jealousy, resentment, frustration and sadness accounted for. I read the book and wanted to be part of what Kev had been part of; a journey that led on to a movement that is the foundation of our sport.

Once I had finished expressing my opinions, Kev looked at me with sadness in his eyes. Initially, he thought I was wrong and almost ignorant for making an assumption without thinking things through properly, but as we both began to explore what I had said, Kevin also went quiet. It was as if he was at a loss to explain how wrong he thought I was. Had the essence of carp fishing been lost to the new breed of anglers that swarm our banks today, and would they ever truly understand what carp fishing is all about, let alone experience that feeling of achievement and satisfaction that the 'old school' anglers who formed our sport lived with, day and night, until their next capture was finally in the back of the net? For a split second, I have to admit, I questioned myself. What am I doing here - is all of this a waste of time?

Moments later, I had a series of bleeps on one of my rods; the bleeps turned into a run and my world went into overdrive as I quickly threw on my waders and hurriedly made my way through the reeds to the rod. I leaned into the fish and as it powered off into the depths I could hear Kev wading out behind me before he spoke quietly into my ear. "There it is, mate. This is what it's all about. It's our eighth proper session on a giant inland sea, and we're fishing for uncaught carp that we believe to be of epic proportions, that have no understanding of the latest rig or bait. We've had to locate them, educate them on to our boilies and here you are now, standing in the middle of this pit attached to the unknown. It's all out there for the taking, Alan. You just need the right mindset. You learn from those before you; and now you are yourself pioneering."

It really was coincidence that before the take we were having a conversation about how it could never be the same as the good old days, and then only minutes later, I felt myself caught up in a world of exactly what the carp fishing legends had gone through in order to shape the future of the sport as we know it. I was honestly speechless when I peered into the landing net and was met with a huge flank of enormous scales, an almost fully-scaled mirror and one that had undoubtedly never visited the bank before.

Fifty years after he began to go carp fishing, Kevin Nash is still on the bank doing it! It was Kev who drove the pair of us to have a go at this water and this was our first proper result, a turning point in my angling with a new realisation that it most certainly hasn't all been done, and it's definitely still out there for the taking. It was at this point that I finally got it – the message throughout Kev's book; work hard and focus to find your own way, and you will get the results you deserve and wish for. Carp fishing may well not be what it was back then, and life does change; the world changes, people change, but passion doesn't change and I, just like so many, will always cherish those special feelings of sharing a capture with someone close to you.

Carp fishing is what you want it to be. It can be as complex or simple as an angler wishes and you can put as little or as much into it as you desire. Each and every person will take different thoughts and lessons away from it, but each and every one of us all have the same drive to go out there and fish.

Enjoy your carp fishing journey, whichever path you take.

Alan Blair

*T*here was a swirl, and then the duckweed parted as it danced and shimmered in the vortex. The boy dipped his net and lifted. He struggled; it was so heavy - much heavier than it should have been for the capture of a tadpole or a newt. He gasped when he saw the fish - and what a fish! Thick-set, deep and armoured with the most golden of scales, its huge mouth opened and closed and its dorsal fin bristled. The boy looked on it in wonder. He had never seen such a beautiful fish and wondered what it could be.

On Monday, after school, the boy visited the village library. He was still thinking about the magnificent golden fish. In fact, that was all he thought about while at school that day. His lessons had been in vain; his teachers' words never heard.

He browsed the library shelves, wondering where to look. Then he saw a book, 'Mr Crabtree Goes Fishing'. He reached up for it, stretching his body from the tips of his toes, barely managing to lift the large book off the shelf. He liked this book because it had realistic drawings, just like his favourite comic.

As he thumbed through the pages he stopped suddenly. There was a picture of Mr Crabtree's son, Peter, with a fish – it was the boy's fish. He read the words and discovered that it was a crucian carp.

He took the book to the library table and commenced reading, his anticipation and excitement growing as every page was turned. He wanted to be Peter and have a dad like Mr Crabtree. He glanced at the clock. He was very late and would have to run all the way home, or face a beating.

It was the evening of the 8th July, 1963. The time was ten to six. At that moment a lifelong fisherman was born. That boy was me.

Kevin Nash

Introduction:
The Pioneering Years

L ife is full of surprises and none more so than finding myself writing this introduction. I never intended to write such a book as this. For years I had resisted the suggestions (read 'nagging') of close friends to write about the pioneering years of carp fishing. I spent countless hours on the bank with Nigel Botherway in the late 90s and early 2000s and as he listened to my carping adventures, he started sounding out and saying, 'Kev, you should write all this down. It is part of carp fishing history.' I guess he sniffed a story, having been a journalist with such respected newspapers as the Sunday Times, but in my own particular stubborn way, I refused to listen to one who is far more of an expert than me.

Then, a woman came into my working life and we all know how women can nag! This is part of a natural evolution, I'm sure. We mere mortal men should note that nature designed it that way and there are times when we should listen to the gentler sex, and Rosie Barham certainly fits the bill there.

Rosie also started to suggest – no, I will definitely say 'nag' this time – when she worked with me in the mid-2000s, but just as I did with Nigel I chose to ignore her until she left, and didn't think of it again. A couple of years ago, a chain of events occurred and I needed an assistant with special editorial skills to make sense of my magazine ramblings, so Rosie came back and the nagging started again!

I had clear convictions about why I wouldn't write a book. I understood that it would be a massive amount of work and that equates to time, which is something I don't have the luxury of in sufficient quantities. Nash Tackle is my business life and so the majority of my time must be devoted to that, and sometimes I have to remember my family, and then, of course, getting out on the bank occasionally is a necessity for me, not only to keep up with current angling trends and get my own thoughts working, but also because I am a lifelong passionate carp angler – it is in my blood, my soul, and has never waned. I need carp fishing like an addict needs drugs; when I can't get out there because of other commitments I become miserable, withdrawn and stressed. It is only when I am at one with the outside, the lake, and nature that I can find peace and contentment. So, I've learned to be as efficient as I can with my time. It is valuable and I have to justify how best to expend it.

I saw little justification in neglecting my day job, my carp fishing or my family, just to write a book that I thought would appeal to so few, but both Nigel and Rosie pointed out that the story would also be about how an ordinary boy had made such a successful business from humble beginnings and sheer hard graft. The theme of how Nash Tackle evolved would run through some of my better, or bizarre, fishing stories, of course, but I was sceptical. I believed that most nowadays wanted to read technical stuff, only a limited number of anglers read 'story books' and who would want to know about building up a fishing tackle company? I did run the idea past the youngsters in the office, though, and was surprised to discover that they were fascinated with the heritage of carp fishing, the pioneering days and the progression and development of baits and tackle. So I was convinced to put that part of my life down on paper, if for no other reason than a hope that it would be inspirational to today's youngsters. I did it, so you can too!

Previous historians of carp fishing seem to have, to a degree at least, overlooked Essex's carp fishing heritage. I'm baffled by the phenomenon as to why Essex can rightly hold claim to being the home of modern carp tackle innovation. Quite why so much has come from Essex, compared to the rest of the country, I have absolutely no idea.

When I started on my carp fishing journey, the carp hotbed was Kent and that may have been because Kent had the edge of a few years of carp stocking, and so more waters were available in that area with access for anglers to pursue carp. It was where the new wave of carp fishing was mainly written about, by such anglers as Bob Morris, Fred Wilton, Derek Stritton and Paul Snepp, who were fishing in and around the county. Kent could also have been perceived as the hotbed because it was home to prolific 'mainstream' angling writers such as Jim Gibbinson and Jerry Savage.

It's reasonable to observe that despite having the edge, Kent didn't follow through with significant tackle innovation, although the bait was a different matter. The tackle crown was placed firmly on Essex and I played a big role in that but it wasn't me alone. At the same time as I was getting off the ground, a guy by the name of Del Romang was converting Optonic bite alarms to more efficient units. Del had a stroke of luck, which I'm sure he didn't recognise at the time. The owners of the Optonic brand, Dellareed, took him to court for converting and improving their product and I'm still baffled by the verdict to this day, but nonetheless they were the victors and that shut down Del's small enterprise, but it didn't stop him from thinking and as I've found in life, you're never more effective than when your back is against the wall. Every cloud has a silver lining, they say, and I would suggest that's never been truer than for Del Romang because when Dellareed, the Optontic owners, closed him down, he introduced a radical bite alarm with vibration sensing, which turned out to be far more innovative and bigger business than his conversions could ever have been.

In this book, I mention a couple of fishing sessions that I enjoyed with Mr Fox, and while he would never be a person I could wish to make a friend, it should be noted that he is an exceptional businessman and is responsible for the company he formed, Fox International, out of Hainault, which went on to become one of the largest carp brands in Europe. Geoff Powell, also a local boy, went up against Fox when he entered the market in bedchairs, and he became the market leader for a time. His JRC brand, which was later purchased by Shakespeare, is well known, and Chub, originally started in Braintree before it was acquired by the northern company, Hardy's.

Not only do companies whose roots were put down in Essex dominate the carp angling scene, but in the early years, Essex also had more than its fair share of embryonic bait companies. The first company to sell carp bait ingredients was Bait 78, which as its trading name states, commenced in 1978. Later, there was my own Happy Hooker Carp Krave range, and Geoff Kemp was immensely successful in his day with his bait company; Dave Hydes Pro-Bait and SBS also sold their share, to name but a few.

I feel that the carp fishing scene has changed so much today and I'd divide it roughly into two groups: those of the old school mentality and that doesn't necessarily mean that they *are* old, and the modern 'instant' carp angler. I am aware of the delicacies of that description and it is challenging to put across what I mean without appearing judgmental or arrogant, but it's important that I explain myself.

As I mentioned, I considered a book covering my carp fishing life from the beginning to have a limited appeal and that it would only be of interest to the carping classification of 'old school' thinkers and there aren't many of them around now; many anglers are in the modern 'instant' carper category. Most writing, publicity and marketing is directed at the modern carper and I confess to being critical of that, but I understand that there is a demand and a need. After all, where do you start when you decide that you want to catch a carp? What points of reference do you use? Where do you find the information? It goes without saying; it has to be the angling press who understand their market and the fact that their readers want an instant fix: tie this rig, and suddenly you will go from a struggling angler to a top rod, or use this bait, like X, that awesome angler does, and you will catch just as many carp as him.

Rarely does it work like that, though, and as a result, there is disillusionment and frustration with the inevitable conclusion - the budding carp angler gives up. Why does he give up? It is simple; it's because he's not catching carp, or at least, not catching them regularly enough to satisfy himself that he's doing it right. I find that really sad when I look back at the massive impact that carp have made to my own life, and let's put aside the unique opportunity that the carp gave me of a working life and concentrate on what carp fishing has given me.

I could list so many benefits; the lifelong friendships I've made, the countries I've visited... but as I write I'm thinking of the little things, like sunrises. For a long time now, I've appreciated that it's the simple things that are the true essence of life, which are missed by the majority as they go about their business in this modern age of materialism. Ask friends or family, who aren't carp anglers, how often they've witnessed a sunrise and watched the sky and clouds turning pink, seen the mist curling off the water and heard the call of the wild as a skein of geese flies overhead. There is nothing in this world that can fortify your soul like being in touch with nature.

Once I finally relented to writing a book, I did so because I'd come up with a kind of working plan to satisfy as many carp anglers as I could, from the newcomers to the experienced. If I was going to document my carp fishing life, I would be specific in the waters mentioned. In other words, I'd miss out many of the lakes that I'd fished if the only point of the story was to record what I'd caught. There would only be tales from the waters where I learned to advance my carp fishing understanding; to portray my 'apprenticeship' right from the beginning to the present day, and yes, I'm still learning!

The early pioneering years and the great adventures we had in those days would be of interest to those who like a good story, and as the book progressed and I began to document recent years with descriptions of the current baits, cutting edge techniques and rigs, I thought that this would satisfy the newcomers. By combining past and present, I hoped that my entire journey would be read and understood in context.

I've been fortunate in life and, I must emphasise, my biggest stroke of luck was being there at the beginning, at a time when we knew so little about carp, when it was such a struggle to come to terms with them and to catch them. The one main difference between then and now is that we had no reference. There were no newspapers or magazines jammed full of anglers holding big carp, and explaining that if you fished in a particular way, you'd catch loads of them. We had to work it all out and had no idea of how poor we were at catching them, so every carp caught was a massive buzz. Even if it was only one or two doubles per year, we had pursued, cornered and landed our Moby Dick, and we only ever felt that we were achieving and were masters at our game, but we didn't have a clue, really, about how to catch these damned awkward things. We had to think for ourselves, unlike today when it's all given to us on a plate, and that is the great tragedy of the modern carp scene. I strongly believe that if you don't exercise your brain and get it thinking, you will never master carp.

As our skills and knowledge expanded, so did our results and I have tried to capture how we were then, which honestly speaking, was young, cocky, top guns! It was the excess of youth - we still had a lot of growing up to do. In our 20s and 30s we were at our physical peak, that time when your whole life is before you and the world is your oyster. Some of my portrayal may raise an eyebrow or two, especially the chapter on Harefield, which was more akin to a rave than carp fishing. I considered long and hard about including Harefield. If I was going to write about the season that I enjoyed there, I should write it factually and document the events that happened. I felt it was essential to include Harefield because of the place it holds in carp fishing history for at least the tackle developments, so you have the whole story, warts and all! Harefield reflects an almost forgotten era of etiquette and comradeship - we were a band of brothers.

As the writing progressed, I realised that I'd underestimated the length of my carp fishing journey and with some dismay became aware that the book would be too big for one volume. There would have to be a cut-off point in the 90s and this left me in complete disarray because, while I hoped I'd produced a good read, I would not satisfy the guys who wanted the latest technical stuff. I started this introduction with 'life is full of surprises' and I was surprised as the point of the book became clear. When I began the writing process, I thought I'd understood the reason for finally writing this book, but I had, in fact, missed it.

In my article writing, I mainly steer away from technical 'how to do it' pieces and rather try to get the message across that you must understand carp in order to catch them regularly, but now here I was, finishing a book in the 90s - now old hat - and it wouldn't end with the up-to-date technical material. Then it hit me; if I had written my adventures and fishy learnings right up to the present day, many newcomers to the sport would just focus on the last chapters, grabbing hold of the last rig diagram, or the bait I am currently using, and go off believing that they had my secrets. They had what Nashy used so they'd catch loads of big carp. I'd be doing them a disservice by convincing them that they had what they needed to overcome their struggle to come to terms with carp. They would still struggle and that would lead to a level of frustration and doubtless, for many, defeat and giving up. They would never again have the desire to watch a sunrise.

I mentioned that I put great value on my time and to the best of my ability I optimise it and make it effective. The message that runs through this book, that I so hope will be grasped, is that there is no shortcut to success. The best things in life come from learning and experience, which leads on to ability and then gratification. I can't say it any clearer than that, and I've tried to put that mindset across from Chapter One.

To master carp, you must understand them and be able to get into their heads. To use a hackneyed phrase, you have to 'serve your apprenticeship'. In our world of instant gratification, most are not prepared to do that and it's why they fail. It is at this point when the readers must make their own decision. Do you want the joy that carp fishing can give you, over decades of personal pursuit, or do you want the instant gratification and the eventual failure that will surely follow; carp fishing today, maybe golf tomorrow, or even back to spending your evenings in front of the box? I can only take you through my journey and point out the basic lessons that led to the wealth of knowledge that I have now.

My carp fishing life started at Wright's, an overstocked, small pool stuffed with carp that were hungry because they'd been forced into an unnatural existence of inadequate food stocks to sustain them. For them, it was a competition to beat their companions to any potential food item in a limited attempt to survive. In this situation, greed is king and overrides caution. It may surprise many readers when I say, with total belief, that small pond stuffed full of stunted carp, Wright's, was the most important water I ever fished. It taught me a number of major lessons, the most important of which was that I could catch carp. You might find it a strange statement but that one lesson has stood me in good stead to this day, because if you know you *can* catch carp then you should question when you are *not* catching them.

One of my key drives when I'm blanking is a repetitive voice in my head. A phrase reverberates around my brain: 'You haven't caught a carp in 24 hours. Kevin, you're fishing like an idiot.' This logic is based on the observation that throughout the year, with the one possible exception of midwinter when on many lakes, but not all, carp do go into a short period of dormancy, there is always a carp looking for food, or at the very least, carp will feed every 24 hours. It is this philosophy that keeps me motivated, working at it, and continually asking – 'Why?'

For most, a blank is an excuse; they weren't feeding...it was too cold...too hot... the wrong wind direction... or most often said, 'they're just not having it'... whereas, to me, a blank is a piece of the jigsaw. A blank should not be considered a failure, but rather a lesson in the journey to success; facts should have been noted and information collated, so that a piece goes into the puzzle. You build up the jigsaw with bits of knowledge until the final piece completes the picture and you get your result.

It was because I mastered those starving carp at Wright's, and could expect a carp more or less every time I fished, that when I spread my wings to more ambitious venues, I realised something was wrong. I could catch the Wright's carp so why was I struggling elsewhere? I'd caught the Wright's carp in all conditions, and for most of the year, so when I moved on I never made excuses to myself for my ineptitude. Instead, I was driven toward a quest for knowledge and thus satisfied the carp gods that I'd toiled tirelessly to understand the carp. I strived to know their habits, where they liked to be in their environment at different times of the day, what their food was, where they found it, where that food became abundant in the lake at a particular time of year, and how I needed to present my barbed delicacy. Once the carp gods recognised the trials and tribulations I'd endured, the lake would pay me back.

Chapter One

Where Did It All Go Wrong?

O f all the places to see George, the last one I would have expected was a bar tucked away among a few dusty, white houses masquerading as a village, in the Alentejo region of Portugal. I was there looking for carp and had driven up into this arid, central area of the country where there are some massive reservoirs more akin to inland seas, that hold immense carp; it was just a matter finding them. The high year-round average temperatures in this region allow the carp to spawn very successfully so the lakes were stuffed with a considerable number of little carp as well as a handful of old, original monsters. I was looking for that handful of originals in thousands of acres of water, and among hundreds of thousands of carp weighing a few pounds. I gave up after several days of touring around, because it really was a needle in a haystack job, and apart from that, the heat was unbearable.

Parched and grimy, I spotted a bar and decided that an ice-cold beer was long overdue. As I entered the dark interior, blinking and trying to adjust my eyes from the bright sunlight outside, I couldn't believe what I was seeing. There, sitting on a bar stool was the greatest British footballer of all time, George Best!

Surprisingly, George recognised me because years before, we'd seen each other more than once on a Southend station platform as we waited for the last train back to London. He was dating a girl from nearby Thorpe Bay at the time. We got chatting; in fact we had a long chat over several hours and I got very pissed - he didn't because this was one of his periods of being on the wagon and he was on orange juice - but despite my inebriated state, an amusing story he told me stuck in my mind.

In his heyday of success, he was dating a stunning, leggy, blonde model. If memory serves me correctly, she was Miss World at the time. They had visited a London casino, he'd hit the jackpot and won about £50K, which was a lot of money in those days. Anyway, they took their winnings back to their hotel room, where George emptied his pockets and threw all his cash on the bed. His girlfriend took off her dress and lay on the bed, chilling, while George decided to celebrate by ordering a bottle of champagne, so he 'phoned down to room service.

A while later, there was a tap on the door and George opened it. A waiter stood there, who George described as being of a significant age, wizened, with white hair and stooping as he brought the tray of champagne into the room – the epitome of the old English butler. As he put the tray down, George saw him glance out of the corner of his eye toward his stunningly beautiful and voluptuous girlfriend, lying on the bed. She was unashamedly in her kit of stockings, suspenders and a revealing bra, and nestled among a pile of £50 notes, which gave completely the wrong impression to the old man.

The waiter poured two glasses of champagne and then cleared his throat.

"Ahem. I've always been a great admirer of yours Mr Best, but I wonder, would you allow me to ask you a question?"

"For sure, fire away," George replied.

The waiter considered carefully for a second or two and then said, "Sir, where did it all go wrong?"

I've often thought of that story when thinking back on the great life that I've enjoyed through fishing. In the early days, I know that my dad often had a similar opinion to George's butler, and wondered where it had all gone wrong for me. There were no fishermen in my family and my father certainly didn't get it; he couldn't understand why I wanted to waste so much time on such a worthless pursuit. It was clear that he was frustrated at my lack of interest in any of the school subjects that might have steered me toward, what he deemed to be, an appropriate a career path. All I ever thought about was going fishing. My father had such an antipathy to my passion that he refused to satisfy my wishes at Christmas or birthdays for

BELOW
My father had such an antipathy to my passion that he refused to satisfy my wishes for fishing tackle for Christmas or birthdays.

fishing tackle, apart from one Christmas when I was presented with an umbrella, but this was only because my dear mum had got her way. She'd persuaded him to give me some semblance of shelter so that her beloved boy didn't keep coming home like a drowned rat.

I must have been 9 or 10 years old when I popped down to Kingston's, a local farm pond, to see my friend, Tim. He'd been fishing for a while, and I got the bug while watching him that day. Kingston's was a small pool of around a third of an acre, with a concrete wall forming a dam along one side, where the branches of an enormous willow trailed in the water. It seemed very deep and mysterious to me and I imagined huge monsters lurking in its depths.

Tim and I sat on the grass chatting, our four eyes glued to his float. The light was fading and bats were skimming the surface as they hunted for flies, and then, suddenly, the float bobbed and disappeared. With an enormous whoosh, Tim struck and a 3-inch rudd arced through the air and landed in the hawthorn bushes behind us. We retrieved it and then, scratched and bloodied, we admired his capture. I can still see the colours now; silvery flanks, a greenish back and the brightest of red fins. We unhooked that rudd and slipped it back – and I was hooked for life.

Times were tough, though, and austerity was rife in England; the pocket money I received would barely buy a bubble gum, or two, let alone fishing gear. There was a tool-hire shop in Rayleigh and the owner must have been a fisherman because he'd stocked a small cabinet with tackle, maybe to test the market. One day, Tim kept him talking while I slid open the glass door and stole an Intrepid fishing reel. To this day, I still carry the guilt of that one and only descent into shop-lifting, but I guess I shouldn't beat myself up too much; I was just a kid, desperately trying to get by. Should the owner of that tool hire shop be reading this, all I can say is, I am very sorry, and get in touch because I owe you nineteen shillings and sixpence.

That reel, attached to the cheapest rod I could find, a tatty old trout fly rod from Woolworth that I'd saved up my pennies for, got me going on a lifetime passion, and began the most magical journey. God, do I feel lucky! I was in there at the beginning of what is now a flourishing and significant carp scene. I was lucky for having been there in those pioneering times; lucky for all the adventures, the friends I have made around the world, lucky that I've managed to make a living and create a great company that not only provides so much brilliant tackle for others to enjoy, but which also provides a living for so many, and most importantly of all, I learned my trade. I served a full carp apprenticeship. My dad never admitted it to me, but I think in his latter years he *was* proud of me and realised that actually, it hadn't 'gone wrong' at all.

I guess I've always been fascinated by water. As far back as I can remember, I was dipping my net in ponds, trying to catch tadpoles, newts, and perhaps the biggest prize of all – a frog. There is a place called The Mount, in Rayleigh, Essex, where a castle once stood. Part of the moat still exists, and one day, as I was wading around in my wellies with a pond net, I saw the duckweed move. Excitedly, I scooped and to my astonishment, I had a fish. It seems that destiny always had me down to be a carp angler, when my first-ever fish was a crucian carp caught in a pond net.

Eventually, I graduated to rod and reel, and fished the local ponds with mixed success. The most my mates and me achieved was rudd, and very occasionally a crucian carp, the predominant species that we found in the local muddy ponds, but my strong desire was to catch bigger and better, and to explore and understand fish. I was obsessed from the first day that I held a rod.

I'd asked my mum if I could cancel my Hotspur comic and have the Angler's Mail instead, and it was in there that I first saw a picture of a proper carp. My mates and I agreed that we didn't want to catch one like that, though. Quite *why*, we decided they weren't cool at the time, I don't know, but it was probably because we thought we had no chance of catching them. We didn't know where we *could* catch these 'proper' carp, anyway, so crucians were still our main target and the fish to strive for. An 8oz crucian is a monster after you've been catching 4-inch rudd!

I started to spread my wings, and my mate, Tim, and I would cycle to the River Chelmer, which was quite a trek for us, some 18 miles each way, and there I caught my first roach of three-quarters of a pound. What a monster that was! Then we heard about a gravel pit in Rochford, called Doggetts and after we were told that it contained pike, we were soon on our bikes. I remember catching my first jack of about 4lbs. I looked at it in awe and I guess I wouldn't feel much different now if I had a great white shark alongside the boat.

Ways of keeping occupied were much different in those days, especially in the short days of winter. There were no computers, X-boxes, or mobile phones. Cubs and Scouts were much more popular then and when I graduated into the Scouts, at the age of 12, I went on a week's camp to Brockenhurst in the New Forest. I nearly didn't go as my parents had planned the annual holiday on the Isle of Wight, and intended to leave on the Saturday, which was the day that the Scouts returned from camp. Eventually, a way was found and it was arranged that my mum and dad would pick me up from Brockenhurst on the way through, and the Scoutmaster agreed to wait until they arrived.

Well, he didn't. My mum and dad were late, so he left me on the side of the road and took all the other scouts back to Rayleigh. Unbelievable to imagine that now, isn't it? At the time, it never occurred to me, or the Scoutmaster, I guess, that my parents wouldn't turn up, but there had been a serious pile-up en route and they'd become caught up in an horrendous 20-mile traffic jam. God knows the stress they must have gone through; not only during that journey, but also when they arrived in Brockenhurst to find that I wasn't there.

After a few hours, a farmer who thought I'd been abandoned took me in and I know a lot of phone calls were made before, eventually, I was put on a train back to Rayleigh. I can still remember that journey because the train from Brockenhurst to London was the last steam train in service in England, so it was quite exciting really. I was accompanied by an adult to make sure that I got home safely and while we waited at Brockenhurst station we got talking, and when asked what my hobbies were, there was only going to be one answer. That kind man, obviously understanding the troubled place I was in on the realisation that the Scoutmaster had dropped me in the shit, bought me a copy of the now defunct fishing magazine 'Angling'. On the front cover, was a bloke wearing a worn, floppy hat and an army surplus jacket, kneeling with two mirror carp in front of him. Thinking back, it was probably Bill Keele or Jack Hilton, and the picture blew me away. I looked at it all the way from Brockenhurst to Rayleigh. I was hooked for life and yearned to catch such magnificent fish, and look like a proper angler.

Meanwhile, my mum and dad were searching high and low in the New Forest looking for me. Eventually, they went to the police station and the desk sergeant informed them that I was heading in the opposite direction, toward home! They had to turn around and drive all the way back to Rayleigh – quite a drive in those days with no motorways. My dad was furious and I can still picture the scene of him dragging me round, reluctantly, to the Scoutmaster's house, and the colossal argument that kicked off. My Scoutmaster was somewhat sheepish, to say the least.

The next week, when I went to the Scout meeting, he asked me if I'd be interested in joining Rayleigh Angling Club; that was his gesture to compensate me for the Brockenhurst debacle. He knew I was mad on fishing, but he'd never told me that he was the secretary of the local angling club. I guess that was probably because although they did have a junior section, he would have preferred it if they hadn't. Junior anglers will be junior anglers, thrashing the water to foam and making lots of noise while the adults were trying to enjoy a peaceful day's fishing; certainly, the seniors gave me a few bollockings over the next few years. I said 'yes', without a second thought.

I had first found out about Rayleigh Angling Club two week s before, when a kid at school had come in with a picture of Moby Dick – a carp he had caught at 5lbs. He was showing it around the playground, so I was on him like a rash to find out where he'd caught it. He told me it had come from a lake called Wright's, and with glee he stated that I would never get in. He had only gained entry because his dad was a member, and they'd only let juniors join on that condition, so I had no chance. I was gutted and I'd written it off, so I just loved going into school the next day and telling him I was in!

Wright's Nursery was owned by Rayleigh Angling Club and is still there to this day. The pond is rectangular, about one-third of an acre, and was re-dug after the original, natural pond was polluted. It was re-stocked as well, and was one of only a handful of waters in Essex that contained carp. These carp, mainly mirrors and the odd common, averaged 3 to 4lbs; a specimen was a fish over 6lbs, and it was rumoured that there was a common in there that had been caught at 8lbs. Monsters of fish! I couldn't wait!

Chapter Two

Wright's Nursery

Rayleigh Angling Club's water was stuffed with fish, not only the carp but also roach, rudd, bream, perch, tench and even chub… there were so many of them that everything was struggling to grow. I couldn't wait for the week to end because my mum had said that I could fish for a few hours after school on the Friday evening, providing, of course, that I was home by nightfall.

My little legs were a blur as I biked at full speed down the steep hill toward Wright's, but when I arrived at the gate I realised that I'd forgotten my key. The barbed wire fence may have been a deterrent to the most desperate POW, but nothing was going to stop me and with torn clothes and flesh ripped to shreds, I was soon over it and sorting my rod out.

I was shocked when, after a mere ten minutes of dropping my float into the pool, it bobbed about erratically, and I found myself attached to a 4oz bream. I'd never seen one of those before, and I remember spending the next ten minutes trying to wipe the snot from my hands onto the grass. I wasn't impressed and I've avoided

trying to catch the things ever since. I've never met an angler who dedicated his life to hunting big bream, but I'd like the opportunity to read the psychiatric report.

I caught a few tench, too, that first season, and they became a favourite fish. They're really spectacular, aren't they, with their greeny-black bodies, paddle pecs and red-eyes? I remember that the first one I caught had a big metal tag on its dorsal fin, and I know that some *were* tagged but I can't remember why.

My problem was tackle. This was toward the end of the era after the war, when the country had been in depression with rationing still in force. Now, in the 60s, times were rapidly changing, but it was still a struggle for most working-class families. I still had the Woolworth's trout rod, which even when new was about the cheapest you could buy and it hadn't fared well in the time that I'd owned it. It was made from split cane; the tip section was bent like a dog's leg and my reel couldn't be secured in the reel seat so it constantly fell off. In fact, that's exactly what happened when I was playing my first tench. As I went to grab my landing net handle, the reel fell off, bounced on the bank, and threw itself into the lake. For those who haven't experienced it, I can assure you that trying to land a lively 1lb tench on nine feet of knackered, bent cane with a reel that is in ten feet of water is problematic, to say the least. With this inadequate set-up, the carp were still a dream away, and it was a dream that I was desperate to make reality.

I had a paper round but the sums weren't adding up and I wasn't getting

anywhere near saving enough for some proper
tackle, so I chatted up the shop owner and was
given the job of marking up the newspapers,
as well as that of relief paper boy. I was up at
4.30am, opened the shop, marked up the
papers, did my paper round, then went
back to see if any of the other paper
boys hadn't turned up – which was
a regular occurrence – and did their
rounds as well.

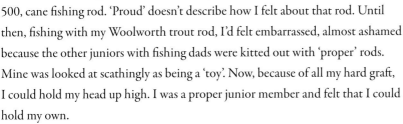

    The funds really started to
flow in when I was 14 because I
became old enough to get a job three
evenings a week stacking shelves in Tesco
and soon, I was the proud owner of a Chapman
500, cane fishing rod. 'Proud' doesn't describe how I felt about that rod. Until
then, fishing with my Woolworth trout rod, I'd felt embarrassed, almost ashamed
because the other juniors with fishing dads were kitted out with 'proper' rods.
Mine was looked at scathingly as being a 'toy'. Now, because of all my hard graft,
I could hold my head up high. I was a proper junior member and felt that I could
hold my own.

    There was a group of three older teenagers who were also members of
Rayleigh Angling Club, and these lads fascinated me. I was in awe of them.
They considered themselves to be serious carp anglers, and just like the guy I'd
seen on the front of that angling magazine, they wore tatty, worn, army hats and
camouflage jackets. One of them was Derek Ritchie and I looked up to him with
a tremendous amount of admiration. I wanted to be like him one day, and be a
proper carp angler, but that admiration nose-dived on the first day that I fished
with my new, shiny, Chapman rod.

    I can still remember that day, my first carp fishing session. I was using a dirty
great monster hook with a lump of Cheddar cheese on it that I'd nicked from my
mum's fridge. My float slid away, I struck and - bloody hell - it felt like I'd hooked a
number 22 'bus. I found that I was good at playing fish. I'd watched the adults and
got it off to a fine art, as I had practised on the odd tench that I caught.

    There I was, confidently playing this monster carp, in full control
and I was winning; it wouldn't be long before she was ready for netting.
Then, Derek Ritchie came round, stuck his hand under my rod, two feet
above the butt, and as he said, 'lift your rod, boy', he pushed. The hook was

pulled out and from that day, Derek was no longer my hero, and he didn't endear himself to me either when a month or so later he ran over my bike! I am pleased to tell you, though, that within a year, I was out-fishing him and his 'proper carper' cohorts, results-wise – I never looked back.

I returned the next afternoon after school and I couldn't wait to get my float and size 2 hook baited with a large lump of Cheddar out to the spot where I'd lost the carp the evening before. This 'spot' was actually only a foot off the bank, down the side of some railway sleepers, next to a bed of lilies. It wasn't long before my float started bobbing and moving around, just like it had the day before, and then, it stopped. I sat there for what seemed an age and I remember thinking, 'the carp must have gone. I'm never going to be able to catch one'. I blinked to refocus my eyes. Surely, I was mistaken because my float had done a vanishing act, but before my mind could work it out, the rod tip lunged over and the unseen monster smashed through the lilies. I was left looking at a piece of line trailing limply from my rod tip. I was shaking like a leaf and so upset I could have cried.

I pulled myself together and set about re-tackling, but my first problem was that I didn't have another float. The one that I'd lost had been paid for with the last of my money when I'd bought the new Chapman carp rod. I'd watched Derek and his friends free-lining, though, so I tied on a size 2, Gold Strike hook, moulded some cheese around it and lowered it in the same spot. Then, placing it on my only rod rest, I tore a piece of tinfoil from the cheese packaging and made it into a little coil which I attached to the line in front of the reel.

Just as I pulled the tinfoil down so that it rested on the ground between my reel and butt ring, it was snatched out of my hand, and the rest was a blur. All I can remember is being attached to a demented rod that was bending alarmingly toward the lilies; then everything went slack and for a millisecond, my heart sank.

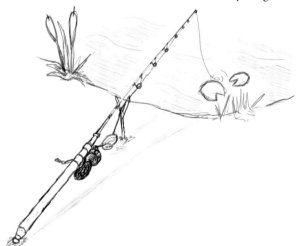

I'd lost another carp. Then the rod tip was pulled around in the opposite direction. I'd stopped the carp from taking refuge in the lilies so it had turned around and roared off into open water. Now, I was in control. I played the carp with confidence and patience as two senior members came round to watch and one of them, Archie Adams, the local funeral director, soon slipped my landing net under this monster carp.

We unscrewed the small triangular frame from the pole, Archie hooked his spring balance onto it and after deducting the weight of the net frame and mesh we calculated that this monster weighed 6lbs 14oz. Actually, it was one of the bigger carp in Wright's and it was some time before I bettered it. A 6-pounder was a true specimen then.

I looked for ages at that carp, nestled in the mesh. It had a row of golden scales along its dorsal that reflected the evening sunlight, turning them from shades of gold and silver to orange. Archie nudged me.

"Come on son," he said. "You'd better put her back."

I think he knew what a magical moment this was for me and had let me linger a bit longer than I should have done, soaking up the vision of my first proper carp. At that moment, a carp angler was almost born, but not quite. I dallied with match fishing.

One of the junior members of the club was Dermot, a big, fat boy who had a big gob and the kid who had teased me in the playground with his photo of Moby Dick. He used to throw his weight around – go back to your childhood, we all knew one – and remind us constantly that he was the junior club champion and was winning all the matches again this year.

I didn't have the confidence to enter the matches because not only did I have to learn how to catch the fish from Wright's when I first joined, but also I felt embarrassed about my tatty tackle. With the purchase of my Chapman carp rod, though, and my growing confidence as a carp hunter, I listened to Dermot shouting across the pool about how he was going to win the last match of the season, I thought 'no you're not' and entered.

I won! My first ever match and I won it with three bream and a couple of tench at a grand weight of 4lbs 4oz. Dermot was second with 3lbs 8oz and when I looked him in the eye I swear I saw fear! Mind you, my late entry didn't stop Dermot taking the junior title and the cup for that year, as he'd threatened, but I made up my mind that I'd enter all of the matches the following year and get it off him.

One night, I was working one of my shifts at Tesco kneeling on the floor, stacking a low shelf, when someone tapped me on the shoulder. I turned round and there was the assistant manageress of my local fishing tackle shop.

"I'm sure I recognise you,' she said. 'Don't you come into the tackle shop?"

"Yes," I said, wondering what was coming next.

"We've lost our Saturday boy," she went on, 'and I was wondering if you'd be interested in the job?"

Is the Pope a Catholic? I was over the moon.

So, with my jobs of marking up newspapers, doing the paper round, the relief paper rounds, three nights stacking shelves in Tesco, and now my Saturday job, I was minted! In fact, my income worked out at nearly half of an adult's wage, but I didn't have any of the outgoings of an adult, and I certainly wasn't going to tell my dad in case he nicked some of it.

I continued to fish the junior matches and the senior ones for a while, winning junior and then senior titles every year. One season, I won every possible cup there was to win and strangely, it was because of the carp. If you're a match fisherman, you want to fish for bream and roach, like everyone else, at least that's how it was in those days. I quickly realised, though, that the matches at Wright's were a lottery. You could be building up a nice little bag of small bream and roach, and then if a competitor hooked a carp, it was game over – they'd won. So, I started to fish for carp deliberately, with maggot.

I had a brilliant approach. As I mentioned I was working in my local tackle shop and I was allowed to take any maggots that were left over at the end of Saturday trading, so because I was in charge of ordering the maggots... you can see where I'm going. I never quite mastered the maggot purchasing side of things and there was always at least a gallon left at closing time, so I'd take them along to the Sunday matches, pour four pints on one small spot in the margin and float fish maggots over the top.

I had so many maggots on my spot that it was not unusual for me to drop my double-maggot-baited hook in and find another one or two maggots curled up in the bend when I retrieved it. The 'mass-baiting with maggots' strategy was lethal. In some matches, I caught four carp and my weight alone would be double the rest of the field. I enjoyed the competition aspect of the match fishing and started to spread my wings. In fact, one year, I just missed winning the Essex Open on the Chelmer, but I was torn between match and carp fishing. If I was going to go out into the open match circuit, that meant commitment and practice. I couldn't do that as well as put the time into carp fishing, so later when I met two guys who were to become my carp fishing companions, I gave up match fishing for good.

The early years at Wright's were magical times for me. It was a great place to serve my fishing apprenticeship and the effectiveness of the maggots is just one example of the lessons that I learned there. Incidentally, I have since caught carp to over 50lbs on maggot.

At that time all of my earnings went on fishing tackle, of course, and I was the envy of the senior members of the club, as I sat behind my pair of cutting-edge, glass, chocolate brown Mark 4 'the bollocks' rods - twinned with Mitchell 300s and sitting on Heron bite alarms. I was it! Even the senior match team members were pissed off, because I had the very best match gear as well, with the highly desirable Abu MK6 match rod and a Mitchell 410.

There was a float company called Ultra, set up by the great Billy Lane who fished for England and won world championships. He used to write a series in Angler's Mail, showing a different float and the shotting patterns each week. I used to cut them out and collect them. The floats he made were works of art and there was only one shop in the area that managed to get them. It was in Southend and I would go down there regularly to see if any had come in, because they went like hot cakes. I made a big, three-tier, float box to house my collection and they were my pride and joy. My mates at school collected stamps, coins, or PG Tips tea cards; I collected Ultra floats.

When I eventually stopped match fishing to concentrate solely on carp, I advertised my float box and collection in Angler's Mail and strangely, a guy drove all the way down from Coventry where Billy Lane's shop was based, to buy them. It may interest some to know that Billy Lane's son, Alan, followed his father into the business of WH Lane and some years ago, Alan purchased Dick Walker's record carp, Clarissa, stuffed and mounted, at auction. Sadly, Alan is no longer with us but Clarissa can still be seen in the shop, to this day.

I found it quite hard to hand over that box of floats, even though the guy was paying me double what the collection had cost me, but I didn't need a box of match floats if I was concentrating on carp fishing and free-lining lumps of cheese or cat food.

Although I didn't realise it at the time, my passion for fishing was influencing my formative years, which would stand me in good stead in adult life. My pocket money was meagre and my dad would never buy fishing tackle for me so I had to find ways of earning extra money and I did it by way of the paper rounds, shelf-filling at Tesco, and the Saturday job in the tackle shop. I learned that nothing comes free in this life, and that's probably why I've been a grafter ever since.

God knows where I would have ended up without the fishing passion. Wherever it was, it certainly wouldn't have been as a result of excelling at school. In my defence, I have to say that it was a crap time to be at school, then. The government had created a split system of grammar and secondary modern schools, so if you had a bit of a brain, was a sissy or a creep, you got into grammar school, where with decent teaching, you'd have a great chance of a reasonable professional career. For the rest of us, who went to secondary school, we got the teaching dregs.

Now, as an adult, I look back and think sometimes about my teachers and I wouldn't give them the time of day if I met them. My maths teacher, for example, who was also in charge of the school tuck shop, was a fat slob of a man. He used to sit at a desk on a raised plinth, so we could easily see the regular pouring of water under his desk as he wet himself. He reeked of stale urine and, throughout the lessons he'd interrupt himself to go to the cupboard where the tuck shop sweets were kept, to grab a bag of something or other. He would then gorge himself noisily in front of us, while at the same time trying to teach us maths. Two and two made five in my maths lessons!

My best subject at school was geography and that was probably because my geography teacher took an interest in me, so instead of me thinking I was stupid and incapable of learning anything, with a little bit of patient teaching, I picked it up rapidly and could have gone on and excelled at the subject. I discovered that the reason for his attention was that he was an angler, too. It was mad. He'd be teaching me geography and then after class finished he would say, "Have you got a minute?" and then tap me up about bait and technique. He even took me and my mate, Tim, fishing a couple of times – me, just a 14-year-old kid – mind you, he damn near killed us as we rolled around in the back of his van as it filled up with fumes from his leaky exhaust. I was gutted when he was put away for receiving stolen goods.

Anyway, that just about finished any chances of me getting anything out of the school system. I have to say, here, that having seen the quality of teaching that my two boys experienced in ordinary schools, today's standard of education cannot be compared with how it was when I was at school. Those who criticise the education system now should look back to how bad it was just a few decades ago, and reconsider.

School did have its good points, though. I've always enjoyed active sport and I loved PE. I can remember balmy summer days when, as soon as we'd got our school dinners down our necks, we'd be down to the changing rooms and out on the athletics track for the rest of the long midday break. I got really fit and loved the exercise. Hurdling was my natural talent; my times got to be at national level and I was invited to run for my county but I turned it down because it would have interfered with my fishing. The athletic field was also the hot spot for pulling the birds. They'd all sit round the edge of the track, brown legs akimbo, allowing a tantalising glimpse of their red school knickers. Shining days!

Once the fishing season opened on June 16th, I would be over the fence after midday dinner break. I twigged that the school tracked us twice a day. Attendance was called before we went off to our first morning lessons and our names marked in the register. The same procedure was followed in the afternoon, but we were not tracked between the afternoon lessons. So once that after-lunch registration had been done, I could sneak around the back of the school block, which concealed the perimeter fence, be over it and away. I could be down on the banks of Rayleigh Angling Club from about 2.30pm and, more importantly, have the pick of swims and the lake to myself before the seniors got home from work and the juniors finished school – well, most days, anyway.

One day, I had a very painful accident while riding at full pelt down the very steep hill on the way to the lake. My rod bag was over my shoulder, the D ring on the strap opened up and the strap became detached. The bag shot through the spokes of the front wheel and I was catapulted over the handlebars. I hit the ground, bounced down the hill and my face and exposed arms and legs became embedded with grit and gravel. I was a right mess and I can still see the shock on my poor old mum's face when an ambulance dropped me off later that night. My big concern was my rod holdall and my rods, of course. The bottom of the holdall had been virtually cut off and I feared the worst, but was amazed and relieved that my rods remained unscathed. I had that rod holdall for another year or two, with a paint tin lid blocking the hole in the base and string replacing the opened D ring of the shoulder strap.

Fishing in those first few years was only done in the summer months. We'd have the odd go for pike and perch in the winter, but we had neither the clothing to keep really warm, nor the inclination, really, because our other great passion was girls. The fishing would stop around November, and I turned to girls, more or less, until June came round again, then I'd become girlfriend-free for a few months. I used to drive my older sister mad because I'd disappear when the season opened. I wouldn't tell my girlfriend of the time where I was because the last thing I wanted was a bird coming fishing with me. They'd be round my house, knocking on the door after school, and my sister would be home by then so she'd cop it from these younger, whingeing girls.

There was one, I guess the first love of my life, Alison, with whom I'd shared lost virginities, who was a lot more determined than the rest, and my sister, remembering the brick incident, told her where I could be found.

One winter, when I was five years old, I found a couple of inches of solid ice at the top of my sandcastle bucket that had filled up with rainwater. I had nurtured this immensely thick piece of ice for several days so I was somewhat distressed when the cold spell ended and it started to melt. I asked my older and wiser sister how I could stop it from melting and she told me to put some salt on it.

The next day, my treasured ice had more or less gone and I was horrified when the extent of her treachery became apparent. She just laughed at me, so in anger and frustration, I picked up the nearest object and hurled it at her; it was half a house brick. I was always good at throwing and pretty accurate, too, so the house brick found its mark square on the side of her head. I was quite impressed but she only wobbled and staggered around a bit; she didn't fall over. I got a real hiding for that, I can tell you, but it was my first lesson of women always bearing a grudge. The old saying, 'Heaven has no rage like love to hatred turned, nor hell a fury like a woman scorned', is only too true, in my experience.

So, Alison turned up at the gate at Wright's one evening and kept hollering, calling my name until it became impossible to ignore her as a couple of senior members attempting to have a peaceful evening's fishing were getting the hump, and so I let her in. Actually, in the beginning she was no trouble. I put up with her coming fishing with me for a while, because she really got into it. All I had to do was to give her my old trout rod set up with a float and leave her up at the opposite end to where I was fishing, and she'd sit there patiently for hours on her own, not bothering me. I chucked her, though, when one morning while we were in our bivvy – a bivvy then was a 45" green umbrella with a sheet of see-through plastic clipped to the ribs – the bailiff came round and caught us snogging, and me with my hand down her knickers. I had to go up before the committee and nearly got chucked out of the club. A big lesson was learned that day. Girls and fishing don't mix!

Chapter Three

Apprenticeship

I swear that the sky was blue every day in those hot summers of my early teens and the sun shone down on my mates and me. It was bliss. I had loads of money to buy what I wanted, and I got the pick of some of the best birds at school because I was drop-dead gorgeous, apparently. I never did get it, and it used to embarrass me, but they said I had a baby face with dimples in each cheek and for some reason it used to drive the girls mad.

It's funny, when I think back to how it's been throughout my life. The knockers have always wanted to pull me down. I had trouble in my young days, too; not only because other boys at school were envious of my bird-pulling ability, but also I was 'the *man!*' I had the dream job, working in a fishing tackle shop and to top it all, I was a member of Rayleigh Angling Club, which as I mentioned, was really difficult to get into.

Apart from a few minor inconveniences like doing schoolwork, fishing had already overtaken my whole life and it was all I thought about. It was my working life and I loved being in the shop on Saturdays. Serving other anglers all day long was a real buzz for me. In fact, I enjoyed it so much that I stayed on as a Saturday boy well after leaving school and taking up my engineering apprenticeship. Fishing also governed my playtime, and everything I read was about fishing, too. I exhausted the library of every book that had a mere mention of the word 'carp', and I bought 'Angling' magazine religiously, every month, just in case I was lucky and it was one of those odd issues when there would be an article on carp fishing.

I began to plug into the scene in this way and whereas the other carp anglers in Rayleigh Angling Club were stuck on the conventional baits of the time, like potato, cheese, and floating crust, I latched on to the 'specials'. This was the first wave of what I describe as modern carp baits. The small band of fanatical carp anglers in England were seeking new baits so such things as sausage meat and cat food became the craze. I quickly realised just how much of an edge a bait could give you. One close season, I spent £50 of my hard-earned money baiting up, more than a couple of weeks' wages then for an adult. I can still remember the look of astonishment on the tackle shop manager's face when he found out how much I was spending, and Malcolm's remark, 'Well, I hope for your sake that it pays off'.

Well, it did pay off when on opening night I caught 34 carp, which I guess was more or less the whole population of Wright's, and I'm sure it was my baiting that had pushed up the weights of these ravenous fish. To the best of my knowledge, I was the only member to catch a genuine double figure carp, and that turned out to be more of a result than you might think. A few years ago, I was given a copy of an old BCSG (British Carp Study Group) magazine, dated way back in 1968. At that time, the BCSG members were the cream of the carp fishing world, and the back cover listed every member who'd had a carp of over 10lbs in that year. A double was a very big fish in those days - equivalent to at least a 30 now.

I left school with no idea of what I wanted to do, but I was expected to get a job. End of. There was no argument. You were expected to walk out of school on the Friday afternoon, and on the Monday morning be working, and contributing to the household expenses. With my scant education, most jobs for me would have been manual and unskilled, but my dad was an engineer so he pushed me into that and I was lucky to get an apprenticeship. My weekly wage for the first year was £6.43, and my dad nicked a pound of that. I was much worse off than when I'd been a schoolboy, which is one of the reasons that I kept the Saturday job going, to fund my carp fishing.

I soon realised how I'd been looking a gift horse in the mouth. While we were at school, all my mates and me talked about was how soon we could leave and how much we hated it. Now I was in the adult world, the working world, in a smelly, hot engineering factory, and I detested it. I thought, 'You prat! All those chances that you took for granted, and now you've blown it!' There were 150 girls in our school and I'd only dated 60 of them; even discounting the ugly ones, I definitely should have pulled more than 60!

There were a couple of upsides, though. I must confess that I got a great grounding in engineering, without which I wouldn't be where I am now and I was to discover that there was another important aspect of working for Helbar Engineering; Bob Poore. It wasn't many weeks before I began to be accepted by the rest of the workforce, although the old hands slaughtered the new apprentices. You got all the menial tasks like sweeping the floors, cleaning the bogs, making the tea... and besides that, they persecuted you, digging you out, and taking the piss, trying to reduce you to tears.

One morning during the first week, I made the tea and took it round to all the engineers. There was a grumpy old sod, called Cyril, who put me on my guard right from the start because he was really scary. I took him his tea; he said, 'thank you' and then reached into the top pocket of his white coat, and pulled out his engineer's rule. Most engineers carried six-inch metal rules in their top pockets in those days and with a sleight of hand, he began to stir his tea with it. Then he pulled the rule out and started shouting at me.

"How fucking strong have you made this tea!" he yelled as he waved a two-inch steel rule in front of my eyes.

On another occasion, they tried to send me to the hardware shop for a skirting board ladder and some sky hooks, but I wasn't *that* thick. I served my time with patience and became accepted. I knew when this had happened because I was invited to join their card school. They played solo during the long lunch break and it had looked so complicated, that I was reluctant to make myself look a prat, especially as it was a game where everybody played against one, and you had to figure out which suits your colleagues were majoring in. In essence it's a team game and I thought they'd thrash me, but I loved it and soon became an expert.

This was how I got to know Bob Poore. He was one of the solo group and it turned out that he fished with a mate named Eric Aris, who worked down the road, and fishing was their life. Bob was ten or so years older than me, and both he and Eric were bachelors. In fact, neither of them married until well into their 30s. At this time, they still lived at home with their parents, had loads of spare money, plenty of spare time and most importantly, from my point of view, they had a car. Now I had access to all the essential elements I needed to further my carp fishing.

For a long time, they had kept a boat up on the Norfolk Broads but were getting bored with it, and I wasn't surprised because it was mostly bream fishing on the Broads back then. I regaled Bob with my stories of carp fishing and my passion for it and one day, he told me that he and Eric would like to have a go. That was the start of us fishing together for several years, and because they had the car, I could widen my horizons.

I'd tap up everyone who came into the shop about the waters they fished and the various clubs in Essex, trying to identify the ones that might hold carp, although they were very thin on the ground at that time. I'd say to Bob, "I think I've found a water," and all three of us would take a drive to check it out.

This was the era for the stocking of carp. After Dick Walker caught Clarissa, interest in carp grew significantly and angling clubs wanted to stock their waters with them. Fish farmers started to rear carp and one of the foremost suppliers at the time was Stambridge Fisheries, just north of Southend-on-Sea, in Essex. This could have been why Essex was at the forefront of the carp 'revolution' and one of the first counties to stock carp in a wide selection of venues..

BELOW
Lake Meadows.

Interestingly, most clubs purchased a relatively small number and this is why Essex has always held a great track record for big carp. I can think of many instances of lakes having stocks of less than ten, so the environment supplied plenty of space and food, which ensured that the carp thrived.

One of the reasonably well-known waters that held mainly carp was Lake Meadows, in Billericay. I guess very few of you will have heard of this park lake, but several of the big names in carp fishing used to fish there, including well-known BCSG members. Most of these names have been forgotten over time, but at least one is still around; this is where I first met Del Romang, of Delkim fame.

Our first meeting was not a happy one. I was fishing one night with Bob and Eric and at around nine o'clock, I saw a figure walking along the dam wall to my left and on the other side. Then I heard a series of loud splashes and saw the water erupting in front of a willow on the corner of an island; someone was baiting up right on top of where I was fishing. I shouted at him and went round, but by the time I got there, the culprit had disappeared. The next weekend, there was a carper who I'd never seen before, fishing off the dam wall to the willow. We had, shall we say, a heated debate about etiquette. Over the following years, I was to see Del on several waters and it's lovely that this fellow pioneer is still out there, and with a great tackle business, too.

There was no such thing as Google then, so I started collecting Ordnance Survey maps, which we would scour, looking for bits of blue. That was how I found

Braxted Park, a 2000-acre country estate, east of Chelmsford, which was then owned by Plessey, a huge electronics conglomerate, and occupied by the Clark family because Sir Allen Clark had been the chairman and his sons held prominent positions in the company. Descendents of Sir Allen still occupy Braxted Park but Plessey was eventually swallowed up by GEC and Siemens in the late 80s. In the grounds is a magnificent, early Georgian house contained within a high brick wall that goes for what seems like miles around the estate; I dread to think what that wall would cost to build today – millions, I would imagine. The estate has always fascinated me as I've driven past it. There is even a church and churchyard within the grounds.

The rear of the churchyard backed on to the lake so we crept in there one night, and climbed over the fence to take a look at it. Huge chestnut trees and the like surround it, and it's one of the darkest and spookiest places I've ever fished. They say that it's haunted and I can't say I ever had an occurrence there but I never felt comfortable fishing at night, although that might have had something to do with the fact that we knew there was no night fishing allowed and the gamekeeper did have a bloody great gun.

Still, to this day, I would say that it was one of the most *boring* places I ever fished. It's a typical estate lake of around eight acres, old and silty, with an island at one end and fed by a stream. Off the back of the earth dam wall, there was a circular brick structure containing a small sunken chamber; it even had a brick lid. The gamekeeper told me that this had been a kind of fridge, or icehouse. Way back in the 18th century, they used to collect the ice in the winter, put it into the brick construction, and then store game in it.

The lake was uninteresting, though, because we never saw any sign of carp. In fact, I believe that the one I eventually caught was one of only two in there at that time. Over a decade later, my good friend, Bill Lovett, had a crack at Braxted and after a lot of effort he also only caught one and that was a different fish to mine. Nowadays, it is a well-stocked water.

The fish that I caught was a monster, but I will never know the true weight because it bottomed my 22lb scales. I can't find the one photo I had of it but it looked massive and had the frame of a good 30-pounder – that would be a 50-plus now. However, being objective and visualising that photo, I remember that my hands were lost in its gut. Clearly, it was an old fish that was empty and flabby and if I had to take a punt at it, I'd say it was probably around 25lbs, which would stack up with the fish that Bill Lovett caught later, which was around 27lbs – again an old fish. I haven't mentioned this fish just because it was such a monster for those days, though, but because it was my passport into the BCSG.

Chapter Four

The British Carp Study Group

I was a sponge, soaking up everything I could learn about carp but the problem I had was finding sources. Despite the fact that I was now stretching my wings, courtesy of Bob and Eric's cars, I had to search for information and to teach myself. To see another carp angler on any of the lakes we chose to fish was as rare as rocking-horse poo, so it was difficult to get information from others. It would have been virtually impossible for me to have learned much from any carp angler I may have met, in any event – the secrecy was akin to MI5.

I was still at school the first time I walked around Boreham Mere, a beautiful, mature gravel pit that is still owned by Chelmsford AA. A customer in the tackle shop had mentioned it to me; he'd told me that it definitely held carp and that he'd seen a couple of carp anglers fishing it. Wow! I had identified one of the few big carp waters in Essex at the time. I reasoned that it must contain big carp if proper carp anglers were on there – like the ones I used to see in Angling magazine with their amazing tattered floppy hats and camo jackets – their uniform!

So, I had a walk round, got to a swim halfway down the lake, and came across a pile of blankets stuck in front of an unbelievable set-up; a bank of three rods were painted in a camo pattern, and even the reels had been sprayed up. The rods were on Heron bite alarms, the first bite alarms I had seen, with electrical cables running back and going underneath the pile of blankets. If it hadn't been for the rods and reels, I could have been forgiven for thinking that I'd stumbled across a tramp on life support. I had discovered my first proper carp angler and I was in awe. I don't think I could have been more in awe if I'd walked up to a live dodo.

From one end of this pile of blankets I could see a very beaten and tatty hat, the trademark of all true carp anglers, and I took that as a reasonable clue to where the head was. I spoke to him.

"Caught anything, mister?"

There was no response, so I said it a bit louder.

"Have you caught anything?"

Still no response, so I tried again.

"Any luck?"

This time I got a reply.

"No. Fuck off!"

Until this time, my only source of information had been angling books, and like I said, I had exhausted the library's stock. Occasionally, Angling Times or the Angler's Mail might carry a carp story, or Angling magazine might contain an article, but it was rare. If I found an article in Angling magazine, it was a real jewel and the best place for me to learn from. From that publication I picked up the fact that carpers were using specials, and that snippet of information gave me a big edge at Rayleigh Angling Club, and the other waters that Bob and Eric and I visited throughout Essex.

I'd moved on from Kit E Kat and experimented by concocting my own recipe that I'm sure I could still catch on today. It was based on liver sausage and liver-flavoured dog food and it was this bait that caught the big Braxted fish.

There was one source of information, though, that I was desperate to tap into and that was the BCSG. The BCSG, numbering some 300 members at its peak in the mid-70s, contained more or less all the country's very top carp anglers. It was the crème de la crème of the carp fishing scene, and the think tank from where everything was coming out, as carpers tried to get a grasp on how to catch these bloody awkward fish.

You've got to understand that until Dick Walker came along, culminating in his capture of Clarissa from Redmire in 1952, carp were considered by all but a handful, as not worth attempting to fish for. For most, it was out of the question anyway, because so few waters contained them, and if they did, the chances of success were considered as bordering on zero.

The consensus was that carp were incredibly intelligent and the only way to trick them was to use the finest tackle and if you did manage to hook one, because of the carp's immense size and strength, it would surely snap your fine line. Indeed, I had read books from the library that contained just that philosophy. However, Dick Walker decided to challenge the myth and prove that carp could be caught by design. I can imagine what it must have been like to have picked up The Angler's News and Sea Fisher's Journal of 4th October 1952 - a weekly at the time – to read that story of Clarissa about a month after Dick Walker's capture, and written by the man himself. I wonder how many were captivated and inspired to catch such a fish, in the same way as I had been on that steam train back from Brockenhurst while reading Angling magazine.

THE RECORD CARP

by . . . RICHARD WALKER

Peter Thomas supports the massive bulk of the 44 lb. carp which has broken all records.

ABOVE
...The pointer came up against the stop with such a thump that we both knew at once that here was a new record...

Extracted from Dick Walkers Article:

The lake was completely still, its surface unbroken by either wind or the movements of fish; and so it remained, except for one heavy splash far out, until some time between 4.30 and 5am. About that time one of the buzzers sounded, and we were both at the rods at once.

STRIKING THE FISH

"It's yours," said Peter. I raised the back of my hand under the rod to feel if line was being taken, and felt it creep slowly over the hairs, an eerie but satisfactory sensation. In went the pick-up; a pause to make sure the line had

been picked up properly, and then I struck hard and far back. I encountered a solid but living resistance, and Peter, needing no telling that a fish was hooked, reeled up his line out of the way. I crouched so that I could see the curve of the rod against the sky - even that was difficult in the extreme darkness - and waited on events. I did not want a fresh, lively fish brought too soon into the 15-yard wide channel between the weed beds, and I determined that if possible the battle should be fought in the deep water beyond.

A SHORT BATTLE

The fish moved slowly and solidly towards the dam. Every few seconds came a tremendous tug; it felt as if the rod had been struck by a sandbag. As the fish neared the dam, I remembered those chestnut roots. Four pounds or forty, it must not get among them, or all would be lost, so I increased pressure. At first it had no effect; then, as I bent the rod more, the efforts of the fish became intensified. I knew only a few yards separated it from disaster, and hung on grimly. The rod bent as never before - I could feel the curve under the corks in my hand; but everything held for the two or three minutes that the fish continued to fight his way towards his refuge. Then, suddenly, he gave it up. He turned and forged into the weedbed between me and the roots, and I was only just able to keep the line taut. Presently he stopped, and all was solid and immovable.

Peter said: "Take it easy. Wait and see if he'll move." I did. Nothing happened. I said: "I'll try handlining." Peter said: "All right, but take it easy. That's a big fish, you don't want to lose it." I had no idea how big a fish it was. I knew it was a good one, but all I could think of then was, 'Maybe another 20-pounder - I hope!' I pulled off a couple of yards of line, so as to be able to get the rod up quickly if the fish bolted suddenly; then I pointed the rod straight at the fish and began tugging. The first few tugs made no impression; then came a frantic pull, up went the rod, and out went the fish into the deep water again. I let him go well out, and then tightened up firmly again, praying for him to move left; and he did. When he was opposite I gave him the butt and crammed on pressure to the limit; and in he came, grudgingly, pulling and boring every inch of the way, but always losing ground, until at last he came to the surface and rolled three or four yards out.

Peter was ready with the net, and as I drew the fish towards it, he switched on the electric lamp. We saw a great expanse of golden flank as the fish rolled. "Common carp," said Peter. The fish rolled again, then righted itself, and suddenly, with a last effort, shot towards me and to the right I could do nothing to stop it, and to my horror it crashed through the fringe of trailing brambles and vanished below the undercut bank. I felt a dreadful sawing sensation on the line where it passed through the brambles; in the light of the lamp I could see the swirls as the fish tried to thrust even farther under; but though I put the rod-point under water and strained it as hard as I dare, nothing would shift the fish, which eventually settled down into an immovable sulk.

Peter climbed out to the edge of the overhang and put the big net, thong down, over the hole in the brambles where the fish had gone in. Then, feeling carefully down the line with his free hand, he reached the fish's nose and pulled it round. I saw vaguely a commotion; then Peter began to lift. He stuck halfway and called for me to take his lamp. I slacked line, put down the rod, and went to his assistance. Once I had the

lamp, he could grasp the mesh of the net, and with a tremendous heave he swung net and fish up and over the brambles and on to the bank.

We knelt side by side looking at it. I knew it was big, and suddenly it dawned on me that it was more than that. It was tremendous! I cut a stick, notched its end, and with this Peter extracted the hook, which was only lightly lodged in the roof of the mouth. Then we put the fish in a sack and lifted it on my spring balance, which goes up to 32lb. The pointer came up against the stop with such a thump that we both knew at once that here was a new record; but we could tell no more; so we tied up the mouth of the sack and lowered it into the water.

Then we re-baited our hooks and cast out again. Peter went into the tent; but I knew I could never sleep, and sat smoking and thinking until dawn. It was then that I resolved that, record or no record, the fish should not be killed. Many, many times I had wondered what I should do if ever I caught a record carp; now I had to decide, and kill it I could not.

At about 9.30 am, after breakfast, which Peter cooked (I think I should have spoiled it!) we were able to get another spring balance, weighing up to 25lb, and by sharing the load between the two we found that, taking into account the weight of the sack, the fish must weigh not less than 41lbs.

Anglers did start to follow Dick and his friends. One, Peter Mohan, from Bristol, organised this new breed of fanatical anglers into a group called the British Carp Study Group. What's more, the BCSG regularly published a magazine containing articles on the very latest cutting-edge stuff from members. The organisation was split up into regions, and each one had a regional organiser (RO). He arranged regular meetings for the members in his area, so giving them a chance to network with each other.

For several years, I thought of nothing else than getting into the BCSG. Other kids carved hearts with theirs and their sweethearts' initials into their desks at school, but I carved 'BCSG' on a classroom desk one day and I wasn't subtle about it. The deep carving filled up the whole desktop, the teacher sussed it was me and I was back in front of the headmaster and another six whacks of the cane.

After I'd caught my first double, I attempted to gain admittance into the BCSG. I took my portfolio of fish along to see the RO at the time, a guy called Les Teager, but I got turned down. There was a kind of unspoken rule that the BCSG would only accept the best, translated by my understanding as 'the best carp anglers in the region.' Say, for example, that I'd walked into a region up north with a pic of a 10lb 2oz common, I would probably have been crowned the king, but in Essex and Kent, that just wasn't quite enough. Half a dozen probably would have done it, or definitely the capture of a couple of big doubles.

With a few low doubles under my belt and the capture of the Braxted fish, I tried again. This time, the RO had changed; now it was a guy called Derek Stritton. Les Teager had lived in Leigh-on-Sea, which was only about four miles from my home, so it was easy for me to get there on a bus, but Derek was a different proposition – he lived in London in Forest Gate. I'd never even heard of Forest Gate and the thought of going to London was really scary. I'd been brought up in the Essex countryside and had only been up to London a couple of times on school trips. It seemed a hellhole to me. My abiding impression was when the train went through the East-End slums, which was an area of such decay, and it stank so much. I couldn't understand why anyone would want to live in such a place without green fields and trees, but at that age, it never occurred to me that most had no choice. Spurred on by the thought of entry to the BCSG, I dealt with my trepidation, went to the station, and got on the train. Getting to Liverpool Street was pretty simplistic. I had no fears of missing it because that was the end of the line, but it was the underground business that completely confused me - all those trains, on apparently different lines, going in different directions. I figured I'd found the right line and got on the train to Forest Gate, only to realise when referring to the map on the carriage wall, that I was going the wrong way.

Even to this day, I hate the bloody underground. Bev, my partner, loves London and so, I get dragged up there occasionally and I will admit that a sunny evening around Covent Garden is a cool place to be, but as soon as we get on the underground, I grab her hand and won't let go; even Essex blokes have their phobias. I'm comfortable with my phobia, though, when compared to one of my mates, whose name I won't mention, Dave Jordison. He'd have no problem picking a fight with a bull elephant and I'd confidently back him to rip the tusks out, but he's a nightmare to fish with. If he finds a spider in his bivvy, he screams like a girl and won't stop until you go in and get it out for him.

Anyway, I worked it out eventually and got to Forest Gate station, then went on a fairly long trek, or it could have felt like that because I was in such a strange place. I found Derek's house and rang the doorbell. He came to the door and while he tried to disguise it, I saw him do a double take. I wondered why and it kind of put me on edge. I was later to find out that it was because he was surprised at how young I was. We chatted, had a cup of tea, I showed him my portfolio of carp, and he showed me his. Bloody hell! I was well out of my depth here. I left some time later thinking there was no chance.

Derek Stritton recalls:

I always find it interesting to read another person's perception of places and memories that are shared, and particularly so is Kevin's view of Forest Gate in the 1970s. Believe it or not, in those far-off days Forest Gate was considered to be the 'posh bit' of East London with the Docklands areas of Canning Town and Custom House being far tougher, more socially deprived and run down. So from my perspective at that time, I lived in a posh place and worked in a rough one. Not too sure what Kevin would have made of Docklands in those days. Anyway, back to the story as they say.

When Peter Mohan asked me to become Essex Regional Organiser for the BCSG, following on from Les Teager, I was still living in my parents' home in Forest Gate. Though a large house, it was a busy household, Mum, Dad, brother Barry and his girlfriend and me living in one part of the house, with another family (lodgers) living in part of the upstairs. That was the way things were in those days, and many East End homes had similar arrangements. Because of this, it could be difficult when I had visitors there as I felt we were invading my parent's space, so I would take friends and visitors to the Spotted Dog, a pub within ten minutes walk of home, so that my family could retain a degree of privacy, while I could get on with day-to-day life.

Peter Mohan had told me that the person due to visit me to be vetted for membership that day had been turned down by Les Teager after a previous application and interview. He also said, in passing, that the person, Kevin Nash, was still young so if it transpired that I considered him unsuitable for membership, he still had plenty of time to re-apply. Sometimes remarks like that register, but the full implication and meaning are lost in the moment.

In reality, it wasn't until the bell chimed and I opened the front door for my first meeting with Kevin that Peter's remark about his youth became clear. The 'double take expression' that Kevin makes reference to and which put him on edge was, in fact, the result of a slightly bewildered thought that crossed my mind, 'What do I do now? I doubt he'll be allowed in the pub.' My recollection of our meeting that day is of having a cup of tea, sharing photos, and talking carp, before walking to the Spotted Dog. Normally, I would have gone straight to the bar, but today I guided Kevin into a darkened corner seat (anyone reading this who knew the pub in those days will know exactly what I mean), before going to the bar to order drinks.

In the hour or more that followed, our conversation convinced me that despite his young years, here was someone who not only had youth on his side, but drive and determination too. He clearly loved his carp fishing, had photos to support his catches and I felt he should be offered membership of the BCSG. Peter Mohan always insisted that prospective members got feedback in writing after interview, probably rightly I suppose, as I guess it could have proved difficult turning someone away if they took offence at a negative decision.

So it was that after guiding Kevin back to Forest Gate station for his long journey home, I returned to my house to contact Peter and suggest we offer Kevin membership of the group. Peter agreed and I subsequently wrote to Kevin to let him know, before Peter's formal letter. Membership of the

BCSG was truly prestigious in those times, and I could tell how much Kevin appreciated that when he telephoned me to say, 'thank you'. It was clear he was surprised but delighted to be in.

In the months that followed, a couple of local BCSG members privately criticised me for allowing such a young person to become a member. I remember remarking to them at the time that I could easily have made a mistake; nevertheless, they should 'watch this space'. Kevin kept in touch with me for a good while after obtaining membership. We spoke regularly on the phone and our conversations continued to convince me I had made the correct decision. I can still recall his early sorties into tackl-e making with stainless steel bank sticks and nylon carp sacks.

Over the years, I have taken some pride in my decision. Not only has Kevin become a very successful and single-minded angler, but also he is probably the most innovative of all our home-grown tackle manufacturers, and I wouldn't say that if I didn't mean it!

Convinced that I had blown my second interview, I was still dispirited and depressed a few days later when a letter popped through the door from Derek. I was in! If I had to pinpoint one factor above all others responsible for where I'm at now, the number of big carp I've caught, creating Nash Tackle... then I would say it's down to one person, Derek Stritton, for seeing something in me. This may come as a surprise to some readers, but without his instinct that I was good enough to make the grade, I wouldn't have got into the BCSG, so I've always felt that I owed Derek a lot.

With the cessation of the original BCSG, Derek and I lost contact, but then some years back I read an article by him, when he told a story about his bivvy letting him down, so I sent him one of mine, a Titan. His surprised response at why I would do that illustrated to me that he's never really understood what a difference he made to my life.

So, at last I was tapped into the grapevine and that stream of knowledge, exclusive to BCSG members. Carp fishing was a secret world. I told you the story of the guy I met, or wanted to meet, at Boreham Mere, and that's how it was on the outside. In the BCSG, though, things were different; there was a free flow of information within the group. For sure, many members were holding back, and just gave out part of the picture, but even that was better than being outside in the wilderness.

In the envelope containing my BCSG membership card was a small pewter badge, as well as several back issues of 'Carp' – the BCSG's magazine, which was only available to members.

Fred Wilton had just written an article, 'Towards the Ultimate Bait' that changed thinking forever. Fred worked in the London docks so quite how a dockie became the leading authority on carp nutrition, I'm not quite sure. I guess it's quite simply that he was interested enough for it to become a passion, and if you are passionate about something then you excel.

Certainly, when I first met Fred I understood that there was a sharp mind at work. Fred became a god to us mere mortal carpers and around him were his disciples, a team if you like, of carp anglers to whom Fred divulged his ideas. It's fair to say that Fred was never a fanatical carp angler in the sense that he *had* to be out there catching loads of big carp; the buzz for him was in learning how the carp worked and so it was that the main beneficiary of his immense knowledge was a small group of anglers in his confidence – such as Robbie Monday, Derek Stritton and Bob Morris, who went down in carp fishing history when he became the first to catch 100 doubles in a season on Fred's baits.

All the members were talking about Fred's article and there was much debate; it was blowing peoples' minds and it provoked a new way of thinking about bait. The main thrust of Fred's groundbreaking article was that carp knew what was good for them so if you gave carp a good food source, they would recognise it as such and so it would be more effective. There were many arguments about that, the main one being, 'That's rubbish! How can a carp know what's good for it?'

Well, if nothing else, Fred got *me* on the research route. I started getting scientific papers through the library and one of these told of an experiment that they'd carried out with young children. The kids were placed in a room for a couple of weeks, which was full of things that kids like; cream doughnuts, sweets,

BELOW
The famous orange BCSG magazine, containing the article by Fred Wilton that changed carp baits forever.

OCTOBER 1972

THE CARP

B.C.S.G.

chocolate... as well as proper healthy stuff, like salads, green vegetables and lean meats, balanced, nutritional food. To start with, they gorged themselves with all the junk food, but within a few days, they'd settled down and began to select a balanced diet because the gorging on sweets and cream-filled cakes made them feel sick. It's obvious, really. If you didn't know, instinctively, what was good to eat and what your body required to maintain good health, you'd sicken and die. I saw where Fred was coming from and the philosophy of fishing with the highest quality food baits has stayed with me.

Mind you, not all the scientific papers I ordered were so influential. I remember receiving one entitled 'The

Locomotion of Goldfish'. It was an enormous piece of research, an inch thick, and must have taken the author years to write. It was a study of how goldfish swim, or more accurately, it was to identify if goldfish swam in one direction more than the other. Interested readers might be fascinated to know that the conclusion was that they do - to the right, if I recall.

For a brief moment, I made a mental note of that in case it would help my catch rate. You never know when a seemingly useless piece of information might come in handy. If I spotted a carp and then it disappeared, maybe I should go to the right to look for it, but then I dismissed the thought with the conclusion that if a fish favoured one direction over the other, surely, it would eventually disappear up its own arse. I've often wondered how many thousands of pounds that 'researchers' receive in grants for such ground-breaking studies.

I latched on to these PYM (Phillips Yeast Mixture - which was a vitamin and mineral conditioning supplement for birds) baits of Fred's and took them to Lake Meadows that first winter. We used to use Lake Meadows as our winter water because it had a good stock of carp so at least there was a chance of a take, compared to the other waters we had found until then, which might only have had half a dozen wild fish. I'd been baiting regularly with the PYM baits and it was only our little team - me, Bob and Eric - who were catching with any consistency, when

ABOVE
*Fred Wilton [left] nets
a good carp for Derek
Stritton. It's 1974 and
few people were ready to
accept the impact that
Fred's bait ideas were to
have on carp waters.*

along came a couple of BCSG members who caught on their first night. I felt that was a bit strange; something was amiss.

There was a regional meeting the following week. Derek used to organise them at the Moby Dick pub in Dagenham. I pulled Derek aside and told him of my fears.

"I'd been baiting Lake Meadows for weeks with the PYM, and I think these other two guys have got in off the back of me. I'm sure they're using the PYM bait, too." I said.

"Make your own label then," said Derek.

"What do you mean? What's a label?" I asked him.

"Flavour it!" Derek replied.

"What with?"

"Something like a cake flavouring," Derek said.

Eventually, I managed to drag out of him that he was referring to almond or vanilla essence from a supermarket. Derek was always like that to me. Maybe it's the teacher in him. I felt he had a bit of a soft spot for me and wanted to guide me but he was never going to make it easy and give it to me on a plate. Derek was a school teacher, so I guess he knew that you have to get kids thinking for themselves. That slightest of nods from Derek was all I needed.

The next Saturday, during my dinner break from the fishing tackle shop, I was walking down the High Street toward Tesco on an almond essence hunt, when I spotted a newly-opened shop. It was the first health food shop to open in Rayleigh and I was fascinated by their window display of health tonics and supplements – the like of which I'd never seen before. It was definitely worth a look, so I walked in the door, and to me it was akin to walking into the best-stocked tackle shop. This treasure trove was bait, though, not tackle. I was looking at all these unusual and exotic beans, and peas, and flours, grains, and stuff that surely it would be worth experimenting with. Best of all was a shelf lined with small, dark glass bottles of flavours supplied by a specialist company. Lane's flavourings offered far more than the basic almond and vanilla carried by any supermarket. That shelf must have been 30 bottles long and held a myriad flavours that I never dreamed you could get; strawberry, cherry, hazelnut, chocolate…to name just a few. I had stumbled upon a carp bait Mecca.

The BCSG pointed me in the bait direction, but it was much bigger than that. I struck up friendships with fellow members who, in their own way, contributed toward today's carp scene; carpers such as Jeff Kemp, with whom I was very close for a while and who later set up a bait company that was highly regarded and successful. One of his mates fishing the same waters was Bill Lovett. He and I became great friends, and we were to fish several waters together. In fact, Bill had an awesome knack of sourcing, or should I say, he had a lot of front. I was the researcher and would say to Bill, 'I've found out about this ingredient. We need to get some' and he'd go for it.

The trouble was that the kinds of chemicals that I was seeking were only available commercially and the companies trading in and using them dealt in tonne lots. Bill would get on the phone, posing as a buyer for some big company and say that he was interested in buying XX tonnes of it. He would ask them to send a sample and, because he'd given it such a big 'un, the supplier on the other end would be eating out of his hand. Bill's idea of a sample would be a 56lb sack, and best of all, most times he'd get it free of charge. More than one of our ideas, combined with Bill's sourcing, helped to get Jeff's bait company going, I'm pleased to say.

At one BCSG meeting at the Moby Dick, a member known simply as 'Brad' to us all brought along a couple of guests, Mick Linsell and his fishing mate, Zenon Bjoko. Zenon was to feature in a big way later on in my carp fishing and I could list many others. Should any of you who used to attend those meetings be reading this, please pardon me and do not feel offended if I've left you out.

Carp fishing for all of us was more than a sport, and still is for me. It was a passion, an all-consuming lifestyle and as such, it was preciously protected. As I said, Fred Wilton was a god among us and for many his words were gospel.

Apparently, Fred had once said that carp fishing should never be commercialised and allow people to earn out of it. I think this may have been because he'd been approached by some company or other to bring out a commercial version of his bait, and despite the potentially lucrative offer, Fred had wanted none of it, believing that the sport might become corrupted, and if you look at today's commercialism, marketing and hype, his stance was prophetic.

Imagine the scene: About 20 of us in the Moby Dick, talking animatedly about all things carp, and there's a new guy there who a member has brought along as a guest. I had my back to him, chatting with Derek, when we all clearly heard him announce that he was going to 'make a living out of becoming a full-time carp angler'. You could have heard a pin drop.

"Who the hell is that?" I asked Derek.

"That's Kevin Maddocks," he said. "He's just got into the BCSG."

I turned and glanced with disdain at the guest.

Well, Kevin did just as he said he would, and was the biggest name in carp fishing in the 80s, writing Carp Fever, one of the biggest selling angling books of all time. Recently, I asked the lads in the office what they knew about Kevin Maddocks, and half of them said they'd never heard of him. That's like young football fans who've never heard of George Best or Pele; I guess if you ask kids today who are mad keen on football about the stars of yesteryear, you'd get a similar reaction.

Fred had another article published about baits that, this time, he termed as HNVs which stood for High Nutritional Value. These were baits made up of everything that Fred thought a carp needed, or as near as damn it as he could get. Fred was the first to write about adding eggs to ingredients and boiling the baits to form a skin on the outside to make them nuisance-fish resistant – the boilie!

I loved the concept of a bait that worked toward providing everything in one round ball that a carp would need. The HNVs were awesome, so I dropped the PYMs and I was the only one to get on the HNVs in my part of Essex. Derek was hitting waters in Kent and around the London edge of Essex, so I had the rest of the county to myself. After chatting with the BCSG members at the Moby Dick, I was sure that the ones on my patch weren't experimenting with the HNVs – they were sticking on the PYM. The reason may have been that two of the key ingredients of Fred's HNVs were the milk proteins, casein and lactalbumin, and they were the devil to source in those days. I tried and tried, going to the library reference section looking for sources, but it was only available commercially in

bulk. I was just a kid and had no way of
approaching big companies to get the
stuff. It was immensely frustrating and
was eating me up, especially as Derek and
his friends, who were close to Fred, were
ripping places apart.

Then, one night, Eric turned up
at my home.

"I've got a surprise for you," he said,
with a grin like a Cheshire cat.

"What?" I asked him.

He was all secretive and wouldn't
tell me.

"Come out to my car and I'll
show you," he said.

I went, he opened his boot, and
there was a 56lb sack of something.

"What's that," I asked.

"Casein!" he said, triumphantly.

"Oh... you... star!" I said.

I was over the moon.

I couldn't believe it. I'd spent the entire winter trying to get hold of casein
and Eric had found it in the factory next door to where he worked. I didn't
understand why a plastic-injection moulding factory would have casein, but who
cared! We finally had the gear and now we could rip lakes apart.

I made up a recipe similar to one of Fred's, but I couldn't get one of the
ingredients exactly the same so I was anxious about how effective the bait would
be. It was the close season and we were having hot weather so I made up a test
batch of bait and took it down to my old hunting ground, Rayleigh Angling Club.
I was no longer a member so I climbed over the fence, threw in some floating crust,
and soon had the fish taking it. Then, I got my new bait out which I hadn't boiled,
but just made into a paste. I pulled small bits off, flattened them into 10p-sized
pieces, and threw them out so they would drift and waft slowly down in the water.
Within minutes, I had the carp feeding avidly. It was like feeding time in a trout
stew pond. I thought the casein worked – at last, we had *the* bait!

This same day, the missing ingredient turned up by way of a small sample in
the post, so I knocked up another batch and the next day, I went back to Rayleigh
Angling Club. Soon, I had them going again on the crust, so I started flicking out

my pieces of flattened paste, but they ignored it. As I threw a piece in, a carp would come swiftly over but as it got close, it would turn. Not one piece was taken. I was gutted and bewildered, but I was convinced that it wasn't the new ingredient that had caused this reaction and this was proven the next evening when I was back with test batch number three, minus the new ingredient. The carp, again, completely ignored it.

That night, I wrote a letter to Fred explaining that I'd acquired a sack of casein from a plastics factory and related the details of my testing at Rayleigh Angling Club. A few days later, I got a letter back from Fred with the answer. My casein was inedible. There are many grades of casein and some that are inedible are used in the production of plastics and glue. I was really disappointed but Fred, bless him, made my day. At the end of the letter he offered to supply me with some of his own casein, and a week later, a big cylindrical tube of the highest human food grade casein arrived. Now, finally, I could use HNVs, but there was still that niggling doubt about the new ingredient, so I had to be sure. I jumped over the fence of Rayleigh Angling Club that evening and baited.

The next day I was back and the reaction was immediate. The carp gorged themselves on the paste and I realised what had happened previously. I had flavoured the original paste with Lane's strawberry flavouring so that when I first offered it to the carp they had hit on the flavour only. Then, when they tried to digest it, their bodies told them that it was crap (does a carp get the shits?) and when I went back on the second day, they wouldn't eat it. With the new version that I'd baited, they'd got on it and loved the stuff. I had the proof that the bait was proper. I was up and running and ready to hit the lakes.

Chapter Five

Star Lane and the HNVs

I n my class at college, where I did day release for my engineering apprenticeship, I got to know a lad called Max. It didn't take long to discover that he was also a fisherman, and although not a serious one like me, he was on a serious water. I'd heard of Star Lane through customers in the tackle shop, although none of them fished it, and it was spoken of in hushed tones. Primarily known as one of the best big tench waters in the area, there were also suggestions that it held monster carp.

The guys who told me about Star Lane had fished it when their club, Prittlewell, had control, but they lost it and then the police took it over. When the police took control of a water in this area, you had little chance of getting in unless you were a copper or a fireman. There was a bigger problem than that, though - Rick Gibbinson, who it seemed, used to have a position of authority within the police club and, I was to learn, had a problem with carp anglers!

I asked Max how the hell he'd got on the Lane and he explained that he was an apprentice at the brickworks, who owned the lake, and what was more, his father was the works' foreman. All employees of the brick works, their families and nearby local residents could obtain a permit to fish the lake.

"I don't suppose your dad would be interested in adopting me, would he?" I asked Max.

"I don't think we need to go as far as that, Kev," he replied, laughing. "My dad's well in with the boss, he's a family friend. I'll ask him for you."

Sure enough, the next time I went to college, Max had been as good as his word and slipped three orange cards across the desk. We were in! Eric, Bob, and I were in the Star Lane Works Fishery Club!

It was a month into the season when we got our tickets and we popped down to Star Lane on that warm July evening. There was one guy fishing on a point, in a camping tent, and by his rod set-up we could see that he was a carper. He treated us with great suspicion and at first was very guarded. He told us he was tench fishing. We allayed his fears by saying that we worked at the brickworks and did a bit of float fishing, and I asked him animatedly about the bream, then, acting a bit thick, I questioned him about what else was in the lake. Eventually, we got him chatting a bit and he admitted that there were big carp and they were what he was fishing for.

"I've been carping on here for a few years," he said, "along with several others, but I've yet to catch one."

"Any been out recently," we asked him innocently, trying to show only the vaguest of interest.

"There were two out on opening day, but none since," he said.

"Cor!" I said. "What were they caught on...and how big?"

"Potato," he said. "A 21 and a 19."

'Wow!' I thought. 'Big carp, and caught on potato! These guys are well behind on the bait scene'.

BELOW
*My 70s set-up on
Star Lane.*

At that time, there were probably fewer than half a dozen waters that I knew of in Essex that had done a 20, and it seemed that with our HNV baits we were in with a very real prospect of catching, so we were all well excited as we wished him luck and made our way back to the car.

We hatched a plan. We would bait the lake with Fred's HNVs for a week and then try our luck. In those days, you rarely fished for carp without first going on a baiting campaign and you would never expect to catch much unless you did. We got into a routine and every evening was spent bait making. Bob and Eric would come to my house, where we would make up a 12-egg mix, and hand roll our HNVs, which I had decided would be flavoured with Lane's strawberry. It smelt gorgeous, and together with the milk proteins, it had a creamy back smell, like strawberries and cream. Bait making was time consuming because there were no guns and rolling tables and it would take several hours to mix, roll and boil a 12-egg mix.

ABOVE
Eric with the Star Lane 20, caught within ten minutes of our first session on the lake.

I would take the baits to work in the morning, and as Star Lane was only a 20-minute drive from where Bob and I worked, and we had an hour for dinner break, we would shoot over to the Lane, bait up, and be back just in time to clock on for the afternoon shift. We were all really excited about the prospect of catching a 20 during the following few months, and dreamed that maybe one of us would be lucky enough.

The following Friday, Bob and I finished work at 4pm, as usual, and were soon down on the lake where Eric was just getting his rods set up. We didn't have any clue about the lake or where to start, but on our initial walk around, we'd each selected a swim, which we had baited throughout that previous week. I was in a lovely bay, with Eric further around to my right, off a point, and Bob around the far bank, midway down the lake. There were no ready-rigged rods at this time, so setting up was quite a slow process, and I was just threading a line through the rings of my third rod, when I heard a shout from Eric, who had cast out no more than 10 minutes before.

I ran round to his swim, to see his rod with a healthy curve and a little later, slipped the net under a carp, thinking 'that is bloody big'. The carp, a mirror, pulled the scales round to 22lbs and we were all shocked to catch such a monster and so quickly, within only ten minutes of being on this new water.

While we were taking the photos, a guy came round who was fishing further down the lake and had spotted Eric in action. I'll never forget his face and his reaction. He almost shouted at us, he was so frustrated.

My first carp from Star Lane, 16lbs.

Any angler feels lucky to catch a fully-scaled, but when it's only your second-ever 20....

ABOVE
*A Star Lane trio caught
on Strawberry HNVs.*

BELOW
*...with photos of over
40 doubles, my 20lb
fully-scaled, and a winter
common of 20lbs. I was
the centre of attention
and it felt good.*

waded out, launched into the water, and pointed myself in the direction of the stranded carp. I was thrashing my arms like a demented helicopter so my swimming technique could hardly be described as graceful, but I got to the fish to find that the line was trapped under a solitary big rock sitting on top of the gravel hump. I released the line, propelled myself back to the bank, took the rod from Eric and soon I had that carp in the net, and what a carp! I'd never seen anything quite like it. Its body was completely covered in scales, but not symmetrical like on a common. It was as if the gods had grabbed a handful of golden scales and thrown them at this carp's body, to stick there in a random pattern that reflected the sun's rays, making it shine like a jewel.

Any angler feels lucky to catch a fully-scaled, but when it's only your second-ever 20 – and a 20 then was the equivalent of a 40 now, at least – it doesn't get much better than that.

The action kept going until the lake froze in the January. This was winter fishing of a level that I can only have dreamed about. We were going down to Star Lane two or three evenings a week after work. We didn't feel it was necessary to fish through the night, but we didn't have to anyway because a picture soon developed; all the action came within four or five hours of dusk. The fishing was

just as good as the summer, just more condensed into shorter periods, and we had multiple catches in an hour or two. I remember one night when Bob had four big carp in 50 minutes. That would be considered pukka fishing, even now.

I went to a BCSG meeting in the March, with photos of over 40 doubles, my 20lb fully-scaled, and a winter common of 20lbs. I was the centre of attention and it felt good.

Chapter Six

Boreham Mere and the Woods Lake Betrayal

We couldn't wait to get back on the Lane the following year, and as it turned out we felt no need to be there for the start as we would now have the lake to ourselves. The previous season when we had first got on Star Lane, word had spread like wildfire when we'd turned up and Eric had caught the 20 within minutes. Several police members were fishing in the ensuing weeks and they watched us all catch big carp, while they blanked – it was clear by their attitude towards us that they were not happy.

One evening, I was set up in my favourite bay, sitting there with eyes glued to my bottle tops, when a guy came strolling purposefully toward me, and announced himself.

"Hello," he said. "I'm Rick Gibbinson."

There was a long pause, as if he was waiting for that to sink in, and for me to be impressed. Well, it didn't, and I wasn't. I'd no idea who this guy was and that I was talking to the brother of Jim Gibbinson, one of the greatest carp anglers of modern times and a lovely man, to boot. Rick gave the impression that he felt he should be equally well known. The conversation was relatively short.

"This is a police water. What are you doing here?" he said.

"I'm in the Star Lane Works Club," I replied.

"Do you three work at the brick plant, then?" Rick asked.

"No," I said. "A friend got us tickets."

Rick was not impressed.

"We only allow people who actually work in the brickfield to fish here." he retorted. "I'm going to get you off."

I was gutted. I'd managed to get on the dream water, had been experiencing the dream, and now it was a nightmare. Rick Gibbinson was going to get us chucked off.

I was so upset that I couldn't fish any longer, so I packed up and went round to Max's house. I was standing on his doorstep telling him about it, when his dad came to the door; Max still lived at home at the time. His dad was annoyed when he heard me retell my story.

"We'll see who gets chucked off!" he said.

Sure enough, he was true to his word and Rick and the rest of the police got chucked off the Lane. I have to say here, that although it seems I'm having a pop at Rick, I've known him for a lot of years now, and there was a moment when we joined up to try to sort out the problems of a club power struggle on another lake. I'm just recounting events as they happened, how I saw them, and at the end of the day, Rick was a copper all his working life. Once a copper, always a copper, eh, Rick?

So, now we had one of the best carp waters around to ourselves. Does it get any better than that? In fact, the only other guy I can recollect fishing that second season was 'Terry the Tench', as I nicknamed him, a guy from the village who also

BELOW
*The beautiful
Boreham Mere.*

had a brickworks permit. He owned a bookmaker's in Westcliff, and for whatever reason, he never took the carp on but was more than happy catching the specimen tench. He had a big soft spot for me and even if he wasn't fishing, he would always pop over, seek me out for a chat, and sometimes, he'd present me with a brown paper bag.

To mount our baits on the hook we used needles designed for threading line through dead baits. They were about six inches long with one end bent over to form a big loop, and we found them ideal for passing the line through our baits, tying a hook on and then pulling it in to conceal it. I used to put the needles down in the long grass and lose one after another. Terry, bless him, would visit my swim after I'd fished it, and hunt around for lost needles until he had a collection, which he would then return to me in the brown paper bag.

So, with the second season on Star Lane coming up and finding ourselves in the amazing position of having one of the best carp waters in Essex for virtually our own exclusive use, we felt no pressure to be there and instead we elected to start the season on another lake I had my eye on - Boreham Mere.

I already knew that the Mere held carp, but my interest was further triggered by a Chelmsford AA newsletter that I was shown. On the front page was a photo; a row of about half a dozen guys, all dressed up in 'the gear' - green hats and camo jackets - and each one was holding a good carp. It was an amazing picture and I'd never seen anything quite like it.

It turned out that they were all members of a specimen group, and later on, two of them would become good friends, brothers, Kevin and Brian Ash. Kevin was to drift out of fishing, but Brian remains as keen as ever. In fact, over the years, we bumped into each other as a new big fish came up and I always knew that one of the first anglers I'd see when moving to a new big fish water would be Brian Ash.

So, my mind was made up. All the pictured carp were doubles, and some looked to be good doubles, and I also knew that Boreham Mere had produced a carp of the magic weight, 20lbs. So I put it to Bob and Eric, and they were equally enthusiastic. We would start the season on Boreham Mere.

We felt confident that anything was possible with the HNVs. It was becoming very clear that when we baited a water, the carp got on to our baits in double quick time and, equally amazing for those days, it was the bigger fish that we caught first. It was as if they saw the benefits of our baits and so were first to get on them. The same pattern had emerged on several waters that we'd fished, and Star Lane had really nailed it. The first carp that Eric caught was actually the biggest of the four 20s in there, so I felt we could take on more than one challenge.

There was another water that had caught my eye, but I knew nothing about it, and didn't know anyone who did, so maybe that's why I didn't take is as seriously as Boreham Mere, which was a 'proper' carp water. Oh, how I rued the day! I had seen a photo of a float angler holding a carp, and it was a monster. It was claimed that it weighed 29lbs and it may well have been the largest carp in Essex at the time, or if it wasn't the largest, it was certainly right up there. I can't understand now, why I didn't totally focus on it, but there you go.

Anyway, as well as baiting Boreham Mere, we also chose to bait Woods Lake, Corringham, the water where the 29-pounder was caught, and if that wasn't enough, we decided to bait Star Lane as well. I can still see my kitchen with piles of eggs and the base-mix powder on every flat surface, including the floor. For the six weeks of the close season running up to June 15th, if I wasn't working or sleeping, I was rolling bait, or driving to lakes to put it in.

Hardcore carpers were beginning to focus on carp tackle. We were reaching out to explore carp lakes, which also led to taking on bigger waters and feeling the need to cast further than was possible with the Mark 4 rod set-ups. I started to visit Essex Angling, a new tackle shop in Leigh, and there was a guy in there, Bill Roberts, a rod builder who had become legendary for his rod development and who had previously worked at one of the most famous shops of its day – Goings of Southend. Actually, Goings was especially known for their sea rods, but Jim Gibbinson was to put his name to The Clooper, a carp rod that they produced in the '70s.

The beachcaster scene was big along the Essex and Suffolk coasts and because of the shallow beaches you had to get out a long way into the deeper water where the fish were. Anglers really got into it, finding ways to cast further and further, and because we went sea fishing in the winter, we got into it as well. It became a natural progression to cross over the emerging beachcasting technology into carp fishing.

I had sold off my Mark 4s, and was now experimenting with glass-fibre bass rods which were considerably more powerful, and by Christ, could they launch a bait and a lead, by comparison to the soft, through-action Mark 4s. With the development of the rods came the necessity to look at our end tackle.

Free-lining was still the preferred method of fishing, when the only tackle on your line was a hook, tied to the main line, and anglers would mould their paste baits around the hook. With hard baits such as potatoes, or in my case, the HNVs, we would pass the line through the bait with a needle, tie on the hook and pull the hook back into the bait. If you really had to punch the bait out, then you would put a cushion of something, like a piece of grass stalk, under the bend of the hook to stop the hook splitting the bait on the cast.

Any resistance on the line, such as a weight, had been looked upon at as taboo until now. It was believed that if carp detected the faintest resistance they would drop your bait, but with the more powerful rods there simply wasn't enough weight in the bait, so carp anglers started to use Arlesey bombs, tied running-link, leger-style. This set-up was relatively resistance free and appeared to offer no concerns to the carp, and it enabled us to optimise on the more powerful rods and get our baits out further than we had previously dreamed possible. It's mad when I think back to our mindset in those days!

Another thing we avoided at all costs was extra knots. If I fished a running rig now, the lead would butt up against a buffer bead that would, in turn, be stopped at a swivel to which would be knotted my main line and hooklink. I came up with a leger stop that didn't need a swivel, and it was the subject of the first article I had published in an angling publication - the BCSG magazine, 'Carp'.

I cut up a used biro tube into inch lengths, heated up one of my baiting needles and passed the needle through the bore and out of the wall of the biro tube at each end. Threading my link leger onto the main line, I then mounted the tube by passing my main line through the bore and out of the hole, wrapped it a few times around the outside of the tube, and then at the other end, passed it back through the hole and out of the bore. Then I tied my hook on at the required distance from my biro stop. It worked brilliantly. It would get somewhat

BELOW
*Early 70s running rig
with minimal resistance.*

distorted during a battle with a hard-fighting carp, but it was never a point of weakness.

As I'm writing this, I look back to those days with tremendous affection. It was great. Quite literally there was virtually no tackle available for carp anglers, and what there was, you certainly wouldn't use today. We were pioneering every aspect of carp fishing from learning how to catch, to the baits, to the tackle. It was quite literally a blank canvas from a design point of view. Rod holdalls were tiny, tubular affairs, capable of taking a couple of rods, a pair of banksticks, and the smallest of umbrellas. If you were lucky, the weight of the umbrella wouldn't cause the strap to break!

The best was a roll-up holdall, made by Efgeeco, the foremost luggage brand in its day, and comprised a flat piece of canvas with pockets at the bottom into which you put your rods, tied them in with tapes two-thirds of the way up, and then rolled the canvas up in the same way as a tool roll. You could get six rods in, which was great, but the D ring on the shoulder strap was not welded, and so it would prise open and the strap would fall off. The umbrella and bank sticks, which went into exterior pockets, would break through the bottom of the pockets, because all that formed them was a patch of leather on the bottom. The points on banksticks and umbrellas would work through the stitching between the patch and the canvas, and you would constantly be walking along picking up banksticks or your umbrella - that is if the bloody shoulder strap hadn't broken first.

It's just struck me that I made my first holdall at the age of 17, and in making this homemade holdall I learned lessons that we use on Nash produced holdalls years later. My first roll-up took the entire close season weekend evenings to make. The canvas I had bought was quite thick, and I also used leather for the patching, so my mum's sewing machine didn't stand a chance! I hand-stitched the whole thing with a leather needle, and it was hard work, I can tell you. I had sore thumbs and palms for months because of the effort of pushing the needle though tough materials.

However, the lessons I learned of how to make pockets so that the contents couldn't break out, stand to this day. I formed an envelope of leather at the bottom, rather than just a patch stuck on to the base of the canvas. Then, I stitched half of the leather patch with the pocket facing downwards (the wrong way) to the base of the canvas, then folded it over so that the pocket was now in place. This made a leather envelope inside the pocket, which was then stitched down along the sides and bottom, a guarantee that no sharp point could break through the stitching. That holdall lasted me for many years; until I made the first Happy Hooker holdall, in fact, and I greatly regret that I didn't keep that item of Nash Tackle history.

Clothing was a big issue in those days. Our source for clothing was the ex-army shops – tank suits and parkas being the favoured garments. A tank suit was exactly what it says; a canvas, one-piece suit that tank operators wore. Mine had a connector in it which was used to connect a pipe to the tank's heating system, but without the tank, and the pipe, the tank suit was about as much good as a chocolate fire guard, insulation wise.

Army parkas weren't a lot better. I remember waking up just as dawn was breaking while doing a night at Lake Meadows. I had slept out, and was white with frost. I couldn't feel my legs, arms, or anything else, come to that. It took me some time to stand, and I only got my circulation going after I had run around the whole lake three times. Thinking back, we were lucky not to have suffered hypothermia.

I decided to make my own one-piece suit, and I did it a couple of years before the first one-piece fishing suit was brought out by a company called Partridge. I bought a sleeping bag from a camping shop, a space blanket, (the aluminium foil survival blankets they use to retain the body heat of casualties,) plus a few metres of green, industrial nylon material. I cut the sleeping bag up into pattern pieces, stitched similar shaped pieces of space blanket to the sleeping bag sections, and then sewed it up. Then I made an outer shell of industrial nylon and fixed it all together.

That suit was a revelation! It was like walking around in a sleeping bag, which I guess it was. There were a couple of disadvantages, though; because of the tinfoil-like lining of the space blanket, you could hear me walking around from miles away, plus it was impossible to sleep in. If I didn't cook, being like a trussed-up chicken wrapped in tinfoil, the slightest movement in my sleep sounded like a herd of elephants rampaging through a field of tin cans. It was a step forward, though, and I was especially proud when later I complemented my suit by making a pair of boots to go with it; if you like, your early moon boots. This innovative footwear was, in effect, platform shoes with a sleeping bag stuck on the top; very cosy, but the devil to walk in.

Really, looking back I made everything except hooks, line and reels. I was moving away from my trusty MK4s, and building my own rods, and it wasn't long

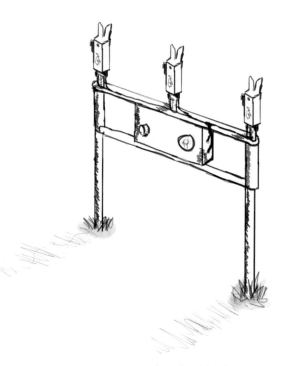

before I started doctoring my bite alarms. The Heron bite alarm was the only device available at the time and it was a crude affair of an antenna in a case, and shaped to a V to accommodate your rod. The line would go around the antenna, which was set off-centre, and if you had a run, this would pull the antenna toward the centre where it would close a relay, making the electrical circuit via a cable from your head, back to a white box with an old mechanical buzzer and a light bulb.

The cables, just like extension boxes nowadays, were always a pain. You could trip over them, or if the swim was muddy you had yards of messy cable to clean up at the end of the session. So, I came up with an idea; I made a bar that had three threads on it to screw my Herons into, one at each end and one in the centre. Attached on the underside of this bar was a box, and there was another bar below the box. Out of the two ends of the bar were two spigots, and inside the box I fitted a GPA speaker, a volume control, and my electronics. I passed cables from the box through the top tube, coming out at each end, and the centre one below the three threaded bosses, and then fitted Jack plugs to the cables, which plugged into the Herons. I took two bank sticks, cut the threads off the ends and by pushing the two banksticks into the ground and locating the ends into the spigots, I had an awesome, rock-solid set-up. Nowadays, they would call that a goalpost. I often thought of incorporating the electronics into a buzzer bar – just think what cute little heads you would have! I guess someone will do it now that I have written about it.

Landing nets were another big issue. The only commercially available one was, again, produced by Efgeeco. It had 36-inch arms which were solid aluminium and while the pole was tubular it might as well have been a solid bar it was that heavy, and the thick mesh didn't help either - that alone must have weighed about 4lbs! If you hooked a carp, you would need a couple of mates to lift this net and to land it for you so I machined up an aluminium spreader block and glued in a fibreglass pole and arms. Compared with the Efgeeco nets, mine was feather-light, and most importantly it was user-friendly. I ended up making a hundred of these, for friends and carp anglers who had seen mine when we were fishing the same lakes.

All kinds of theories and ideas were tried and one of the crazier ones that I experimented with was loading my rods with mercury. The theory behind this was that the mercury would be in the butt and as I compressed the rod, and followed the cast through, the liquid mercury would flow up the rod, increase the weight of the tip and thus the power, in the same way as a slide hammer does – well, that was the theory, anyway. It was a bit like having six ounces of molten lead inside your blank.

To test my theory, I first had to overcome a big problem and that was obtaining the mercury. It's not only highly poisonous but also highly expensive and with limited applications. I'm not quite sure how it came about, but someone knew someone, who knew someone else, who worked in a dentist and apparently, dentists use mercury for fillings. I still don't know how it's used, or why, because it's about as poisonous as cyanide, but whatever. Soon, I was the proud possessor of a pint of the stuff, which I poured into the butts of my one-piece, 11-foot bass rods.

I felt sure that this was going to be awesome. It would put miles on my cast, and I visualised the mercury flying up the rods, increasing the tip speed phenomenally as I hammered out my baits. I couldn't wait to try out the theory on the carp, but as it was the middle of winter I settled for a piking session at Abberton, the massive reservoir dug to provide drinking water to south-east Essex.

All my friends watched with interest as I swung a dead bait over my shoulder and launched it with all the power I could muster. The rod went through its arc and the mercury flew up the blank with such force that it blew the tip ring off and followed itself through, straight into the reservoir. I kept my head low and my eyes on the news for weeks after that, but thankfully, I never heard of a mysterious bout of mercury poisoning from our county's drinking water.

There was a craze for one-piece rods, because we figured that some of the action and distance was taken out of the rod by putting a spigot joint in it, so we'd drive around to lakes with our rods tackled up and the reels left on. We'd have one-piece, 11-foot rods strapped to the roofs of our cars, sprayed up with camo paint, and in my case, I'd found some huge three-inch butt rings. I cut the ring off the colossal foot/cradle, turned up a neat little male/female thread, and brazed that to a standard ring foot, so that I could screw them on.

Did my set-up look cool, or what! Everyone who came round stopped in their tracks and looked at it when I was fishing; rods at waist height, with three-foot drops, a bottle top with an isotope sticking out, and an immensely tapered rod. At the butt end they probably weren't far off an inch and a half, and with the camo'd paint job, camo'd Mitchell reels and the three-inch butt rings, they did look the part and capable of casting to the moon.

That was how I set up on the afternoon of June 15th on Boreham Mere, sharing a swim with a carp angler with whom I'd kept in touch since the Rayleigh Angling Club days. You'll understand as you read on that it's best I don't reveal his name so let's refer to him as 'The Noddy'. He was always in the tackle shop and occasionally we socialised with our ladies. He was still carp fishing but was never really successful, mainly because he didn't keep up with developments, like keeping ahead with the baiting technology scene as I did, so he struggled to catch. He also did a lot of sea fishing, which was his other passion.

His wife was of Jewish descent, and it was her wish to go to Israel, I guess to get closer to and understand her roots and culture, so they were going to spend at least a year on a kibbutz. He was really in two minds about this, and clearly felt that he'd miss his fishing, so as a kind of goodbye gesture, I thought it would be great to let him fish with our team and have the opportunity to catch some great carp before he went off on his travels. It could be that I'd never see him again. Bob and Eric weren't particularly enamoured of this individual so it took a bit of persuading, but eventually they agreed reluctantly to him joining our team.

We were so excited as dusk drew in and the time was ticking toward midnight. Out in front of us was the Mere's island, and between the island and us, just off its margin, it was like a Jacuzzi as fish bubbled and fed avidly on our baits. Rods were cast out bang on the midnight start and at 12.30am, my Heron screamed, (did they scream or did they squawk?) the bottle top glided smoothly up toward the butt ring, I struck, and my rod hooped over into a healthy curve. I

BELOW
The shallows at Boreham Mere.

was in, and obviously to a good carp. Then the tip sprung back, the hook had pulled out and that was it for the session, well, carp-wise, anyway. For the rest of the night, bottle tops were going up and down like yo-yos. We were striking like demented lunatics and I think we landed four fish that night; green things with red eyes. We were well and truly tenched out!

We hadn't learned yet about boiling our baits so hard that tench would find them difficult to eat, but doing that wouldn't have worked

anyway. At this time, we were pre-hair rig or side-hooking, and we completely buried a hook in the bait to hide it. Our baits had to be soft-skinned enough to pull hooks through; after all, if the carp could detect the hook in any way, you'd never get a bite – or that was the thinking back then, and in retrospect I probably lost that carp, and others, because we overlooked the issue of pulling the hook out of the bait with our new long-range set-ups.

Boreham Mere turned out to be my jinx water. A week later, on a lovely sunny day, I was up in the shallows and looking for carp. As well as baiting with bottom baits, we'd been feeding floater cake in during the close season, and I had really got the carp going on it, despite the lake's other carp anglers telling me, 'they'll never take floating crust here, mate'. How many times have I heard that since!

I spotted two enormous commons sitting deep in a hole in the weed, maybe three or four feet down from the surface. We reckoned they were both 20s and the bigger one was an absolute monster of about 25lbs. I hooked on a corner of a floater cake - the toughest and biggest piece, at that, because casting free-line was going to push the limits of my cast; we never used or even considered controllers back then. I made it out there, though, and the strawberry-flavoured HNV cake put down a few inches into the surface weed on the other side of the hole where the carp were sitting. I inched it back until it settled in the hole.

Bob was alongside me watching through binoculars.

"Kev!" he said, excitedly. "The bigger one - it's coming up!"

I saw its shoulders break the surface as Bob screamed, "Strike! Strike!"

I struck with all the force I could muster and the water erupted as the big common torpedoed across the surface, scything through the weed in a desperate attempt to get out into the main lake. My clutch screamed and then stopped abruptly. The line went slack and I reeled in a hook, still with the floater cake attached. The point had barely gone through. The barb was still in the cake and I hadn't managed to pull the hook out of the cake properly to hook this monster.

That was the last carp that I was to hook at Boreham Mere until I returned several years later, but 'The Nod' was more fortunate. One morning, he got the carp taking floater and caught a mirror of 20lb 2oz, which was only the second 20 ever to be caught from Boreham Mere at that time; again, testament to the results of our awesome strawberry HNV bait.

Bob, Eric and I left the Nod to plug away for a few more weeks at Boreham before he also gave up. Clearly, we hadn't got it right on the Mere. We hadn't boiled the baits hard enough, so only a few of the carp had got on our HNVs and all we really managed was to feed the big head of tench. We were getting fed up with catching them, especially knowing that we had Woods and Star Lane to have a go at, so we pulled off the Mere and turned our attention to Woods.

My first session on Woods was in a swim with the end point of the island in front of me. In those days, there were certain rules of etiquette that don't seem to apply nowadays. If an angler was baiting a particular swim, then other carpers would keep well away from it, and it was no different with me, Bob and Eric. If any of us were baiting a swim, the others wouldn't fish it, so I concentrated on a swim out to the pointy island and Bob and Eric had their fancied swims, too. It was a red-hot sunny day, one of those days when you don't expect much on bottom baits until the sun starts to go down. Nonetheless, I had a screamer and soon landed a common, a long, lean fish of 10lbs or so, and later that afternoon, I caught another one of 6lbs, so the omens were good.

While I was at home that night, The Nod came round and explained that before he left for Israel, he wanted to have a final goodbye fishing session with an old mate. The Nod hadn't joined Woods so he asked if I would lend him my ticket and get one off Bob or Eric for his mate, so they could do a night there. I was a bit reluctant to do this and knew Bob and Eric wouldn't be happy, either, mainly because The Nod had declined to join Woods so had taken no part in our close season baiting efforts. Nonetheless, he softened me up and eventually, I agreed and told him the three swims we were baiting and fishing, so that he would avoid them.

I was at work a few days later when he came in to see me, all excited, after his previous night's session on Woods. He had caught the big mirror of 29lbs and some ounces, and then he went on to tell me something that left me in complete bewilderment, disbelief, and growing anger. To make matters worse, he said it so nonchalantly; he just didn't get it.

Firstly, he told me that he'd caught the carp from the very swim I'd been baiting, and then he dropped the bombshell. He'd let a certain individual take this fish away to his own private lake, and in return, he would be allowed to fish the lake himself. It was rumoured that this water was stuffed full of carp, and because only the owner fished for them, they were amazingly easy to catch.

I was beyond speech and couldn't believe his treachery. How could he stitch me up and so selfishly blow mine, Eric's and Bob's chances, not to mention other Essex anglers who would now never be able to catch that carp. In fact, I ended up having a big row with Bob and Eric, and it nearly split up our team because, as they pointed out, they hadn't wanted him to join us in the first place.

The Nod was to repeat the exercise later, with what may have been the Essex record at the time. I say 'may' because the paradox is that this saga bit The Nod in the arse. It could well be that he broke the Essex record when he investigated a report by his brother that there were big carp trapped in a pool at a local gravel pit during a drought. The Nod caught a huge carp, allegedly, but he couldn't keep his mouth shut and it leaked out that this fish also had 'walked' to the same lake as the Woods carp.

ABOVE
I landed four carp, two over 20lbs and another two 20s the following week.

However, a well-respected angler, who was a friend of the private lake owner, got mixed up in it. He was worried that his own reputation would become tarnished, so possibly to save his embarrassment, he discredited the claim by saying that the fish had died a week or so after its move, and had weighed some 8lbs less. This raised questions about whether the carp had truly been as big as The Nod maintained. Whatever, the weight was irrelevant, but my relationship with The Nod had been seriously fractured.

Author's note: This book, in a small way, documents some of the carp fishing history in Essex, so I believe that it's only proper that the weight of The Nod's carp should be fully scrutinised. At the time, Malcolm Freund, the manager of the tackle shop in Rayleigh where I'd worked was a good friend of mine, and The Nod's, and I consider him to be honest. When The Nod caught his carp, he rang Malcolm who went out

for the weigh-in and photos, although when I recently discussed this with Malcolm, his recollection of the weight was different to that claimed by the Nod. Nonetheless, it was still a monster carp. I'll just say that I trust Malcolm and so it's my belief that The Nod did catch an absolutely monstrous carp, for its time.

It's funny how carp travel around, even to this day. I had done some research on the Woods Lake mirror and had noted how strange it was that this fish was such an exceptional size compared to the other residents. There was a pond next to a fire station in Hadleigh, Essex, from which they used to fill up the pumps and when the pond was eventually drained and filled in, they found one carp. How that carp had got in there is anyone's guess, but I wouldn't mind betting that one of the villagers had put it in there when it had outgrown its garden pond. This was the very same fish that was then taken to Woods Lake. Anyway, that was Woods blown; there was nothing much else in there beyond low doubles, so it was back on to Star Lane.

My first session at the Lane was on a Friday night and what a session! I landed four carp, two of which were over 20, and then I had another two 20s the following week. It turned out that our HNV baits had increased the weights of the carp in the Lane, and now eight of them were in the 20s! It seemed that luck had returned, or maybe the carp gods had decided I'd been tested enough with the sagas at Boreham Mere and Woods. I couldn't go wrong. I finished that year on Star Lane with ten 20s, eight different fish and two recaptures; a rare achievement in those days, but I didn't think much of it at the time. We didn't notify the angling press; we just fished for ourselves, and to gain credibility within the BCSG.

There was another important event that was to be significant on my journey toward understanding carp. I was in the health food shop, picking up some more Lanes' flavourings, and I started checking out all the beans and pulses that I'd walked past every time I went in there. I'd never seen chickpeas, black-eyed beans, red beans… before, and I thought, 'why not give them a try?' So to start with, I cleared the shelf of 20 or so bags of chickpeas and took them home to experiment. It's only just struck me how lucky I was! The pulse I'd picked just happened to be one of the best particles there is for relatively hard-bottomed gravel pits, which exactly described Star Lane.

The dried chickpeas were rock hard so I soaked them overnight, but they were still hard, so I boiled them. That didn't make a great deal of difference, but at least I could put a hook through. I baited with them for a week, in the same way as

OPPOSITE PAGE
Probably two of the first carp to be caught in the UK on chickpeas.

we had with the HNVs, and then gave it a try. I hadn't had a rod out five minutes before it roared off and soon I had a good double on the bank, and I was to get three more that night. I told Bob and Eric of my success, gave them some chicks from my bucket, and they both caught first time.

The HNV results had been petering off, so we all switched to chickpeas, we had a couple of great months' fishing, and we never blanked. Those carp loved the chicks. Then, just as with the HNVs, the run rate dropped and instead, I kept getting twitches. I tried striking at some to no avail, put it down to tench and assumed that the bait had blown.

One night, my mum dished up some beef and tomato soup. It tasted really good and as I was eating it, I wondered what would happen if I cooked my chick peas in soup. So I boiled up a big saucepan of chickpeas with beef and tomato soup and some red cochineal colouring. The results were epic; bright red chickpeas that smelled lush, all beefy and tomato flavoured. The carp thought so, too. We were back into the runs – screaming takes, one after the other.

I was learning that the baits would blow and so when the runs were replaced by twitches, jerks and the odd take, I was better off switching baits to get the runs coming again. At this time, it just never occurred to us that there could be another way of keeping the takes going, but that was a lesson I was to learn in later years.

Chapter Seven

Braxted

Terry the Tench from Star Lane had several times referred to a reservoir in Braxted, a small village near Witham in Essex. He was a member of a London club, Barking AC, who leased this water and he told me that five years before it had been stocked with small carp, mainly of 3-4lbs and the odd one up to seven, he said. I assumed that, at best, there might be a few good doubles in there, so it wasn't really of interest to me, but then this water came up again.

In the BCSG, I'd become very friendly with Geoff Kemp, who was friendly with Bill Lovett. They both lived around the Harold Wood area and so found themselves at times on the same waters. While not necessarily fishing together, they kept in touch, and as Geoff and I became close, it followed that Bill and I connected up.

Bill told me about a water that another well-respected carp angler, Jimmy Eldridge, had mentioned, and that Bill and his friend, Bren, were going to bait. It was the reservoir that Terry the Tench had told me about. I told Bill that I didn't think there would be any carp approaching the magic 20lbs in there, and so I lost interest.

Bill and Bren targeted another water at the start of the season, but a couple of weeks in, Bren popped over for a day session on Braxted and in a few hours he'd caught a couple of good doubles and, for its day, a massive mirror of 27lbs-plus!

Bren would have been the first carp angler up on Braxted reservoir. It was controlled by Barking AC, which was one of the old-fashioned, coarse angling clubs that regularly held matches for the members. Quite how a London club so far away got the rights to a section of the Essex Blackwater and this reservoir, I haven't a clue, but it did work well for us, I realised later. We rarely saw any of the members, except on match days, from recollection one Sunday a month in the summer. The club had an old 1930s bus, which would clunk its way down to the Blackwater where they would hold the matches, and once every season they held a match on the reservoir.

It was funny; Braxted reservoir is on a hill, on farmland and accessed by a long concrete road. The first time I was up there when it was match day on the lake, I wondered what was happening. Gradually, I became aware of a noise. It was like the drone of bees at first, and so distant that I was hearing it almost subconsciously, and then it got louder and louder until suddenly, my mind snapped alert as a crescendo of metal studs hammering on concrete erupted in my ears. I shit myself. The last time I'd heard a similar sound it had been when 100 skinheads had chased my two mates and me up Pier Hill in Southend, but that's another story. Quite why studded waders, designed for salmon anglers wading in rivers, were the preferred choice of footwear of the Barking club match anglers, I have no idea.

BELOW
Braxted reservoir.

Anyway, Bren recounted the story of his big carp to Bill, who later rang to

tell me, and I was blown away. We didn't know of a bigger carp than 27lbs in Essex, other than at Layer Pits, which had produced a 30 to an angler fishing worm. Layer was a lake that I was fishing, on and off, but in those days, it held a very small head of carp which were seldom caught and it was also a challenge because you couldn't night fish. It was restricted to daytime fishing and a long drive for me, just to fish days. Braxted was also days, only much closer to home and the carp were unfished for, so I didn't even need to think about it.

Bill and I moved straight on to the res. Because of the naïvety of these previously uncaught Braxted carp, they were very receptive to our methods, and we had some great fishing that summer, with carp up to just over 20lbs. In fact, other than Star Lane, it was the best fishing I'd had, in terms of the numbers of big carp.

This carried on right up to the winter freeze-up when we jacked it in until the last few days of the season in March. We were hardly surprised that we blanked; the last gasp efforts we had every year in March always bore patchy results and really, it's no different today. The carp haven't properly woken up most years, unless there's an early winter.

The close season was a time of immense expectation as we planned a baiting campaign at Braxted res. This was my – and Bill's – mission, with Geoff Kemp on the periphery. It was still immensely difficult to find good bait ingredients, especially the essential casein, but we were making progress. One great ingredient came by way of Kempy's employment with Cow & Gate. If the Cow & Gate baby milk went out of date, it was effectively scrapped, so Geoff was able to get us good quantities of this baby milk and it became a basic ingredient of our HNVs.

The real break came, though, when Bill became lost in London while looking for a business premises and stopped at a phone box to check it out in the Yellow Pages. As he opened the directory he saw a page with an advertisement for a supplier of high- protein milk powder. By then, Bill had not only become a great salesman but he'd sharpened his blagging techniques, too, so he got on to the company and explained that he was setting up a production line to manufacture high-protein biscuits for athletes. The guy on the other end of the phone was immediately hooked and promised to send Bill a sample of their very best Irish lactic casein.

"Some sample," I suggested wryly to Bill when he showed me the 56lb sack he'd received. We added a cream flavour to our magical mix of nutritious ingredients, baiting commenced around mid-May and about 30 mixes were put in up to the start of the season. Looking back, that would have added up to no more than 5000 baits, or so; very little when compared to the volumes that we bait with today. If only, I'd realised then! Over the years, whenever an unfished carp water

came up, I'd observe that the biggest challenge was getting the carp to recognise that our baits were a food source. I'm convinced now that this was purely down to the volume; quite simply, we didn't introduce enough baits to get the carp on them.

We stuck to our baiting rota and either Bill or I would pop up to Braxted every other day to bait. Bill had elected to do the off at Braxted, but I didn't fancy it. I loved the traditional start and the build-up, arriving on the lake at least on the 15th, and getting set up with the growing anticipation of the midnight chuck.

As night fishing was positively banned at Braxted, I opened the year's campaign at Star Lane along with Geoff Kemp, and then late morning of the 16th, we pulled off and made our way to the res. I was quite content to have a few days on the Lane, but Geoff wouldn't have it and told me that he wasn't

staying a minute longer. Star Lane was a nightmare for mosquitoes, and I understand that it still is. To this day, I've never fished a water in the UK where the mosquitoes are such a problem, and it's not only the numbers, but their size - they are enormous, more like B52 bombers, and do they pack a punch! I guess over the years I have got used to them, if that's possible, but for Geoff it was a new experience and one that he couldn't hack. He got bitten to death, despite sleeping with a carp sack over his head. I did have to laugh at his swollen mess of a face when I saw him in the morning.

So, we pulled off, and when we arrived at the Res I was surprised at how quiet it was. There was just Bill and three other carpers, and one of them was the guy who had told Bill about Braxted, Jimmy Eldridge, who I'd never met. Bill was very happy with himself as he had landed an 18¾lb mirror, which was soon to be joined by a common of around 11lbs.

Meanwhile, this Jimmy Eldridge character and his two cohorts were having it off. I watched them from a distance; bottle tops going up and down like yo-yos, a twitch up, a twitch down, a twitch to the side, then whoosh! - a smooth glide into the butt ring and off it went. I lost count and as I packed up in the fading light, I reckoned that they must have landed at least a dozen carp. Bill had two; me and Kempy had blanked.

I went back to Star Lane to sulk and get my head round it, and meanwhile, Bill and Geoff went back to the res and Bill had a 15lb leather. That was the last carp we ever caught on the cream, a bait that had ripped other lakes apart.

I went back to the res a couple more times over the following weeks, but each time I had to put up with a blank while I watched Jim and his friends having it off. I couldn't buy a take. All I got was a series of twitches that never developed into a positive run. I tried striking at them but without success.

Later, I found out that the main reason for Jim and his friends' result was down to a massive baiting campaign, the likes of which we'd never seen or considered. Quite literally, they put tens and tens of thousands of boilies in, which if I recall, were based on Munchies cat biscuits. On open day alone, they baited up with 3,000 boilies. It was no wonder, the carp were so hooked and they caught so well, but it still didn't explain, to my mind anyway, why we couldn't get a take and instead the best interest we could expect from the carp was a two-inch twitch. Why didn't the twitches convert to screaming takes?

Bill disappeared to somewhere or other, leaving me and another guy I'd teamed up with, Phil Wilson, to try to figure out why we couldn't catch a carp when Jimmy and crew were God's gift, seemingly. Taking my lesson from Star Lane, I switched baits to my beloved chickpeas and I didn't mess about either, I went straight in with my number one chickpea flavour; the beef and tomato soup. This produced a handful of doubles for me, and then I was down to catching small carp, with loads of twitches in between.

Interestingly, and unbeknown to me at the time, Bill had moved back on to the res in the autumn with a similar idea to bait heavily with chicks. He set sail one night in a kid's Mickey Mouse dinghy so small that he couldn't sit in it and had to kneel, with a tennis racket stuck into a plastic bag as an oar. This blanket baiting of

chicks produced similar results to my soup chicks but after a few fish, Bill was back to twitches only. This res was really beginning to do my head.

Word was really getting out now. More and more anglers were hearing about Braxted res and it was only a matter of time before it was mobbed, so I made up my mind, despite this place continuing to kick me in the balls. I was going to sort it and catch the big mirror. Fellow BCSG member, Brad (as he was known), had moved on to the res by this time. I'd met him at Layer along with Stuart Demon. Stuart had caught a 30 at Layer, which at the time was the Essex record. He was a hippy-type guy, really laid back, and we were like chalk and cheese, but became really close friends. He decided to join me on the ressy for the start.

I commenced baiting it a month before with one of my favourite flavours, cherry, in an HNV mix. I had seen the effectiveness of Jimmy Eldridge's mass baiting, so while I couldn't match it in volume, I did my best. I rolled six mixes, three times a week, which would take me about six hours, and then drove up to the ressy, which took three-quarters of an hour, spent an hour putting it in and looking around, and then drove the three-quarters of an hour trip back. In short, I was putting in about 25 hours a week just baiting alone, but I was determined to make it happen. I gave some of the mix to Stuart who popped over a couple of times and baited so he could feel he'd done his bit. Mind you, I thought he cheated because his mix consisted of just ten baits the size of oranges. Clearly, he'd minimised his rolling time!

The opening started with a tense word when the secretary came stomping along the bank in his studded waders, suggesting that I'd started well before dawn. At what point the faintest glimmer of light qualifies as 'dawn' is a matter of interpretation, though, and I thought I'd smoothed him over.

Soon after, Stuart was into one and I couldn't believe it. He'd gone back in time. There was me, fishing my ultra-sensitive link leger rig, with the latest trend of black Spider Dacron hook links, so the carp wouldn't detect the mono line, and Stu's free-lining a cherry-flavoured boilie, but unlike my 'cherry-sized' ones, his was the size of an orange.

I slipped the net under his 18½-pounder, feeling a little miffed with him. We were supposed to be the ultra-cools, on the edge of the carping revolution and innovation, not fishing like Mr Crabtree from the 50s. I cheered up a little an hour later, when a much more intelligent carp of around 12lbs fell to my cutting-edge rig. After that it was all downhill, though. Stu punished me that day, landing two more doubles, but much worse was the fact that despite all the hours of effort, and pounds and pounds of bait I put in, we didn't catch another carp on the cherry mix. I have never applied myself so hard and invested so much time and money into catching carp, only to fail so dismally. I just didn't know what to do next. I did know that I needed my confidence back, though, so I pulled off in search of more well-adjusted carp that didn't have these mental issues.

I had other pressures, too. Strangely, a serious girlfriend ended up being the cause of a completely different source of pressure, hassle from tackle shops. I'd started a fishing tackle business with the ambiguous name 'Happy Hooker', which I'd taken from the title of a book written by an American prostitute. I was really into literature! The name that I chose for my 'business' gives you an illustration of how seriously I took the enterprise.

The story of Happy Hooker started when I went to a night club one night to meet up with a couple of mates after a football match. This time, we were there for the social and not the birds, but as always at the end of a club night, the slow songs would start and the crowd round the bar cleared as everyone rushed to the dance floor. I glanced up from my mate's Spurs v West Ham programme, and my eyes beheld a huge pair of breasts bulging out of a very tight dress. I could never resist buxom, shapely women, so I thought I'd go and introduce myself.

It turned out that Linda came from Chigwell, quite a trek just to see a bird. For me, that was a good hour's drive, but she was good company and I was intrigued by her so we started dating. Her father was very wealthy, which you had to be to live in Chigwell, and he'd financed her and her sister while they attended college to study textiles and design, and then bought them a shop where they produced haute couture ladies' wear. This business was never really successful for a couple of reasons; firstly because the two girls weren't early risers, and normally wouldn't set off for work until after 11am, and secondly, their 'couture' dress shop was next to a scrap metal merchants in Hackney. I have to say that I never saw many posh birds strolling down Hackney's Morning Lane!

One afternoon, I visited the shop and while waiting for her to finish up - after all, it was getting on for three o'clock and well after her normal going home time - I spotted a roll of black material. As black was the cool carp colour then, I went over to investigate and immediately noticed the open weave. We were using carp sacks made from industrial nylon, which were considered to be a significant improvement on the old hessian, potato sacks that carp anglers had used to retain their captives overnight. Hessian gave no oxygen or water flow, though, so there was always a risk that your carp would have suffocated by the morning. Industrial

nylon sacks with punched holes were a big step forward, but even so, my friend, Eric, had a carp die one night. I picked up on the potential of this seemingly strong nylon with a much looser weave than the industrial stuff and as I held it over Linda's sink in the shop kitchen and turned the tap on, the water just fell through it.

The next week, after some cajoling, I can tell you, because Linda and her sister had 'a blouse' to make and there just were not enough hours in the day, I got Linda to knock me up a couple of carp sacks. Then, I obtained some nylon cord and threaded them up but needed a device to close and secure the opening so I milled up a toggle at work from a piece of laminated, fibrous material – branded Tuflon - with two holes to lock the cord when I closed the sack opening.

My carp sacks were an immense success, far beyond my expectations, in fact. Eric and Bob watched me as I lifted my first carp in my new sack from the lake, and we all marvelled at how the water just fell out, whereas with industrial nylon sacks we'd have to wait minutes for it to drain. Eric and Bob were quickly on my back to make them sacks too. I just hoped that the blouse was nearly finished.

I'm only covering some of the more relevant waters in this book, but there were dozens of others that I fished, or visited briefly. In a way, me, Bob and Eric had become a bit of a hit team and it's probably fair to say that we may have been the first posse of carp anglers in Essex to visit waters, catch the carp in quite a short time and then move on. Anglers generally stuck to the same water for years because results were so meagre that it could take a very long time to come close to capturing a good number of your chosen lake's inhabitants.

That mindset changed for us, though, because of the baits; most notably, Fred Wilton's HNVs, but the particles also came in handy. We had a system that either worked, or it didn't. When it worked it was great. We'd arrive at a lake after baiting it for a week or two with the HNVs and start to catch from the off, and as we'd found previously, the early captures were often the lake's biggest carp. It really was plain to see that the largest carp in the lake had reached that size for a reason – they recognised a great food source and got on it first. We hit a number of waters and went straight into catching the lake's big fish, which got the locals twitching, I can tell you.

Conversely, we strangers could turn up at some lakes and blank, leaving the locals feeling rather smug. Half a dozen blanks were normally enough for us, though, and we'd move on. Looking back, it's easy to see why we weren't successful on all waters. It was simply down to location. We'd turn up cold on a new lake and bait the spots we fancied, without any previous reconnaissance to establish that the carp were regularly using those areas.

OPPOSITE PAGE
...so I pulled off in search of more well-adjusted carp that didn't have these mental issues...

So I was coming into contact with an unusually large number of that rarity of all fishermen, the carp angler, because of our being 'on tour' as it were. Carpers would see my sacks and straight away ask me if I would make some for them, so I saw the potential for an earner which was much needed at that time, I can tell you. This posh bird from Chigwell was expensive to run and never helped me out with the petrol.

Word spread on the carp grapevine. I started to get phone calls from carp anglers who were miles away, and I took a sample of my sack to a BCSG meeting. Everyone wanted them so I soon had a proper little venture going. I was doing a four-day week at work, which released me for three days fishing, and in the close season that meant I had three days a week to make carp sacks. When I started the carp sack business, Linda was quite enthusiastic to help so I'd go up with her to the shop on Friday morning, she would sew up the sacks and I would punch holes to further increase the water drainage, string them, fix the toggles and bag them up. She soon tired of this, though, partly because there was a hint of another 'blouse' in the pipeline, and I was struggling to get her help on the stitching side of things, so I got her to teach me how to sew.

I worked four days in the engineering factory, and drove up to Chigwell in the evenings to see Linda. Well, I have to confess here that Linda wasn't the main attraction; it was her mum's cooking. I'd worked out that the cost and aggravation of fending and cooking for myself didn't stack up with Linda's mum's great Italian fare. In fact, she was so good that I got her to teach me some of her best dishes which had been passed down several generations and I still have a bit of a reputation for my Italian cooking to this day.

On Fridays, when I wasn't working in the factory, I'd drive up to the shop in Hackney and more likely than not, I would be alone because with the blouse finished, the girls were happy to dwell on their success for the forthcoming months so I would cut and sew up my carp sacks and be back at Linda's in time for more of her mum's luscious food. We'd go out that evening, or stay in and watch TV, and at some time, Linda would go to bed. Then, my production line would commence in earnest and through the early hours of the morning, I would cut my drawstring cords to length, melt the ends of the nylon over a candle flame and then mould them into a point using my fingers. I can still feel the pain of that molten nylon. I'd thread up the sacks, attach the toggles, knot the cord behind the toggles so that they didn't come off, and often, Linda's mum would help me to fold them up and bag them. Really, Linda's mum was beyond price. Looking back now, I realise that I definitely looked a gift horse in the mouth. Not only was she an awesome cook, but she was also an insomniac and a great packer. I'd pulled the wrong bird – or maybe not. In the past, her husband had numbered the Krays among his acquaintances.

With the sacks all bagged up, I would grab a few hours sleep, then be up at 7.30am to start my round of delivering carp sacks to the ever-increasing number of shops in the Essex and London area who had contacted me for supply. Deliveries were done by 11am, and I'd be back just as Linda would be getting up.

This system worked well until the fishing season started, but then it was difficult to produce carp sacks, go carp fishing, and see Linda so something had to give. A decision had to be made. In retrospect, it should have been the bird, but I chose to shut down my carp sack production through the summer months. Shops were doing their nut, constantly ringing me for more supplies but I told them that I was sorry, I was too busy. The pressure grew as demand and my reputation spread, though, so as I didn't know where to turn, to find a solution to catch the reservoir carp, I figured that I was better off making some money, eating pukka Italian grub and getting some bird time.

The summer came to an end and the pressure from shops dwindled so my thoughts turned back to the res and soon, I was back with Bill and undertaking another baiting campaign - some people are gluttons for punishment. This time we were on a lovely, sweet, spicy-smelling flavour called Spice B, courtesy of Geoff Kemp. Bill did the honours of putting in a few hundred baits and then we fished and I have to say, from my point of view, without my usual confidence, so it was a pleasant surprise when we both caught a couple of fish that first session.

It was no surprise when a couple of sessions later the takes dried up and we were back to twitches again. It was on one of those lovely, mellow, sunny autumn days with carp occasionally showing in front of us, in some 12 feet of water, that Bill decided to try the old method of anchored bread crust. On this occasion, though, the bread was replaced with a piece from a loaf of Spice B-flavoured floater cake he had made the night before. He mounted a piece of cake onto his hook and with a three-foot hook link and a running lead, he cast it out, leaving his bail arm open so the cake would float up to the surface. His floater cake was around mid-water when suddenly, the cake was grabbed and line began to snake off his spool at a rate of knots.

Once Bill had overcome his surprise, with bail arm closed, his rod took on a satisfying curve and shortly afterwards I netted a double-figure common. "Jammy sod," I said, but another four carp later, I began to think otherwise. Bill and I couldn't wait to get back the next day and we were back on as the sun began to rise.

We had to be very careful using three rods on this water and at weekends it was just too risky, with barking mad committee members going out of their way to drive over in the forlorn hope of catching us out, so we chose to fish one rod with Spice B boilie and the other with anchored floater cake.

The day before, all of Bill's carp had taken the bait well below the surface. He elected to fish his mid-water, but I'd already seen movement as carp swirled sub-surface so I thought I'd give it a try just a foot below. We were both soon into carp. It was amazing! What a difference between now and then. In previous years, I'd been hitting my head against a brick wall, but now, I almost lost count of the takes.

We had four takes that day and we were elated, but what bothered me was the success rate. With the hooks buried in the cake, Bill and I landed one carp each, two out of four just wasn't good enough. I tried exposing the hook from the cake but the small amount of point and bend protruding from it was masked.

Bill and I couldn't wait to get back the following day; me, especially, because I'd been thinking about the landing rate and had decided to try something that went completely against the thinking at that time. I'd try a sea hook, a massive size 1/0 and stick it right out of the side of the cake, so when the carp grabbed it, and from whatever angle, I would be sure that the hook would catch. You have to bear in mind that until now, we'd been brainwashed into hiding the hook in our baits, so the carp couldn't detect them, but I was in experimental mode, mainly because of my experience with the particles.

After discovering and catching so many carp on the chickpeas, I began to question the old-fashioned folklore of concealing the hook because at least the point around to the bend was exposed when I fished the chicks. I had experimented, trying to discover whether one or two chicks on a hook was more effective and I caught on one chick rammed right up over the eye, which exposed the entire hook – point, bend and shank. My interest in these Braxted carp had been heightened; it struck me that we were getting takes on a floating bait, Spice B, which was the same make-up as our bottom baits that had apparently blown. Could it be that the issue had never been the bait at all, but that the carp were sussing how we were presenting it?

It was an amazing moment when my indicator cracked into the butt as I caught my first carp on a dirty great size 1/0 hook, sticking proud of a piece of floater cake that barely covered half the shank, fished 15 feet up from the bottom, in 16 feet of water. This was my first carp on a side-hooked bait and as Bill was to muse later, if only I had gone on to try this 'side-hooking' approach on our bottom baits, we would have struck gold. The method was amazing. In fact, I was so confident that I invested all my rods in it and unbeknown to me, I was discovering a rig that although I didn't name it, others have since called the zig rig.

I did much experimenting that late summer and autumn to establish the ultimate depth to fish the sub-surface floaters, but I never found a pattern and now understand from zig fishing that there isn't one ideal depth. I would go up to the ressy, and if it was safe to fish three rods these would be cast, feeding the line out until the cake surfaced. Then, I'd pull the first rod down one foot, the second two feet, and the third three feet. I did establish that there would be a depth on the day so once I had a take, I would put two rods at the same depth and leave the other slightly higher or lower, in case the carp switched feeding level.

The method was a complete turnaround and so consistent that now I expected at least a couple of takes every time I fished the res. I never experienced twitches like the bottom baits, but did start missing takes again, and after bumping a fish, feeling that it was on, then off, I realised that I had to find a better way of ensuring that they stayed on the hook until I could strike. I came up with the idea in the most painful manner.

As I swung my rod in and grabbed the cake, the lead slid down and wrapped around my bite alarm. At the same time, my hand was moving in the opposite direction and the size 1/0 hook sank into my thumb, up to the bend. After I'd sorted out the hook removal, mopped up the bloody mess and calmed my nerves a bit, I had to admit to myself that I was well impressed how the snagged lead had driven the hook in, so I decided to fish the lead, fixed. Unbeknown to me, I was now very close to using what would later become the very successful side-hooked bolt rig. As Bill observed – not only was it a shame that I didn't side-hook my bottom baits but also that I didn't fix my lead.

The difference was amazing. The first time I tried it the take was so savage that my rod was launched off the rod rest, so I had to sort out my set-up to stop that happening again. Aborted takes became a thing of the past; every take was a screamer and well nailed. My confidence in this new method was total, but the problem was that I didn't have another one. It was coming into late autumn, early winter, and of course the carp wouldn't be on the surface or in the surface layers then. With the colder weather, they'd go to the bottom, or so I thought, so I would need to fish bottom baits, but what was the point of that if I couldn't get a take?

I kept fishing my floating cake rigs right up until the freeze. The take rate slowed but there were some surprises, especially one really foggy night at the end of October. By this time, I was fishing the nights as there was no one else on the res except Bill, and with some covert parking we could fish right through.

On this particular night, I fished up near the dam with baits around 16 feet in 18 feet of water, so my floater cake baited rods were presented just two feet below the surface. The fog was so dense that I couldn't see the end of my rod tips and yet I caught two carp between midnight and dawn. That memorable incident has stayed with me all these years because, as experienced carpers will tell you, autumn/winter fog is one of the worst conditions for catching carp. Maybe the blanket of fog has a warming effect and it's just a simple matter of presentation. Instead of fishing bottom baits, perhaps we should be fishing near-surface zigs.

Chapter Eight

Baiting Up

O ver the years, I have undertaken a great many baiting campaigns with varying degrees of success from mega to complete failure. It's worth analysing the reasons for failure so that they can be understood today.

Along the way, I've learned that the two key elements of a successful bait introduction are to put it where the carp will eat it, and to put in sufficient quantity so that they know it's there and at some point, understand that it is edible. There is more to the second part of that simple statement than you might think.

We're dealing with the location aspect, firstly. I believe that some of the reasons baiting campaigns failed in the early years were simply down to location and it's very difficult and rare to be able to pull carp into areas of a lake with the promise of food, when they don't want to be there, or use it as a regular feeding area. When we were a hit team with our HNVs, I'm sure we failed sometimes simply because we didn't take the time to locate the carp before we started baiting, rather we just worked on our knowledge of watercraft and guessed where they would be. Of course, occasionally we got it wrong. So, to optimise a baiting campaign, it's important that you have prior knowledge of the areas where the carp most like to visit and feed.

The volume of bait will also be an issue. You can bait an area that the carp visit frequently with, say 50 boilies, and then in the next 30 minutes, the coots could move in and eat them all before any carp arrive. Conversely, if you baited an area that the carp did not frequent regularly, and it stayed there until they did, then in theory, you might get them on it. The whole topic of bait volume is a fascinating one. I've lost count, over the years, of the number of times I've been asked how much bait to put in, and there is no simple answer.

Every situation will be different, but the amount of bait you use is the very essence of how successful you will be. Get it wrong and it can go badly, but get it right and it is so amazing that I've been stunned on occasions at how easy the carp were to catch. There have been three times in my life when I've got the bait in so perfectly, that (and this is a term I use) the carp are looking for it. In each of those instances, the usual prime reason for carp fishing success – location – more or less went out of the door. I could have turned up blindfolded, cast anywhere and it wouldn't have been long before a carp sought out my bait. You're on a roll. Every time you turn up, no matter which swim you fish, no matter how crowded the lake is, you will catch, and it feels good!

If I had to point toward one reason that we struggled in the early years, it would be that of bait recognition. I saw a pattern develop, especially on rich waters with only a small head of carp. It could take three years before they would really get on to boilies and I don't think it had anything to do with time, rather that in the first instance, we simply didn't put enough bait in for the carp to recognise it as potential food. As we started to catch the carp, word got out so that more and

BELOW
My current water. Mega difficult – one of the main issues is that it's stuffed with natural food and they don't recognise bait.

ABOVE
*I sat on a slope above
the lake, looking
for signs of carp.*

more carp anglers moved on to the lake. It stands to reason that much more bait went in and the carp began to recognise the boilie as a food source.

There are many factors that get in the way of bait recognition. Around the mid-70s, I moved house to within minutes of a small gravel pit and while I was concentrating on Star Lane at the time, this lake did hold an attraction in a different way. I could be on it in five minutes and back home in a similar time, so I could sneak out for a couple of hours and get away with it with my new bride, Hazel.

This water had a reputation for being very difficult and, indeed, good local anglers were really struggling on there, with just one or two fish to show for the season. I joined one evening after work and chose to get a feel for the water and figure out an approach. It was a small pit of two acres, with many reedy areas, and intimate bays, and I sat on a slope above the lake, looking for signs of carp. In the couple of hours that I sat on that hill, I saw four anglers who came over one at a time, walked round the lake quickly, baiting as they went and then they were off again without breaking stride, presumably to get home for their tea.

If those four carpers had lingered a while, they would have seen the coots move out of the rushes with glee, straight to the spots that had been baited, and gobble up this heaven-sent opportunity of free food. What a waste! There was not only the money element to consider but also, remember in those days, you had to roll your own and rolling 100 baits and tidying up could take you a couple of hours from start to finish.

So, I made a plan. I would have tea with my wife, then pop over to the pit and bait under cover of darkness, hoping that the coots wouldn't see me baiting or find out where I'd baited. I did this for a week and after catching up with Hazel, and having tea, I'd pop down to the pit.

One particular night I took three rods with me. I was back two hours later, early enough to watch a bit of TV with the missus and keep her happy and smug enough with the memory of an 18¾lb, gorgeous-looking mirror in my mind.

Over the next three weeks, I fished that lake nine times. I caught on every occasion and ended up with 15 carp, one of which just scraped 20. Really, there wasn't much else to be caught; the other members only had six, all year.

The whole point of relating this story is to demonstrate my absolute conviction that if you want to get carp on to your bait, they have got to be able to find it, recognise it as food and eat it. It is this whole issue of 'finding' which can end up as a car wreck for you, if you're not careful. You must always endeavour to ensure that your bait stays on the bottom long enough.

I had this conversation many years ago with Rod Hutchinson and I remember him saying, 'the bait's got to sit there until they get fed up with looking at it, so they'll eat it'. I think Rod's simplistic take on it hits the mark. The determination of length of time is the key factor. I've watched carp swim countless times with complete indifference over a bait that they've never come across before

BELOW
Black boilies; a way of minimising coot and tuftie detection.

and then, on the 99th lap, something triggers them, they drop down to check out this foreign substance, try it, and from then on it's heads down.

Obstacles can get in the way of this necessary process, and I mentioned coots and other diving birds that can be an absolute pain in establishing your bait. Apart from covert baiting in darkness, using camouflage baits that don't stand out on the bottom or the surface is another alternative.

Over the years, I've had good success with black baits that are much more difficult for the birds to see. However, I recommend that you only use this approach on waters where the carp already recognise boilies as bait. You are baiting to get the carp on your particular boilie, while attempting to avoid the coots, so should you be lucky enough to find a virgin carp water, then vision plays a significant role in carp recognising food and bright baits. In my experience, yellow and orange baits are the first colours of boilie to be effective because they are particularly easy for the carp to spot.

The third option is a tactic I employed at the Snake Pit. There was no way I could stop the coots diving on my baits there, so I spent a day counting how many they would take. Based on the fact that the birds are territorial, I knew I could get a pretty reliable figure, in the breeding season, at least. To this figure, I then added the amount that I hoped the carp would eat.

Birds are one thing, but of course there are other boilie eaters. Nuisance fish,

ABOVE
*Attract the food source
and the carp will follow.*

such as bream can mainly be sorted by ensuring that your baits have a hard skin; tench are not so easy and can be a pest, so alternative baits, or mixing boilies together with particles such as tigers can help. Tigers seem to be pretty nuisance-fish-proof on most lakes. Okay, you'll pick up the odd tench, but I've yet to fish a water where I've been slaughtered by tench on tigers. Crayfish are an entirely different proposition; bloody things are a nightmare. The worst thing of all is that no rig is safe from them, so even if you decided to fish a bit of plastic, they'd still do your rig.

A few interesting observations regarding crays, though: If you had to pick one flavour proven to be head and shoulders above any other when looking at the big picture, not only in the UK but also in Europe, I'd suggest it's Scopex. More often than not, when fishing abroad on virgin carp lakes, Scopex was the first boilie that the carp picked up, on crayfish waters in particular.

A long time ago, I sussed that providing you use a ready-made type of base mix, i.e. mainly flours, rather than meals, if it's flavoured with Scopex, the crayfish aren't keen and will certainly leave you alone if there is other more interesting food available. This became a major successful method for me on some of the enormous French reservoirs. I took the view that if I could attract the food source, then the big carp would follow, so I used to attract the crays by baiting with sacks of trout pellet and then scatter Scopex boilies over the top, as well as using it as my hook bait. I've had some mega hits with this approach and been cray-free, but put another flavour boilie on the hook and you'd get slaughtered by the crays.

There you go, just an insight into some of the factors you should consider, and ways to approach a baiting campaign for a successful outcome.

Chapter Nine

Braxted: Despair

That winter, Rod Hutchinson had come down to my area in search of work. He was a scaffolder, and there wasn't much demand for his trade in the Lincolnshire area. They never built houses more than ten feet high, in case they blocked a view, so he, and his like, would travel great distances seeking work.

Bizarrely, our relationship started with me writing a letter to him telling him how pissed off I was that he'd blown the particle thing wide open. Unbeknown to me, though, when I'd first discovered chickpeas, and was using them with great success, Rod had also (or should I say more so) put a great deal of work into particles, trying many different ones and experimenting with how best to prepare and fish them.

So, there was me thinking I'd got an awesome bait that no one else knew about, when I picked up the latest edition of Angling magazine in which Rod had started a series of articles on particles. I vented my frustration at him for letting 'my secret' out of the bag, and then he explained how much work he'd put in and how long he'd been experimenting and using particles successfully. Other anglers were about to blow it wide open, so it was only right and proper that Rod got the recognition. I realised that he was so ahead of the game that I couldn't blame him for opening up on particles. We became good friends after that and swapped information, which was very useful to me as I got different slants and angles to think about. We Essex boys were experimenting and going down completely different routes to Rod and his friends anyway, at the time.

When Rod told me he was coming down to work on an oil refinery, along by the Thames, I invited him to stay at my house to save money on digs and I have many fond memories of those months. Rod was older and a lot more worldly than me. He took me for my first curry, as Indian restaurants had just begun to spring up, and he also gave me my first joint, which made me violently ill. He told me afterwards that there was a bit more than cannabis in it, though, and I'm indebted to him, because it put me off the stuff forever and gave me a great fishing advantage.

If you ever want to cream a water and be top rod, just find a big-fish lake fished by full-timers who are all dope heads. Not only does regular use of the stuff, rot the memory cells, but also the lethargy induced by the 'weed' in others gives you a massive fishing edge if you use their lack of energy to your advantage. Make sure you're up at dawn, find where the fish are and move in on them while the dope heads are still stoned and out of it, fast asleep. The real long-term dope users, for whom paranoia really took hold, could easily be wound up and upset until they all disappeared, leaving you with the lake to yourself. I think they should legalise the stuff. It's a real fishing edge!

BELOW
*Rod Hutchinson,
the particle guru!*

Rod and I would while the night away, just talking carp, or playing the guitar because Rod had become my guitar teacher. One night, I told him about my experiences at Braxted and the sub-surface floater rig, the exposed hook and the lead fixed on my line. He gave me a really funny look and I guessed he knew something and was reluctant to tell me at first, but I kept at him and eventually, he divulged the particle rig that he was using with immense success. The first thing that struck me was the length of the hook link. He was using an incredibly short six-inch hook link, whereas our bottom bait rigs were 12", but the main point was that he was using barrel leads.

For those of you new-ish to carp fishing, barrel leads are what the name suggests - a long, barrel-shaped

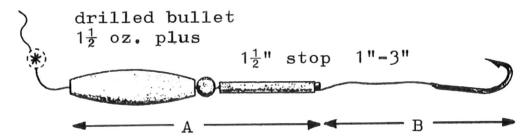

ANTI-TANGLE SHOCK RIG FOR LONG RANGE

```
drilled bullet
1½ oz. plus
                      1½" stop   1"-3"
```

Length B must be less than A, to prevent hook length tangling round main line during cast.

✳ If baits are taken well down, or bite-offs occur, pinch a swanshot on the line about 1" behind the leger weight.

lead with a bore throughout its length. They were designed for salmon anglers fishing above prawns and the like, so they could cast reasonable distances keeping the prawn down in the current. It wasn't the barrel lead revelation that interested me, though; it was more the fact that Rod was using barrel leads so he could plug them with a cocktail stick to fix them to the line. We had both come to the same conclusion, that for centuries, carp anglers had got it wrong. It was not the case that you needed to fish a rig that would offer no resistance to a carp, or it would drop the bait. In fact, it was to the contrary; if you offered them resistance, it would scare them into a bolting take. What I'd missed, though, was adapting my floater set-up to a bottom bait rig. I felt that I'd really got it now, and couldn't wait to try out Rod's rig.

Bill and I decided to pool resources and really sort out the Braxted carp once and for all, the next season. Despite the previous failures, we decided on a massive baiting scheme, hoping to mimic the results of Jimmy Eldridge and his friends by putting so much bait in that it became an accepted food source. We figured that at this time, Braxted was so rich with natural food, that this had been the reason for our past failures. We simply hadn't put in enough bait to persuade the carp that it was worthy of their attention in preference to the easy pickings.

To guarantee our success, we elected to use Rose d'Orient flavouring, which had become my number one choice. The base mix was also our best shot – an expensive blend of the very best cascin, lactalbumin, meals and vitamin

ABOVE
Rod's barrel lead particle rig.

supplements. I was confident and Bill, as always, was super-confident. He was, and still is, the ultimate optimist. We could have been baiting the M25 and he'd still have expected to catch! We chose three areas of the ressy that we knew were feeding hotspots, and over the following weeks we rota'd so that one of us baited every day.

We'd been getting a bit of friction from the club officials the previous year. They felt that we were breaking the rules...what us? never!...and it was very obvious by their increased presence as they patrolled the res that they were gunning for us. It was always that way in the early years of carp fishing, and indeed, this discrimination toward carp anglers from the old guard, match club types goes on to this day. For some reason that I've never quite understood, they just don't like us. Maybe the battery of rods and the flash kit intimidates them, or perhaps it's the modern (to them anyway), high-tech thing that they don't get. They seem to think that unless you're sitting on a box, watching a float, you're not practising the piscatorial art. As I write this, it's just struck me that it could be an inadequacy thing. Them with their one little rod and us with our three big powerful ones – little willy/big willy.

The previous season, I'd had more than a few surprise visits by bailiffs. I had my ticket checked so many times by one particular committee member, that it was verging on harassment and I must admit to getting arsey. One afternoon, on being asked yet again for my ticket, I said, "Surely you recognise me by now! Oh, and by the way, while you're spending all your time wandering around Essex looking for me, me and your missus are getting on great guns!"

I don't think that warmed him to me, somehow, or his colleagues on the committee, for that matter.

With the days counting down to the 16th June, we decided to clear it with the secretary regarding what time we could start. As I mentioned, the previous season I'd had the secretary in my swim accusing me of starting before dawn. It seemed as if we were walking on eggshells so we went along to the AGM and when we walked in, the temperature plummeted. It was abundantly clear that they wanted us off. Bill and I didn't want to put a step wrong, so I went out of my way to confirm a start time that would satisfy the secretary. He told me two o'clock and I didn't argue, but that was exactly the same time that he'd bollocked me for starting the year before. The moron!

Club secretaries and angling committee members are of a certain type, mostly. Me and Gary Bayes once summed them up, (grouped with others like VAT officials and Special Constables), late one night when we'd had a big result and stayed up all night drinking tea. We concluded that they are 'little people' who have particular personality traits and are deliberately put on this planet to piss off 'proper' men who have nothing to prove. That's why there is a natural inclination for little men to gravitate toward angling club committees. It's one of the few times in their lives when they are in a position of power and can bully and pick on others. Normally, there's not much opportunity in their ordinary working lives, sweeping factory floors or filing papers in an office. In fact, they are so boring that the highlight of their lives is dying. You may gather that I have a strong point of view when it comes to the little people, and yes, I am aware that I might find being granted membership to some of the clubs challenging in the future!

The start was getting ever closer and Bill and I were very excited. It was always that way for me with carp fishing, especially when I'm hitting a brick wall and then a solution pops up. It never occurs to me that the solution might not work. Confidence is key to successful carp fishing and on this occasion it was no different. I had the answer, and with the new fixed-lead rig, I was going to hammer those Braxted carp.

I drove down the country lane that goes over a bridge crossing the river Blackwater. It's then a short drive up a hill, through the farm, and up to the reservoir. It was 1.55am as I crossed the bridge and caught sight of the secretary's car, hidden behind a hedge in the entrance way to the field alongside the river. I thought, 'you sneaky bastard', but laughed because I was clean. It would be another three minutes before I parked up at the reservoir and by the time I'd got my gear out and walked up there; it wouldn't be before 2.05am, at least. As I pulled up in the reservoir car park, so did Bill, and as soon as he got out of the car he said, "Did you see Paul?" We both pulled a face; you know the one – the 'little man/prat' face.

I had chosen to fish off the dam wall. There was a nice deep margin along there with a warm breeze blowing into it, so I knew carp would be right in the edge and I elected to fish close range. This worked out well because I'd found out that Rod's rig was prone to tangling on the cast. There was no problem here, though, with just an underarm swing which laid the rig out perfectly as it hit the surface. Stealth was the name of the game, and indeed, as I pushed my banksticks quietly into the ground, a carp rolled just a couple of yards out in the dawn gloom. Pukka, I thought! I'm going to have a result.

Suddenly, there was an almighty flash of light, and a searing pain penetrated my iris, seemingly probing deep into my brain. What the...?

A voice shouted, "What the fuck do you think you're doing, fishing here before daybreak?"

I was fuming. "If you don't get that fucking spotlight out of my face, I'm going to ram it down your neck," I said.

Then, an almighty argument kicked off with the moronic secretary who had been hiding down the road, behind a bush. For the second year in a row, he accused me of breaking the rules and fishing before light, after previously confirming the time with me - also for the second year in a row.

My fishing was wrecked as he exercised his Nazi tendencies with his torch, which clearly he'd salvaged from Stalag 13. The margins were awash with light, he was stamping his feet like a spoiled child in a tantrum, and both of us were hollering at each other. In the end, I'd just had enough of it.

"Fuck off," I said, "Get out of my swim. I'm here, now and I'm staying for the day, but if you give me back my money, you can stick your club and I won't come back."

He agreed to do that. "... and the best thing you can do now," I went on, "is to get out of my way because I'm *really* about to lose it." Possibly luckily at this point, Bill Lovett turned up and pulled him away. If he hadn't done so, I'm sure I'd have chucked him in the lake.

I was incensed. I'd come within an inch of decking the club secretary. I'd banked so much on this opening day and this cretin had ruined it for me. Rods and baits were out, but I just couldn't be arsed. I should have moved, because there wasn't a carp within miles of the dam wall after the fracas, but I couldn't be bothered. I just didn't want to be on Braxted any more and I'd actually come to terms with the fact that I wouldn't be after today. I was a bit skint at the time, and thought, 'Oh well, at least I'll get the membership money back' so, with the fishing trashed for me, I tried to calm down and chilled in the sun for the rest of the day. I planned to go to Layer Pits for the rest of my week off, and fish with my old mate, Stuart Demon.

Bill came round after the secretary had gone, and tried to console me.

"I'm sure it'll blow over, Kev," he said. "You'll be able to stay in the club."

"They can stick their club," I replied, which upset Bill a bit because he was going to lose his fishing mate, but I was still so angry that I was past reasoning with, and so Bill wisely retreated to the other bank.

I saw the secretary come back around lunchtime, and although he gave me a wide berth, he did go round to Bill and they spoke for some time. Then Bill came round to me.

"Kev, it's all sorted," he said.

"What's sorted, Bill?"

"The secretary's prepared to forget it and I've got your membership back."

"Do fucking what?" I was fuming again.

Bill, bless him, thought he'd done me a favour by taking an ambassadorial role, calming the waters and getting my membership restored, whereas I thought differently. I hated the water, the club, and their cloth-capped, small-minded mentality and now I was having my second row of the opening day, but this time with my dear mate, Bill Lovett, who really didn't deserve it. Then again, he should have known better than to interfere with a very pissed off Nashy! As well as that, the expected carp bonanza wasn't working out for Bill either. He'd had six aborted takes that day, eventually landing a small mirror, hardly what we'd envisaged; maybe we would have been better off baiting the M25.

That was enough of Braxted for me, so I packed up and went home. Unbelievable – it was the first time in my life that I'd pulled off a water on the first day of the season. I sat at home that evening feeling sorry for myself, but still fuming. This wasn't right. What was happening here? There was I, sitting at home watching drivel on the telly, while all my mates were out on carp lakes.

I phoned Stuart, to get the gen on Layer and he said it was absolute bedlam, rammed out, and it would be pointless going there, unless I wanted to get in the queue for the car park, which was a mile long at four in the morning to be assured of a place when the gates opened at six. That wasn't really my scene, so the next day, I reluctantly decided to go back to Braxted. After all, Bill, bless him, had restored the membership so as I wasn't going to get the money back, I might as well get some value out of it, for the first week anyway, until Layer calmed down. There was always the big mirror, which was the whole point of me being on there in the first place and it was still eluding me. I only had six days of my holiday left, and then I would turn my back forever on the reservoir. I didn't rate my chances.

My mindset was so negative that I couldn't even be bothered to get up to the res for dawn, especially as no one could tell me when dawn was, apparently. In the end, I had a lie-in and rather ashamedly, got up at 8am and so didn't get to the res until 11 o'clock. By then, it was scorching and Bill was stripped down, shirtless. Ominously, he had nothing to report and said that no one else had caught, so I fished toward the dam end. Anglers were now disturbing the margins so in the searing heat, not imagining that carp would be on the bottom, I chose to whack out three of my anchored floater rigs to the middle, fished one, two and three feet below the surface in ten feet of water. I used three rods in the hope that the club secretary, would come back and catch me. I wanted to make recompense for the day before and this time, I'd actually deck the bastard! In short, I just didn't give a shit.

Then, I stripped down to my shorts, slapped on the Ambre Solaire, and lay back in the grass with the radio rocking in my ear. As you can tell, I really was on it, totally focused on the possibility of catching, eyes glued to the lake, ready like a coiled spring to strike at the slightest rod tip tremor, or should I see a sign

ABOVE
*Braxted's big mirror.
The heavens opened
and it rained, hence
no Ambre Solaire and
the one-piece suit!*

of carp elsewhere, (highly improbable from my prone position) I could up sticks and move in a millisecond, probably. I could spend a week basking in the sun at Braxted, no trouble.

Suddenly, I was brought round from my sunbathing reverie by a screamer on my middle rod and I thought, 'I'd better hit that'. I blinked the sun tan oil from my eyes and after a short, boisterous but uneventful fight I slipped the net under Braxted's big mirror. She was down on her top weight because she had spawned, but she was still a big fish for the time at 24½lbs. Funny how things work out, isn't it? All the maximum effort and focus that I'd put into this place, and on the day that I'd given up and was completely distracted, I caught her!

Many years later, other captures of sought-after carp occurring when my mind was completely off the thought of catching, got me thinking. Is there something in it? I firmly believe that in my case, at least, I give off some thought wave that the carp pick up on. Readers who have doubted my sanity will have their fears confirmed when I tell you that now if I think a big carp is in my swim, I will deliberately try to occupy my mind with other thoughts; maybe pick up a book or get on the phone. In fact, I've lost count of the number of big carp I've caught while making a cuppa, or getting a phone call.

Chapter Ten

The Zig Revolution

I'm not quite sure when a sub-surface rig became termed a zig rig, or even what zig actually means, but I suspect anglers at Layer may have had something to do with it. The idea was taken to Layer, from the results that Bill and I had enjoyed at Braxted with some considerable success, refined from there on, and the word spread. It's interesting to observe how a solution to a fishing problem gets grabbed by others and developed. I remember once having a conversation with Rod Hutchinson, when he said, "We come up with the ideas, and the kids develop them!"

Through the pioneering years we were hitting our heads against the proverbial brick wall at times, and then we would crack it with a particular method or rig but - and this is the key point - that didn't necessarily mean we would take that method along to other waters because the next challenge might have a completely different set of problems. So, I forgot about the sub-surface rig after Braxted.

While on that subject, later on I overlooked another profound rig development - the slideable/adjustable helicopter rig that I developed while fishing Waterways in Cambridgeshire during a break from the Snake Pit. This rig came about in order to deal with the carp that were cautious of feeding on clear spots, so I had to go after them in the weed. Funnily enough, this was the subject of an article that I wrote for Carp Fisher. Soon after its publication, Jim Gibbinson commented on its ingenuity, but I moved on and forgot about it. Nowadays, not so dissimilar rigs are called the chod.

I hasten to add that I am in no way suggesting that I was the inventor of the chod rig, or indeed the zig. I have no doubt that other anglers around the country could have been experiencing the same problems and coming to similar conclusions. I'm only portraying the carp fishing scene in Essex and its possible relevance to today's techniques and tackle.

Anyway, back to zig rigs. Anglers have been dabbling with zigs for some time and it's fair to observe that it's only in the last few years that they have gained in popularity. It's taken a long time for anglers to consider the zig as a useful part of their rig armoury, and I think the reason for that is confidence, or rather a lack of it. Most anglers are aware of zigs; they have seen people writing about them, or possibly someone catching on one, but because the method seems too alien and unlikely, most only tie up a zig when they are struggling.

You know the scene: 'It's Sunday morning after a weekend blank and fish are sighted swirling on the top, so I chuck a zig out. What have I got to lose? I'm blanking anyway!' This is not the way to fish zigs. To understand zigs and optimise their effectiveness you have to commit yourself to the method with all of your rods. In fact, I can't think of a method where this is more important. The more rods you have zig fishing, the more chance you have of identifying the key cruising depth. This is the essence of zig fishing; the margin of error for setting the depth of your zig can be finite.

Generally, 6-inches either way can mean a blank, but sometimes it can be as little as two or three inches. If you cast out one rod on a zig it is much harder to identify the feeding depth, or at least, it will take a lot longer because you fish it until you deem that you have got the depth wrong, and then you wind in, adjust, and then try again. Committing all of your rods, let's say three because this is the number most of us are using these days, you will see that you have much more chance of taking the error out of zigging when three rods are searching for you.

I will give you an example of how I do it: It's March and the carp are starting to move around, but they are mainly off the bottom in that strip of sub-surface water which is their comfort zone; perfect conditions for zig fishing. The lake is ten-feet deep, so from experience I guess they will be in an area a little above mid-water. How much above mid-water depends upon the strength of the sun, if any, and the chilling effect of the wind. So, I set one rod at 6', one at 6'6", and the third rod at 7'. Should I not have any action, then I will drop the 6' rod to 5'6" and lift the top rod to 7'6", adjusting the zigs as and when, down and up, until the hoped-for take materialises.

Once you have cracked it with that first take, it then gets a lot easier.

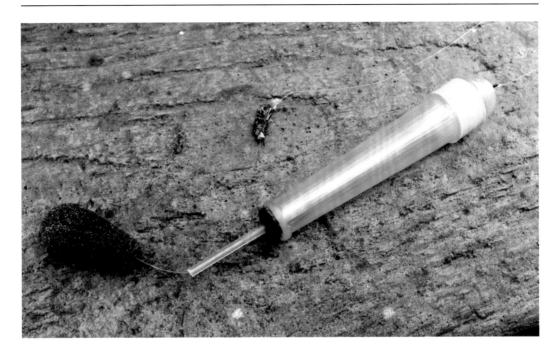

Depending on how confident I am, I might fish two rods at the 'magic' depth, and use the third rod as a 'seeker', dropping it six-inches below the zone, or lifting it six-inches above. Alternatively, I may use my second rod as a seeker too, so in that instance I have one in the zone, and one six-inches either side. The reason for this is that the first take is rarely the best depth, for me at least; maybe it's just luck with one carp, and with a little bit of fine tuning you discover that the consistent take zone is actually a little higher or lower.

I don't put all my rods at the magic depth. I always have at least one searching around, because the effective depth may vary from hour to hour, as the carps' comfort zone varies in specific weather conditions at the time. It may be a dull day, and then a strong cold wind gets up chilling the surface layers, and so they drop down deeper, or the sun may come out and the wind drops off so they lift up in the water seeking the band that is slightly warmer.

On observation, most anglers seem to prefer to tie a fixed-length zig rig, bolt-rig-style, and I confess that this is my favourite method too, but unless you are confident of your depths, it's a lot more messing about because you have to keep on bringing in your rods and retying your hooklink. The adjustable zig is the most efficient way, by far, to find the zone. It's a simple task just to let out a little line to increase the depth, or wind in a little on to your spool to reduce the depth.

However, a lot of anglers worry about the float on their line, and the possibility that it could spook carp. One way around this is to fish the longest hooklink that is achievable, after all, your zig bait is buoyant, and will float up

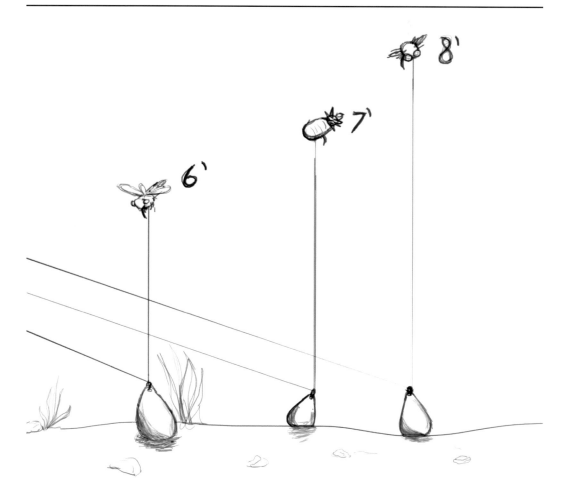

anyway. So, if the shortest depth you think you are likely to fish with a zig is, say, eight feet, then why not get the float right down near to the bottom and fish a seven-foot hooklink?

In the past, I've noted a number of times when I've just had a single bleep, and on occasions when I've flavoured my zig baits with bug juice, I've had a bleep and then the surface ripple has flattened off above the rig as the oil in the bait has been disturbed and risen to the surface - a missed take!

One reason for aborted takes, particularly with more buoyant hookbaits, is that the carp is just above the zig. It goes down onto the bait to try to suck it in, but because the offering is on a taut link between hook and lead, it cannot easily take the bait back properly into its mouth, so the hook doesn't take hold and you miss it. I was shown a way around this problem by Jack Brown, who ties an elastic element into his rig by the lead, to enable a little movement, but I prefer the method that Alan Blair showed me, whereby you have a short length of tungsten tube - I use four-inches - on the rig side of your fixed lead. This short piece of tube

pinned on the bottom, provides a little bit of movement as it lifts up when they take the bait.

    I am finding the subject of zig fishing increasingly fascinating and I'm beginning to get it now. It's fair to observe that until comparatively recently, carp anglers have fished mainly on the bottom, with the next most targeted feeding zone being the surface, but it's reasonable to suggest that the amount of time anglers have spent surface fishing is minimal when compared to the time they spend fishing bottom baits.

    Wherever you fish for carp, they become aware of that area and the hazards that they face. We condition them to be wary of the potential danger, and actually, it's not just a question of depth, or the bottom or the top; it could be an area of the lake. For example, if there is a sanctuary in a lake that never experiences fishing pressure, then the carp will deem that area as safe and be off their guard. I have seen examples of this on lakes where a bait can be looked at, in the very least, with extreme caution, or it is blown, and yet if you present that bait in an area of the lake where the carp have never been hooked, it will be like it's the first time they have ever seen it. They eat with relish and you almost mug them.

    Incidentally, this is why I believe the chod rig has been so effective in recent years. Actually, I don't rate it as a good hooker, rather I think its effectiveness has nothing to do with its hooking ability, a chod enables anglers to fish a reasonably presented rig over areas where the carp have not been targeted previously with any great effectiveness.

There is one massive amount of water in any lake where, until now, the carp have been able to go about their business more or less unmolested; between the bottom and the surface, which as it happens, is where they spend the majority of their time. For this reason alone, zig rig fishing should be taken seriously because, so far, the carp have not been hammered like they have on the bottom.

I think we are on the verge of a revolution as our understanding increases of how to catch carp mid-water and the most exciting thing for me about future zig fishing is Nash Tackle's recent introduction of Zig Bugs. Rather than a hookbait or a piece of foam, now we are presenting bug imitations, recognising that the carp are feeding on aquatic creatures as they cruise around sub-surface. We are imitating the natural food that they have eaten without fear of being caught since the beginning of their time on the planet.

I can visualise a revolution taking place when carp anglers will swap their tubs of bait for boxes of trout-fly-style imitations, and zigging will become an art form which few will crack. I suggest this because of the effort and energies that will be required, but those anglers who work at it to identify not only the feeding depth, but also what the carp are feeding on at that particular time - which could be as varied as a particular type of hatching insect rising to the surface, a beetle swimming sub-surface, or a tadpole - and then present a suitable imitation, will have it off.

Since writing this chapter my head has been in overdrive and I have become a zig addict. Indeed, dare I suggest that I have understated the potential of zig fishing? I will give you an example: On my own Church Lake, the first 20 carp caught this spring were all on Zig Bugs, and what I have found really interesting is that several of those carp caught on zigs were crapping boilies and particles. Despite anglers fishing bottom baits, there was not one carp caught. I think this illustrates my point above - that the sub-surface zone is deemed to be safe by the carp and while they are managing to avoid bottom bait rigs, even when consuming the freebies, they then rise to mid-water and get caught.

I've been doing a lot of work on designs of Zig Bugs; from doing my best to imitate insects accurately, to the opposite extreme of visual attraction, going down the path of iridescence; i.e. bugs that will catch or reflect the light in the way a bluebottle does - and even bugs that glow in the dark for night zigging.

I confess my obsession with zig fishing is quite new. This is because, I guess, I am old school in the way that I love to get a bait established and working, and I get

ABOVE
The next step in baits, imitating the carps' natural diet.

the most satisfaction from captures as a result of that process. I saw zig fishing as opportunist, without creating feeding situations. How wrong I was! Feeding Riser Pellet on the surface, and then fishing zigs a foot down has proved lethal, which then goes on to another very effective avenue - surface imitations.

The area of development that is exciting me the most is my work on groundbaits that produce a stream of food items as they break down; pellets, dried insects, shrimp etc. which rise up to the surface and fall back down, or even suspend sub-surface. So now that you have food throughout, you can fish a bottom bait to catch the ones out on the bottom, and zigs alongside to catch the ones in the rest of the water column.

I have just come back from being dragged out reluctantly to the chore of some DVD work for our 2013 Tackle DVD. I confess, when fishing, I want to get into just that – and I really hate being filmed. Still, I have to do my bit. Alan Blair wanted me to do a section on how I would approach an ordinary club water that I had never fished before - the kind of situation that many anglers find themselves in. I spoke about location, which of course is the most vital element, and then I did a piece on how I would approach a lake zig fishing.

This club lake contains a 40lb common and I have to say that I was delighted to catch it only 22 hours into the filming on a prototype glow-in-the-dark Zig Bug

ABOVE
*First session; 22hours.
Job done! Thanks
to a Glo-Bug!*

fished up in the water column, and baiting with my aforementioned prototype groundbait. The common was a little down in weight at 38lbs something, but it was an immensely satisfying capture, nonetheless. Was it luck? Well, I think we all need a bit of that, but really, I believe it was caught by design and this old warrior got tripped up because I had got out of the box and did something different from the rest, which is the message throughout much of this book.

Chapter Eleven

Braxted: Revenge

With the successful capture of the big mirror, my old enthusiasm returned. It was time to wreak my revenge on the ressy. I wasn't going anywhere until I'd emptied it, which surely I would do now. Nonetheless, I didn't feel that I'd cracked the water and consistency is important to me so that I can measure my achievement. As the saying goes, one swallow doesn't make a summer, and catching a lake's biggest inhabitant doesn't illustrate that you're a crack angler – and what's more, I could hardly say that catching the big mirror was a well-deserved result!

It was time to prove to the Braxted carp that they'd met their match, so out came Rod's bolt rig. As I swung it out, Bill fell about laughing.

"What the fuck have you got on the end of your line, Nashy?"

He couldn't get his head around the concept that you could catch carp on rigs that offered resistance, but I proved him wrong and caught a few good fish on it. It wasn't to last, though, and soon I was back to twitches and one to three-inch lifts of the indicators.

I was so close to cracking the side-hooked bolt rig, although I didn't realise it at the time. With the benefit of hindsight, it's now clear that the rig would have worked for Rod in his particle fishing, especially as he more than likely used it in silt with a short hook link because the fish were digging into the bottom. It would have got his presentation right, as well as prevented bite-offs. With the lead buried in the silt, creating resistance, and the smaller, sharper hook point and bend sticking proud of his particles, he had a much better chance of pricking a carp than I did with my over-sized, thick-wired hook sticking out from the side of my boilie.

My 2oz barrel lead just wasn't heavy enough to offer the necessary resistance to prick the carp, and as well as that, the long shape meant that when carp picked up the bait, and tensioned to the lead, just one end would lift up, so not even the whole 2oz of lead was coming into play. This alerted them to the resistance, but as they weren't pricked, they dropped the bait – hence all the twitches. It was really frustrating and doing my head. Later, I went on to red dari seed with a smaller, sharper hook. It caught me a few more carp, but then once again, the runs died away. I am convinced, looking back, that rig would have worked with a 2oz bomb, if only I'd got rid of that bloody barrel weight.

I think it's important for the reader to have an insight into the rig evolution we were going through then, because it will help in your fishing today when the runs fall away. Recently, I took some kids fishing on a very prolific lake - we're talking 20 runs a day – and as an experiment, I tried one rod with the old side-hooked bolt rig, a rig that was later to be incredibly successful for me, and I blanked. I just couldn't buy a take on it, even on a water rammed full of starving carp, because they had learned how to avoid this once lethal rig.

To be successful consistently in these modern times, it is essential that you understand that you're educating the carp to avoid your rig set-ups, so you must keep ahead of them. When you think about it, though, it's not so much the carp you need to keep ahead of, but the other anglers. Find an effective rig that other anglers haven't used on your lake, so the carp haven't come across it and been educated to the dangers, and you will fill your boots.

So, I was back to the res, back to twitches again and I was losing heart. I fished the reservoir less and less, and spent my time at Layer instead. I kept in touch with Bill, though, who told me that Jimmy Eldridge was back on the ressy, and on one occasion, while Bill blanked, he watched Jim have four screaming takes and land four carp. I said to Bill, 'He's doing something. You need to check him out' but Bill still put it down to bait.

That winter, even Bill had enough of Braxted and decided to have a few sessions on Waveney Valley in Norfolk. I have to mention here, that considering Bill only had his Friday night through to Saturday afternoon session every week, it's a tribute to his passion that he drove all the way from Chelmsford to Wortwell in Norfolk several times, just to bait up. He caught the odd fish here and there that I guess justified his efforts but even he was beginning to realise that something was wrong. Every time he fished, soon after casting out, his indicators would start to twitch away, and he became convinced that it was carp after he hit a lift on his bobbin and momentarily came into contact with one.

One night, Bill met Nigel Dennis. Nigel joined the BCSG around the same time as me and lived in Norfolk but then moved to Bristol and for some time gave up carp fishing. He left Bristol under circumstances that I dare not reveal and returned to the family home in Norfolk where he dusted down his carp rods and started fishing at Waveney. Bill and Nigel chatted into the night and the subject of twitches and aborted takes came up. Nigel also had a feeling that something was going on and he'd heard rumours that some anglers, including those at Darenth where Jimmy Eldridge fished, were on to something. They were getting loads of screaming takes when those around them were blanking while suffering twitches. Nigel was friendly with Len Bunn and Dick Weald, two of the best carpers in Norfolk, so he told Bill that he'd pop round to see Len to find out if he knew anything.

Bill saw Nigel a few weeks later on the last day of the season at Waveney. He hadn't yet visited Len so they both popped round to his house the next day. Len clearly knew something but wouldn't give them all the answers. He advised them to think about using heavier fixed leads with the hook point exposed. He also made some strange comments about fishing with the bait, *not* the hook, which completely mystified Bill and Nigel at the time.

On Bill's return to Essex, he got on the phone to me and related the conversation. "Bloody hell," I said, as it all became as clear as day. I remembered something else Bill had said when he told me about the day when he'd watched Jimmy Eldridge smashing the reservoir, 'Jim was fishing his rods really high with lines tight out to the middle and he wasn't getting any twitches, just screaming reel-churners.' Immediately, I thought, 'to make a line tight, you need to anchor it with a heavy weight. I was gutted in one way, because I'd been so close but now elated that I'd put the final piece of the jigsaw in place; I just needed to use big, heavy leads. I was content that I had the answer and was sure that I would finally sort these carp out.

Meanwhile, Bill was bothered by Len's comment about fishing with the bait and not the hook. We discussed it at length but unless it meant sliding the bait up the hook link, which I didn't think would work because I'd already tried it, we couldn't really see where Len was going. Bill wouldn't let it go, though, and eventually, he phoned Tony Howells who had taken over from Derek Stritton as regional organiser of the BCSG. Tony was a really great bloke, a bit of a character and most importantly, as RO he talked to all the other members and so was well tuned into the grapevine.

"What Len's talking about is the hair rig," Tony said. He'd heard about it because, apparently, when Kevin Maddocks and Len Middleton were fishing up at Waveney, Kevin had cast a rig into the far margin on D Lake, but he overcast and it landed in a tree. As he tried to retrieve, his line snapped and the rig was left among the branches. Dick Weald was on Waveney at the time and watched this event with great interest. Kevin Maddocks and Len Middleton were ripping Waveney apart and it was clear to Dick that it wasn't due to of the golden tint of their bollocks!

After Kevin and Len pulled off, Dick took the boat out and retrieved Kevin's rig which amazed him because hanging off the bend of the hook was a piece of line with the bait attached; on the line and not on the hook. Unbeknown to Dick, this strange set-up that he was holding in his hand was the hair rig.

The story of the hair rig is worth telling. Len had set up a huge fish tank with carp in it at home so that they could experiment with baits and rigs. The legend goes that one night Len plucked a hair from his wife's head, tied it to the bend in the hook, and then attached the bait to the hair. The rest, as they say, is history.

One evening, my phone rang and there was a very excited Mr Lovett on the other end, going on about hairs and things. Quite how much he'd been drinking, I wasn't sure, but the concept of sticking a 'fuck-off big rabbit' on my rig was of little interest, I have to say. After further discussion, I got it, though.

"Oh, you mean 'hair' not 'hare!'"

We were really on a roll now, with all this amazing new rig technology. I felt particularly confident with the side-hooked baits and bolt rig because I'd lived with this, been so close and knew the potential. I was thinking that all the zillions of twitches I'd had would now be converted to steaming runs and carp – and when they started sussing that, well, there was always the rabbit rig. Our personal rig revolution wasn't to end there, though.

Bill came round to my house and showed me a new possible hooklink material. I'd never seen anything like it; it was so very fine and subtle. At that time we were on hooklinks produced from Dacron, and the most used make was Black Spider – really thick for its breaking strain. This stuff that Bill showed me was so incredibly fine and supple by comparison; it was dental floss. I didn't even know what dental floss was at the time, but I was on it in a flash. I tied up a rig, tested it on the scales and I could get between 8-10lbs on it. I would have preferred over ten, but as we mainly used 12lb line, anyway, I thought I could fish it with reasonable confidence.

Next, I tied on a hook, side-hooked a boilie and flicked it into a sink full of water. The dental floss became almost gossamer-like and the threads separated. It was virtually invisible, and when I stuck my hand in to feel it, I could hardly feel the floss. Carp could detect our hook links, like the thick Black Spider, but I felt that they'd have little chance of detecting the floss, and if they did feel something they'd probably think it was silkweed. I was so impressed that I decided to use it the following week when the season started at the reservoir. I couldn't wait to get there.

Bill was positively gagging and was so excited that he hardly slept for the ten nights, or so, up to the start. You could say that we'd had a few disappointments at the ressy, and so we should have curbed our enthusiasm, but we just knew that this start was going to be different. We had the rigs, but as well as that, we were massively confident on our bait choice.

Nigel Dennis had got himself a job as a McVities sales rep and was given the territory of Essex, and Bill had told him that I'd just bought a new house. Sadly, Hazel and I had called it a day a couple of years before. We had been going through a rocky patch, she said that she wanted some time on her own and I took that to mean that she didn't love me anymore. Incidentally, that was the wrong assumption, as she told me when she contacted me out of the blue and we met up some 26 years later. Put simply, we both had issues at home and to escape them, we married far too young. It was particularly hard for Hazel because her dearly beloved father had died, leaving her with, shall we say, a 'challenging' mother. At the time, though, I didn't understand all that. We lived apart, albeit in the same house because the housing market had gone through the floor, and eventually we managed to sell the house and go our separate ways.

I only had my income and the price of even the most run-down of properties meant that I'd be on the breadline unless I could find a lodger to help with the rent, so Nigel rang me and quickly took up residence. Pukka, eh? I had a top class carper to share my house with, spending countless hours talking about carp, and it was much more interesting than sharing with a bird; apart from the obvious which only a bird can provide, but that element was covered with a drive to Chigwell.

One evening, Nigel showed me a bottle of flavouring that Len Bunn had told him about. This was ultimately to tear up many of the UK's best carp waters, including Savay. It was a maple flavour but you'd never believe it was maple, it smelled more like a bad night at a curry house. It was seriously pungent. More than a few times, I'd be fishing and people would come along, pick up the scent of the maple from ten yards back, and say 'What *is* that curry smell?' I loved the stuff immediately and just knew it was a big carp catcher.

Bill came down to my new home one night for the first time and thought he'd gone to the wrong house as he smelt the terrible, sickly odour when he walked up the garden path.

"What *is* that disgusting stench," he said as I opened the door and the cat made a bolt for it, gasping for fresh air.

He took his words back when I put a boilie in his hand. Nige and I had knocked up a bird food-based boilie that when flavoured with maple smelt fantastic. We just knew that there wasn't a carp out there that would be able to resist it.

When we were fishing with it, and rolling it at home, we became almost anaesthetised to the odour and that was fine, but a year later, Nigel moved on and I needed a new lodger. I put an advert in the local paper and I'd see a car pull up and a prospective lodger walk up the path, but before reaching the door, they'd do an about-turn and walk away. I figured that the smell had ingrained itself into the walls and paintwork so I spent a weekend scrubbing. It helped, but there was still an odious smell. The only way that I eventually got rid of it was to skip all the carpets and curtains; it proved to be an expensive bait!

At last, the day of reckoning had arrived and despite me being barely able to contain myself, I actually turned up at the ressy with daylight nearly upon me. Conditions seemed perfect, with a light, warm north-westerly blowing into our bank. I just couldn't wait to get stuck in. Strangely, I found Bill in a more sombre mood. As I mentioned, he is normally the eternal optimist, but he wasn't quite so on this opening day. I guess it was realisation time and the disappointments of the past had come back to haunt him. Me? I was having none of it. I was going to cane them!

Despite the hair rig revelation, Bill and I weren't sure that it would be the rig to use because there was a light covering of silkweed blanketing the bottom of the lake at this time. We could just imagine a carp trying to suck in the boilie and being prevented from doing so by the hook snagging in the weed, so we both chose to use side-hooked bolt rigs.

I had discovered a really super-strong pattern of hook, so unusually for the day because we mostly used size 4s, I elected to go down to a size 8. I wanted to try really small boilies and that hadn't been done before. To my size 8 hook I tied two feet of dental floss to which was fixed a 2½oz lead. I didn't realise it at the time, but I'd taken another step forward; hooks were nowhere near as needle sharp as they are today. These tiny hooks would be sharper than the usual size 4s because the wire was that much thinner, and this meant that there was much more chance of the carp being pricked against the resistance of the lead.

With the sun just threatening to poke out over the horizon, I cast straight on top of a fish that I'd just seen roll, and I was just baiting my second rod, when it ripped off. There were no twitches here, just an absolute screamer and Bill was on hand to do the honours, slipping the net under a 17lb common. Years later, this same fish was to be a much sought-after resident at over 40lbs. After a couple of hours, I landed a 21lb mirror, and if I wasn't made up already, I would be by the end of the day with a further three carp falling to my rods.

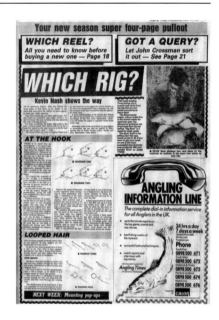

Maybe Bill had a sixth sense for not sharing my confidence as he only chipped in with one low double, but nonetheless, it was still a result as no one else caught. This fact was not only relevant but also, I have to admit, extremely satisfying because on this opening day, there were some big guns up there; Jimmy Eldridge, Brad and Stuart were back on, as well as Nick Lindsell and Zenon Bojko, Brian Ash... in short it was rapidly becoming a who's who of carp fishing – and they'd all blanked, except us! We were both absolutely buzzing. We knew we'd cracked it at last and nothing could stop us now.

What a difference! By the Friday of the second week of the season, I'd caught 14 carp and it didn't seem possible; the number didn't equate when compared with what had gone before. The lake was paying me back. Finally, I'd cracked it. Heaven knows how many carp I would have had that year had I stayed, but the carp gods clearly had other plans for me.

When I arrived for my next session, I found a stranger on the lake, a local of questionable ability. I say that because as I walked up to him, he was casting, swinging his rod over his shoulder without looking - he hooked his pink golf brolly and tried to cast that out, too. Nonetheless, I paused for a polite 'hello' and was quite taken aback when his first sentence was that he'd just seen a monster carp caught 'up the road'. He told me that it was 34lbs and had been caught at Silver End, a lake just a few miles away from the reservoir.

I couldn't settle into my fishing. All I could think about was this monster, if it was true. Ironically, my grandparents had lived in Rivenhall, the village next door to Silver End. My grandfather was a great bloke, and when I went to stay, he always gave me his time. As a small boy I was captivated by the outdoors and the wondrous sights and smells of nature, so we would go on long walks, all the way up the road toward Silver End. Firstly, I would dip my net in the lake at the big mansion at Rivenhall, and then we'd walk further up the road to a magical wild and overgrown pool, which was now, apparently, the home of what could be the largest carp in Essex.

Actually, I had looked at Silver End one day when I was driving past it a

couple of years before. This was because of a guy I'd met on Layer. He was a vermin controller, who travelled all over Essex in a futile attempt to keep the rat and mice populations under control. He told me that he'd seen bigger carp than the ones in Layer and as the biggest known carp in Essex at this time *was* in Layer, this was quite a statement to make. Silver End was one of the two lakes where he'd claimed to have seen massive carp.

When I visited Silver End it was a hot day and I would have expected to see good fish, had they existed, but all I saw were several small, wild-looking commons. Factoring in that this guy did seem to need some friends, and I felt it was very likely he had exaggerated just so that fellow anglers would show an interest and listen to him; he was probably talking crap. Now, though, I wasn't so sure. It was too much of a coincidence. I made up my mind. I couldn't leave this alone. I had to be certain whether this monster carp existed or not, so after all the years of heartache and pain trying to crack the reservoir, and just when all my hard work was bearing fruit, I turned my back on the res and walked away, never to return.

I shot off to the local tackle shop to buy a ticket for Kelvedon Angling Club, and with the ticket purchased, I pulled into the car park of Silver End at 4pm that same Friday afternoon.

Chapter Twelve

Silver End:
The Night of the Moon

S
ilver End didn't quite live up to my childhood memories of a magical pool. Firstly, it was a gravel pit and, like most pits, it is a scar on the landscape, but nature had done her damnedest to repair her wounds and it was very mature, or at least it was when I fished it. A few years afterwards, the club decided that this small, intimate pool would make a good match venue, so they bulldozed the track along the bank and filled in the shallows.

In those days, it was only the entrance that let it down and because of this it was easy to miss its beauty and charm. As you passed through the gate, you entered an area of rough, neglected gravelly ground, which was the car park. Glancing to the left, you would have a glimpse of the lake, but only by looking along a bare, gravel bank, which at first impression, wasn't particularly enticing. If you stepped out of the car, though, walked to the steep edge and looked down, you soon realised that it was a pretty, intimate pool. The pit is L-shaped; imagine that the L is upside down, so your feet are at the top of the L as the water stretches away in front of you, with the bottom part of the L as the main pool, kicking left.

The shallows were crystal clear because of the vigorous weed growth. From the high vantage point you could see right down to the bottom, except where the potomogeton beds covered the surface. The shallows fell away into the main pool where, from memory, the depths went down to about 12 feet. The right-hand bank was also very steep, mainly grass with the odd small bush clinging precariously.

Should you be able to climb down without slipping and breaking something, you would be at the water's edge.

There were three spots that could vaguely be described as swims, if for no other reason than you could set up and the bank was dry. Part of the way down the right bank, I was to discover a kind of plateau, an area which was to prove very productive for me. The back and left banks were lower than the cliff-like right bank, with just a slight gradient and were heavily wooded. The back bank had the largest potomogeton bed in the pit, which was overshadowed by a mature oak tree, a great climbing tree to look down into the potomogeton bed, a favourite place for the carp to chill, out of the direct rays of the sun.

I had a good walk around for a couple of hours, or so. The lake was deserted and this was now Friday evening, when you would have expected someone to be turning up. So, the doubts were creeping in again. Surely, if a 34 had been out, someone would be on here? Nonetheless, I was determined to stay and have a crack.

With not a sign, or a clue, of where to start, where should I start? I have a little theory that I've observed over the years. Often one of the most, if not *the* most, productive areas of a lake is the first swim to the access gate or car park. It's more than a coincidence. Why? It can only be conjecture, but the most reasonable suggestion I can make is a simple one; it's the area most fished, so it's where the fish can guarantee to find food that the anglers have discarded at the end of their session. I had nothing else to go at, so it was near the car park for me. I pitched up halfway along the bare gravel on the left-hand side at the point where, by plumbing around, I'd deduced that the shallows dropped away as the water got deeper into the main pool.

My approach was simple; right-hand rod in the shallows, middle rod on the slope and the third in the deeper water, on the bottom of the slope. Rig-wise, all rods were on the hair rig. Despite my success with side-hooked boilies and the bolt rig at the beginning of the season at Braxted, I did experiment with the hair and soon was convinced that it was far more effective than side-hooked baits. My concerns about it snagging in the bottom debris and silkweed were unfounded, probably because I'd found the most effective hook link length was 15" of Dacron; I had ditched the dental floss because the separating strands got tangled in the weed. My hair rig consisted of a size 6 hook, with 1½lb mono tied to the bend, with a hair length of an inch and a half. My lead choice was 3oz and fixed.

ABOVE
My version of the
original hair rig.

Bait was the mega maple and bird food boilie. I was set up by 8pm, and sat for the last two good hours of daylight with my eyes peeled to the lake. I didn't see *anything* – and I mean anything – not even a small fish, like a roach. I was beginning to have my doubts again and finally got my head down at 11pm, thinking I would set my alarm for an hour before dawn so I could be back on the ressy at daybreak. I was absolutely exhausted having had a hard week of work and then driving up to see my girlfriend in the evenings, so it was prudent to set my alarm.

The next thing I knew, it was midnight and with absolutely no recollection of being woken, extracting myself from my sleeping bag and hitting the take, somehow or other I found myself holding my rod. It was bent into the most alarming curve as if something of quite awesome power was roaring off to my left toward the deeper water, with seemingly unstoppable force. What a fight that was! As I write this, it's still vivid in my mind. There was a full moon, and it was almost like being on a football pitch with floodlit illumination. I could see my line cleaving through the water and the swirls as the carp fought for its freedom. After what seemed an endless time, I slipped the net under a huge fish, or at least I could see its incredible length clearly in the moonlight. With the adrenalin of the fight, but I think more the excitement and mystery of hooking a monster from this lake of secrets, I was shaking like a leaf. I sat on the gravel with net handle in my hand, allowing myself, and the fish, to have a brief rest and restore my nerves before the formalities.

It turned out that this carp wasn't quite a monster but at 18¾lbs, it was a big fish for its day, and a very special one, as the first one from a new lake always is. It was a leather and while being very long, was equally very lean, more like a torpedo, which accounted for its speed and strength in the fight.

I slipped her back and I'll never forget it. I lay back on the gravel, my head resting on a tuft of grass, looked up at the stars and bathed in the light from the full moon. I was buzzing, I'd caught my first Silver End carp and I just knew, instinctively, that this lake was going to be my home for a while and that there would be many more epic battles ahead.

I didn't have long to wait. An hour and a half later, the same rod was away. This fish, again, moved to my left, but not at the same lightning speed of the first. It felt heavier and more ponderous and I felt sure that this was a significantly bigger carp. It was just as I had that thought that my line went slack and I wound in to find that my hook link had 'parted' a few inches up from the hook. I was sure of the strength of my tackle and the pressure I could apply and felt that I'd been within my limits so I was perplexed as I studied the end of my hook link, especially as the break was so clean. It was as if it had been cut through with a knife. Had the carp cut me off despite the fact I hadn't felt a snag?

Just as dawn was breaking, my right-hand rod in the shallows was away with another fast take and no warning; no twitches here like at the res. I picked up the rod and it hooped over as I leaned into the fish, and then sprang back as the line went slack. I was speechless as I wound in only to find that, yet again, my Dacron braid had 'snapped' a few inches above the hook. I'd stopped using the dental floss over at the ressy because it was a difficult material to use; if you weren't careful it

BELOW
I lay back on the gravel, my head resting on a tuft of grass, looked up at the stars and bathed in the light from the full moon. I was buzzing, I'd caught my first Silver End carp...

would easily tangle in the bottom weed. The hair rig was such an immense edge that it worked brilliantly with the Dacron, so I had reverted to a Dacron braided hook link of around 15". It had proved to be a trusty and reliable rig at Braxted, so I couldn't understand why it was letting me down now.

This second incident was exactly the same as the first and the line had been cut through like a knife. What the hell were the snags in this place? Then my mind flashed to teeth - were they bite-offs? Could it be that these uncaught carp were taking my maple boilies so confidently in their mouths, right back to their teeth, that they were biting me off?

I wound in all three rods and shortened my hook links to around 12", casting back out to make the most of my last few hours, but no more takes came my way before I had to pull off. I'd promised to go to a party that evening, but before that, I wanted to track down Bill and tell him my news. I couldn't contain myself. I'd had three takes on my first session, despite knowing zero about the water, so how many carp were in here? I felt convinced that the rumour of the 34-pounder was true and I couldn't wait to get back.

Chapter Thirteen

Bite-Offs and Hooklink Mechanics

O ver the years I have experienced the problem of bite-offs on several waters. In the early days, it was because the carp were so naïve to our tactics, and in particular the grub we gave them. Carp that had rarely, if ever, been caught were being presented with manna from heaven; lovely, irresistible food. Couple that with the possibility that a carp may have had a few mates with him when he came across my baits, and as greed kicked in there would be competition to get the tasty grub down his neck as quickly as he could before his companions did.

Nowadays, bite offs are a much rarer phenomenon, and certainly on waters where the carp have been fished for regularly and for some years. They are much more cautious in appraising a potential food item to ensure that it hasn't got a dangerous, hidden agenda, so it's fair to say that bite-offs are rare; they are not non-existent, though.

I'd lived with this problem for decades, and it had almost become an obsession to ensure that I had 100% strength in my tackle, so when I *do* suffer an inexplicable occurrence of a parted hooklink, my radar is up.

The last time this happened was in the 90s, just when I was beginning to understand that the carp were avoiding clear spots on weedy lakes, so I had to go after them in the weed, and I was doing exactly that when I lost a fish. On winding in, I discovered that my hooklink had been severed, and I suspected a bite-off.

There are a couple of indicators that you can look out for; the hooklink will

normally be cut a couple of inches above the hook, and the cut is as clean as if it has been sliced through by a very sharp knife. I was fishing a 10-inch hooklink and I was sure that the reason I had suffered a bite off was because I was fishing PVA bags in weed. There are two ways of going after carp in weedy swims; you can present a bait on top of the weed as most do, or you can go after the carp where the natural food is, and where they are feeding, i.e. in the weed.

This is a favourite tactic of mine when fishing in shallow weed up to a couple of feet deep. A heavy lead is used and put inside the PVA bag with the bait and rig, which is then punched into the weed. The carp burrow into the weed seeking out the bait and as the bait and rig are close together, the carp's mouth is right on the spot, so it gulps the lot down without browsing the swim or turning its head. There is a very real risk of a bite off, and in this situation, I would recommend being aware of the potential danger, and using short hooklinks of 4 to 6 inches, maximum.

I am not a lover of such short hooklinks and it is only when I want to present my bait in deep weed, or to punch it into the silt, that I use them. I mention this because there is a trend for short hooklinks currently. They are being hyped up, and of course they do work, especially if every angler on the lake is on short rigs - the law of averages dictates that carp will get caught on them. However, over the years I have experimented with hooklinks from two-inches to four-feet long, and I've identified a clear pattern that generally, short hooklinks do not catch the big old girls. This may be because of their frame size and deep bellies, which means they must make more effort in order to get down and suck in a bait on a short rig.

I am always aware of and experimenting with hooklink length. I am looking for the shortest possible length that enables the carp to take the bait back a decent distance into its mouth. At that critical moment, tension comes into play by way of a fixed lead, or the friction in my running lead set-up, which turns the hook

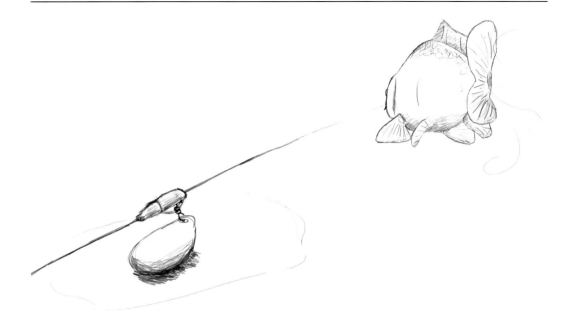

and pricks the carp. Too short a hooklink, and the carp won't be able to take the bait and hook in properly. Too long a hooklink, and it may well be that the carp sucks the bait in, feels or senses that something is wrong, and because the hooklink hasn't tensioned and thus the hook hasn't pricked the carp, it blows it out without concern. If it is feeding greedily, there is the real danger that it will take the rig back over its throat teeth, and you will experience a bite off. There is an even greater danger that if the carp can't bite through your hooklink, then bait and rig will continue on their journey down into the carp's gut, where the hook will catch; this could lead to its death.

A few years back, I was enjoying a great deal of success on a syndicate lake, and in an experimental frame of mind. I decided to fish four kilos of boilies as tight as I could, with the hope that one solitary, big, old mirror would come across this feast and get its head down. My four kilos of boilies were put on a spot no more than a foot across. I'd been having some exceptional results against the other members by fishing two-foot hooklinks, and it was a rig with a two-foot hooklink that I put on this spot.

I had a screamer in the middle of the night and found myself playing what appeared to be an extremely heavy carp. I struggled with that fish, but I just couldn't get it up off the bottom and I was sure that it was the lake's big girl. After a lot of heaving, to-ing and fro-ing, I was relieved finally to slip the net under her, and that was a bit of a saga in its own right because it was a pitch black, moonless night and my head torch batteries had died.

Once the net and carp were on the unhooking mat, I probed into its mouth for the hook with the intention of unhooking it, getting her sacked up comfortably and safely, and then sorting out the weight in the morning. As my fingers followed the hooklink into the mouth, probing for the hook, I felt sick. My fingers were as deep as they could reach into the carp's mouth, but I couldn't feel the hook; all I could feel was line. I had a flashback of that carp gulping down my four kilos of boilies tight on the spot, as well as my two-foot hooklink, and now my hook was fatally stuck in its gut. With no torch, and in total despair, I cut the hooklink just outside of its mouth and sacked the carp up in the hope that I could save the fish from my stupidity in the morning, and that maybe I'd see the hook deep down in its throat, and be able to extract it.

BELOW
Lucky or what! Landed, but only just. To my mind, a clear indication of a hooklink that is a couple of inches too short.

BOTTOM
This hook position is an indication that the hooklink may have been too long.

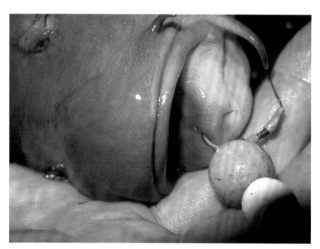

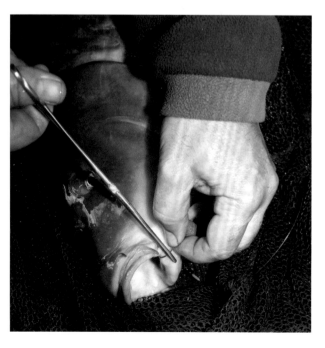

I was gutted and lay on my bedchair cursing myself for my carelessness. I really should have known better. I was out of my sleeping bag as soon as there was enough light to see what I was doing and as I cleared the sack away from the carp, I felt something in its belly, a few inches behind the pec' – it was my hook! The hooklink went back under the gill plate into its throat, and was still hanging out of its mouth. I was amazed, and extremely relieved, I can tell you. Of all the thousands of carp I'd landed, I'd never had one take a rig and bait in while sorting out its food from the bottom debris and then blow the hook and bait out of its gills so that the hook stuck in its belly; but then, I'd never used such a long hooklink on an extremely tight bed of bait before.

Over the years, I have found the best all-round hooklink length to be around 10 inches. As I mentioned, at this length you have enough play for the carp to take the bait and hook into its

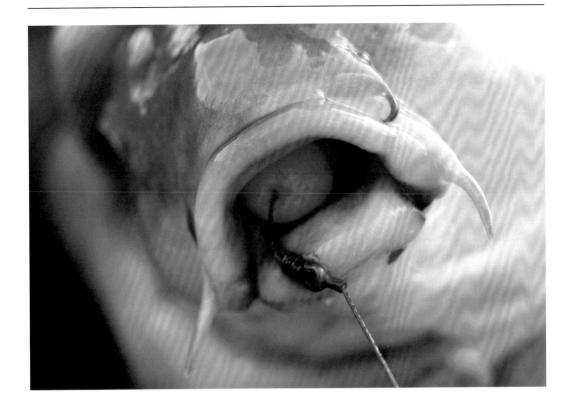

mouth properly, and for the rig mechanics to work for you, i.e. pricking the carp. You may have to fish hooklinks longer than 10 inches to get your presentation right on the lakebed, or because that's what the carp insists upon on that day, but there will be some occasions - when fishing in weed as I described, for example - when a shorter hooklink is required.

It must be perplexing for a newcomer to carp fishing to decide how to arrive at the optimum hooklink length, so here are a couple of pointers:

Check every hookhold of each carp you land. If the hook has only just caught in the lip, then it may be that your hooklink is too short, preventing the carp from taking it in properly.

It's also worth mentioning that if you're bending out or snapping hooks, then providing you are using a recognised strong pattern, the reason for hook failure is most likely down to your presentation preventing the hook from sinking properly down to the bend. It may well be that your hooklink is too short, or you need to increase resistance in the set-up/weight of lead. If just the hook point penetrates then all the pressure is on the point, and there isn't a carp hook on the market that can take that pressure from a hard-fighting carp. Another reason that hooks may bend or snap is unavoidable poor hook holds due to mouth damage.

When landing a string of carp; if you note that the hook is caught in the corner of the mouth consistently, then this is an indication that your hook link is over-length. The carp sucks in your rig and then because of the overlong hooklink it is able to move freely without the hooklink tensioning. It is only when it has moved its head sufficiently to the side that the over length hooklink comes under tension and the hook catches in the corner of the mouth. You know when you have achieved perfection, and the optimum hooklink length, when you are consistently nailing the carp in the bottom of the mouth, an inch or so back.

Chapter Fourteen

Silver End: The Demon Eye

After pulling off at Silver End, I went to the ressy and sure enough, there was Bill. When I told him about my result, his jaw dropped. Just like me, he'd fished the lake in the past, some 15 years before as a teenager, but unlike me, he didn't have childhood memories when every stream, pond and ditch seemed to be magical and mysterious through my young eyes. Bill's memory was of a barren, scruffy pit where all he caught were minnows, sticklebacks and small perch. I'd kept the best bit until last when he asked me why the hell I'd moved on to Silver End. When I told him about the rumoured 34, he said, "That's got to be bollocks!" Despite his doubts, though, he decided to pull off the res and take his chances with me. When I got home I told Nigel and he was up for joining, too.

With my four-day working week advantage, I was back on the Thursday evening and, as you do, set up in a swim where I'd enjoyed my success the Friday before. This night, however, was different. I didn't get a twitch. I spent the Friday morning having a good look round but with a cloudy sky and a cooling easterly, conditions weren't exactly great for fish spotting. As I walked further along the bank to the point that looked over the main pool, though, I did see a fish roll to my right, halfway to the far bank, so I moved my kit down to this spot.

The margin was very deep so I elected to fish a rod to the left down the margin, the centre rod was cast directly out in front of me, then I put a third rod out toward the far right-hand bank where I'd seen the fish roll earlier. I didn't

have long to wait before the right-hand rod was away to what was proving to be an amazing bait – the maple boilie. I hooked the fish and it moved off to my left and then the rod tip sprang back and the line went slack. On winding in, I was horrified to see, yet again, that the hook link had parted an inch above the hook. I was absolutely gutted. A little over a week before, I'd been on such a high when I'd landed the 18¾lb leather; now I'd lost three on the trot, and life didn't seem so good. At least, I felt sure that it was bite-offs, and as the line had severed closer, only an inch above the hook, I reduced all my hook links a further three inches, down to nine inches.

I'd just got the rods back out when Bill and Nigel turned up. They didn't stay chatting for too long, partly because they wanted to get stuck in but I would guess mainly because I wasn't particularly sociable – I had the right hump! Despite us all fishing, this and the next two weekends, no more takes came our way. The positive start was certainly not living up to expectations. I kept on the maple boilies but Bill, being Bill, was off in all sorts of directions and I know he used luncheon meat and I'm sure tried some more archaic offerings – potatoes and marshmallows spring to mind. Eventually, I got our little team back on track by suggesting that we try a baiting scheme for the following week, and as Bill lived only 20 minutes down the road, it seemed reasonable to me and Nigel that he should be elected to undertake this project, which Bill did in his usual enthusiastic manner.

Then, I had a serious accident at work, when my white work coat got caught up in a lathe. I damned near had my head chopped off, so I was lucky to live. I escaped with just a badly strained back and cracked ribs, nonetheless I was signed off by the doctor for what was eventually ten weeks. Damn! I so loved work. This was an opportunity not to be missed and I grabbed it with both hands, fishing the pit five days and nights a week, on average, only leaving to make bait, stock up with provisions and occasionally, very occasionally, to see the bird.

My next session after the baiting was fishless through the Thursday night and Friday, but some time around midnight, fishing the Point where I had my third bite-off, I had a take on the right-hand rod from the same area. After a short battle, I landed what I knew was a better fish. Nigel and Bill were on the far side and Bill shouted across – "How big is it, Kev?" Funny, my reply stuck in his mind and he repeated it back to me years later – I said "Safe to say, it's a double". That was a little conservative because I knew it was close to the magic mark. I just prayed that this was in fact a 20. Bill saw through my modest reply, though, and was round like a flash.

On the scales, this pretty mirror went just over 20lbs and I was elated – my first 20 from Silver End. I gazed at her flank in the light from Nigel's torch.

OPPOSITE PAGE
... the point that overlooked the main pool...

Among the larger scales, she looked like she'd been sprinkled with stardust, which was in fact the tiniest of scales so I named her 'Stardust'. This lovely mirror is still around today, albeit not in the same lake, and I understand that she's now called The Ghost. When the club attempted vainly to turn this intimate pit into a match venue, Stardust was moved to an adjacent lake. This old lady now comes out at around 27lbs. I wonder if today's captors know of her history and how old she is.

On my next session, because both my last two takes had come from my right rod, cast toward the right bank, I moved over there to concentrate my efforts. I found that the water was a lot shallower on this side, falling away to a flattish area, like a plateau. I had another take on the maple boilie and the fish snagged me in deep weed, but it didn't seem to be a great distance out so I waded until I was quite literally up to my neck in water. By stretching forward, as much as I could without the water going up my nose, I managed to get the rod directly above the fish, so I wound down and heaved until the fish came out of the weed. I was soaked to the skin, but well satisfied with what turned out to be a well-deserved 15lb leather. After my run of bad luck, now things were seemingly looking up.

As I netted that 15lb leather, cheers went up and I turned round. On top of the high bank were three dog walkers, a fisherman who was the local milkman, and a lovely old boy who was the bailiff. It was like I'd just scored a goal at Wembley. In the bailiff's eyes, this event made me his hero. Whenever I was over, he would make a point of asking me when I'd be back and always came over to see me. I thought 'this is a bit nicer than the ressy' but he didn't reflect the club's viewpoint. In his own way, I think he was a bit of a rebel himself, but it was certainly good to have him on side as I got wind of rumblings within the committee, especially as someone had clocked me

using three rods. He warned me to be careful and wind in my third rod when other club members turned up. Now that's what I call a proper bailiff!

One day, the milkman was fishing and rather jokingly, I said 'When you come past on a Friday morning, you can drop me off a pint of milk, then.' The next weekend, I heard a 'clink' and when I got up, I was somewhat surprised to find a pint of gold top on my bivvy doorstep. This was to continue. If the milkman saw my car in the car park, I was guaranteed a fresh milk delivery.

Later on, a youngster from the village would come round and he really wanted to get into carp fishing so we would chat and I would answer his long list of questions. Nigel was the paper boy. He took a bit of training, though, because the first weekend that he left my paper outside it had rained before I could get to it, resulting in a soggy mess. In the end, we worked out that the best 'letter box' was to slip the paper under the side of my bivvy. I was sorted.

Later on, actually the next season, it got even better for a very brief spell. There was a pub up the road and I was driving past it one morning when I saw what turned out to be the landlord cutting the grass. He was wearing a pair of shorts and no top apart from an enormous pair of strap-on false tits. I'd only seen them out of the corner of my eye as I'd driven past so didn't realise they were false, or indeed that they were attached to a bloke - I nearly crashed the car! Anyway, we got talking. I told him I was fishing the pit down the road and rather cheekily said, "I could do with some dinner and a pint at lunchtime if you fancy bringing it over." He did, and continued to do so for about a month or so but sadly, he tired of it after that. Some people, eh!

I didn't get any more takes over the next two weeks and thinking back to Braxted I began to worry as my mind returned to the experiences on the reservoir. I wondered, even though I'd caught a few fish, if the carp weren't really getting screwed down on the maple boilies. Maybe I hadn't put enough in for the fish to identify them as a food source. With the hard fishing and seeing my girlfriend in between, I couldn't go on a massive bait-rolling exercise so I turned to my trusty chickpeas, figuring that this way I could carpet the bottom with food, without the hours and hours of preparation that I would have to spend with the boilies. Surely, there would be more chance of the carp noticing hundreds of small round peas on a lake bed, rather than the odd round brown ball.

For once, I was right. I couldn't fail. Every week I was catching. I'd worked out that if I went into a swim and caught, I didn't get a take the second night, but if I moved out, and fished somewhere else and baited the original swim before I left, and then went back, I would catch, more often than not. I'd identified three 'going' swims – the aforementioned Plateau, under the oak tree on the bottom bank where the largest bed of potomogeton was, and opposite on the point where I'd caught Stardust.

The most consistent swim was the Oak Tree and the Plateau next. So it would work like this: I'd do a night in the Oak and catch; the next night, I'd move to the Plateau with a 50/50 chance of catching. The next night I was over at the lake, I'd go back to the Oak with a very good chance that I'd catch. If I went back to the Plateau so soon after I'd last fished it, I would blank, so the next night, I'd fish the Point with a 20% chance of catching... and this is how it went on, moving backward and forward between the swims, keeping them baited.

In the beginning, I just fished two rods with chicks and the third with maple boilies, but the carp were so on to the chicks that I gave up on the boilies. Meanwhile, poor old Bill couldn't buy a take. I was so in tune with the water, having spent so much more time there than him, that I could almost sense which swims to go to next. I was catching every week and Bill, now also on chicks, was blanking. All he could catch was tench, which strangely, I never caught. He did however, have a couple of funny occurrences when his hooklinks broke. I did mention to him that I suspected they could be bite-offs, but I'm not sure if he ever accepted that.

One weekend, I couldn't go and as Bill and I chatted on the phone about his prospects for his forthcoming Friday night session, I so wanted him to catch. I told him which swim I thought he should fish and exactly where he should put his baits. I just knew that without me there, hogging it, he was going to catch, so I wasn't surprised when on the Saturday evening, I picked up the phone and it was Bill.

It wasn't a happy Bill, though. He was effing and blinding, really not a happy chappy. Perhaps I should let Bill tell his story.

'One dark night, I had a screaming take on a close range chick-pea fished on a 2-inch fixed bolt rig. As I closed the bail arm the rod slammed right round and the fish tore off along the margin parallel to the bank. After a tremendous scrap lasting about ten minutes, the fish became firmly embedded in marginal weed. The entire weed bed, at least three-feet long, was moving, and I truly believed I'd finally hooked a carp of massive proportions. I

managed to dig the landing net through the weed, and hauled net, weed bed and fish into the margin. I looked on in amazement as the dim light of my small torch revealed the prize which lay covered in weed in the landing net – a bloody great pike which turned out to weigh just under 23lbs! Fed up with tench-trouble, unexplained snap-outs and night-feeding pike with a taste for chick peas and 2oz leads, I decided to leave the place alone for a bit.'

This really was the last straw for Bill. He decided to lick his wounds and move on to Layer. Nigel had also stopped fishing the pit and gone to Layer, so now I was 'Billy No Mates' – pukka! In one way, it was great that I had the pit to myself, but Bill and Nigel absolutely ripped Layer apart. They were the first on there with the hair rig and our awesome maple boilie but apart from that, they fished at long range and were the first anglers, for sure, to present this mega combination of the rig and bait in the centre of the pit, where normally the carp would remain unmolested. I had to put up with Nigel at home midweek on the odd evenings that I didn't fish, telling me of how many dozens more fish they'd caught that previous weekend. I did crack once, though, and instead of fishing Silver End, Nige and I went to Layer. We had 60 takes in a day. Unbelievable fishing! Nigel had an absolutely cracking common of 26lbs, to boot, but despite this awesome fishing experience, nothing could keep me away from Silver End.

On my return, I found that another guy had turned up, a really strange individual. I don't know what he'd been crossed with, although I have some theories. He was to prove to be a right pain over the forthcoming months as I discovered that he must have picked up a chickpea that I'd missed. I was usually so careful, searching the swim for any peas that might have flown out of the 'pult, but I must have missed one and the secret was out. What didn't impress me was the fact that he'd left loads behind when he'd been in the swim, so other anglers saw them, and got on them. Worse than that, though, he wasn't cooking them. I felt that I had to try to, at least, get him to cook the chicks before he blew it for me. I explained the process but I'd have been better off talking to the oak tree.

I turned up one Tuesday night in the middle of October and fished the back bank ten yards along from my favourite Oak Tree swim at a spot where the potomogeton bed thinned out. On the session before, I'd seen what appeared to be a big carp roll along the bank to my right, tight to the emerging bough of a sunken tree. I'd fished this bank a few times without success, and had more or less given up on it, but I don't need telling twice when I see a carp roll. From this new spot, I

ABOVE
*...The next thing I
remember is waking
up to a white-out...*

could cover my favoured area in front of the oak as well as casting one across to my right, where I'd seen the fish.

Bill had not only caught the pike on an extremely short 2-inch fixed bolt rig, but also he'd been doing well on Layer with this set-up. It wasn't lost on me that Bill was on a water where he could enjoy loads of action and he was experimenting so there had to be something in the 2-inch bolt rig. I decided to give it a go on my right-hand rod. I'd started to have twitches on what were now my standard 9-inch rigs and while catching regularly, I had noted the twitches and with the experiences in the ressy firmly burned into my brain, I started experimenting, too.

Two rods were out to my left and the third, I have to say, was a great cast to the right, tight to the tree bough. There was just something about that cast and spot that made me feel confident. I was enjoying the evening with anticipation when 'Uncooked' as I'd named my chickpea bandit, turned up to ruin the tranquillity. He set up dead opposite me, on the point, noisily bashing bank sticks in, and catapulting chickpeas in a random fashion in front of him. I'm sure just as many went down his boots as in the lake. I should mention that no matter the weather, rain or heatwave, he always wore wellington boots. I could have done without him on this particular night, but I'd caught carp before, despite his antics, so with darkness falling, and me having to go to work in the morning as sadly, my ten week 'holiday' (ahem) I mean sick leave had come to an end, I got my head down, still feeling confident.

The next thing I remember was waking up in a white-out. There was dense fog and I couldn't see further than 10 feet, let alone the far bank where Uncooked was. I'd been woken by a screamer on my right-hand rod. I lifted into it and the rod thumped over in the most satisfying curve and stayed there. I panicked as I wondered if the carp was snagged around the dead tree but then it moved slowly out and away from the snag, thank God, toward the middle of the lake. By this time, I am sure that I'd caught more or less the lake's entire population, bar two or three, and in some instances, more than once. I'd never felt a weight like this, though, and I just prayed that it wasn't Bill's pike!

There was another bite alarm screaming and it took me a second to figure it out. This alarm wasn't registering in my head as a tone I knew and as well as that, it seemed to be muffled and distant. Then, I realised. The noise was coming from out of the fog on the other side. Uncooked was also in. I heard a lot of scuffling and clattering, then a muffled 'whooosh', that I thought was an ambitious strike. There were a few seconds of silence, as he played his quarry, I imagine, and then an almighty 'splosh!' It seemed that Uncooked had just fallen in!

My carp had decided to wake up a bit so I forgot about whatever antics Uncooked was up to and applied some side pressure before I got done in the potomegeton bed to my left. This worked and the fish plodded back out in front of me. I heard splashing and although hidden from me in the shroud of fog I knew the fish had surfaced. I could hear it and see the waves lapping toward me. Then the fight seemed to go out of it and I could feel the fish just wallowing on the surface.

Those of you who may have experienced this relatively rare event will understand where I was at this moment. Having a fish some distance away from you that has blown its tanks with the fight ebbing out of it, wallowing on the surface is a difficult situation to be in. You have to apply pressure to ease the fish slowly toward you, and pray. The whole bulk and weight of the carp is on a tiny piece of metal – the hook. I was certainly praying, or perhaps a better way of putting it in my Essex parlance, is 'I was shitting myself', when out of the mist emerged an enormous light flank. This just had to be the big girl. Slowly, I eased her toward me. She was coming in head first and I could see my hook embedded in the bottom lip and the three-ounce lead hanging down, just two inches away. Slowly, oh so painfully slowly, she came toward me. I eased off the pressure as she kicked a little and wallowed on the surface and she took my breath away when I saw how wide she was. She was enormous, like no carp I'd ever seen before and so wide that I could almost have put a saddle on her.

I kept up the pressure as she inched forward. Now, just a few more feet and she'd be mine, and then she saw me. Violently, she jerked her head to the left in an

effort to break away and make for the sanctuary of the potomegeton. The surface erupted, spray flew through the air and one drop hit me square on the forehead. My rod tip sprang back, as the lead and hook were catapulted toward me. She just lay there, eyeball to eyeball with me. The drop of water ran down to the tip of my nose and dripped off; I could have sworn she smiled as she slowly sank into the depths.

This was to be the last time that I'd ever fish such a short fixed bolt rig, so that the carp could use the heavy lead to bounce the hook out. I was gutted and in despair. I sat on the bank with my head in my hands, beside myself, a dark depression and feeling of foreboding fell about me as I relived the fight. The intensity overwhelmed me and I could still feel her stare as it burned through my skull like a laser into the centre of my brain. All I could see was that carp's eye. It was as if, at that moment, she had possessed me.

After about five minutes of this mammoth sulk, I parted my hands and looked out across the lake, back to the spot where I'd last seen her sink away, praying that I was in a dream and that this nightmare wasn't happening and she'd still be there waiting for me to net her, but no, it wasn't a dream. She'd gone. In her place was a bush hat, floating on the surface.

'God! Uncooked!' I thought. The last I'd heard of him was the almighty splash, which, unless he'd brought a pet cow with him, must have meant that he'd fallen in. I was concerned because the margin was deep. Why hadn't he gone out and recovered his bush hat? Despite the fact that he wasn't my sort of bloke, I was very worried so I went round to see him. His swim was empty. There was no sign of him. Now I was really anxious. I walked all along the point bank, back around to my swim and right round to the other side where the plateau was, and then, up to the shallows. There was no sign of him anywhere around the lake but by now, the sun was beginning to burn through the fog and I could just make out the car park where my car and his were still parked. It seemed more than likely that Uncooked was now 'Cooked'.

I ran as fast as I could back to my swim. The ground was wet and slippery from the moisture drenched fog and as I went around the corner at the bottom end I slipped, going down too heavy on my left knee. God, that hurt! I struggled up with mud layered on my trousers and arm. I could feel the damp and cold of it working its way through my sweatshirt and penetrating through to my skin, but I kept going. I got back to my swim, breathless, chest heaving, and I could feel intense burning in my lungs and the sour taste of bile rising in my throat. I fished out some coins from my wallet kept in my rucksack and although at the limit of my endurance, I knew I had to keep going as Uncooked's life may now depend on it. I pushed on, back up to the car park intending to drive to the village telephone box to summon help. It's a funny thing, when you're in a 'life and death' situation; the panic, stress and emotion can play with your mind. I was in a quandary. Every second counted; who I should call first? The police and report Uncooked's drowning? Or should I call the ambulance service? He could just still be alive somewhere.

As I ran past Uncooked's empty car, I saw a pair of wellies sticking out from under his rear bumper, so I bent down and was stunned when I saw that Uncooked's legs were attached to them. Clearly he was sodden, wet through so it seemed the last place he'd want to be. I said 'Are you all right?' and got some kind of garbled response that he was.

"What are you doing under your car?"

"I fell in and I'm drying off."

I found this a bizarre response, so I said,

"Riiiiight. Okay... but wouldn't you be better off drying off IN your car... with the heater on?"

Uncooked clearly wasn't 'Cooked'. I had mixed emotions; relief verging toward homicide. I had just worried myself half to death, and run myself into the ground to a point almost beyond endurance, only to find this idiot, soaked through and lying underneath his car.

He went on to explain the folly of my logic. If he'd got into his car, he would have made his seat wet. Instead, standing outside and reaching in, being extremely careful not to drip on his seat, he turned on the ignition and ran his engine until both engine and exhaust were hot. Then he lay underneath the car where he could dry off without making the mistake (that someone stupid like me would have done) of getting their car seat wet. I applauded him for his sensibility and as I walked away, I made up my mind that next time he fell in, fuck him!

Chapter Fifteen

Silver End: Possessed

D espite the loss of the big girl I continued to fish on, only stopping when the lake froze in late November. I decided to call it a day for the rest of the season because I'd been avoiding the phone since the start and needed to placate my customer base.

During the previous close season, I had doubled my range of Happy Hooker products with the introduction of two sizes of weigh sling. These had been a massive success and the orders had flooded in. It was a somewhat stroppy Jack Simpson, the owner of Simpsons of Turnford, who I visited the next weekend, but after a few sarcastic remarks all was forgiven and Jack placed a nice order for more sacks and slings. Fishing forgotten, my non-work days were now spent producing carp gear.

Before I knew it, the season was nearly upon me again, the orders were just piling up as word got out, it seemed that the postman had to double the size of his post sack and I would soon need an extra telephone line. Because of all this, I never got my act together like I'd done in previous close seasons, with a planned baiting campaign, military style. I couldn't rely on Bill and Nigel, either, because Layer had hooked them. I was disappointed that Bill seemed to have lost interest in the pit, but that's the difference between us; I hunt the biggest, Bill loves just catching carp.

So, I turned up at Silver End on the morning of the 15th expecting to have the lake to myself. I knew Bill and Nigel wouldn't be there, and as no other carp anglers had turned up the previous season, I was hoping that word hadn't got out, so I was surprised and devastated to see a brolly set up under the oak and another a little way along the bank, completely tying up my favourite area. 'If this is Uncooked and a mate,' I thought. 'I'm going to kill him!'

As I approached, a guy who seemed really old to me, even though he was only in his late 40s but certainly helped by the fact that he wore an old, holey cardigan and carpet slippers and was smoking a pipe, greeted me in a relatively high-pitched voice.

"Helloooow. 'Ow are *yooo?*" as if we were old friends from years back.

It was Roger Smith, a legend in his own kettle. Roger had been around the carp scene for donkey's years. In fact, at one time he was married to the daughter of Tom Mintram who ran the Redmire syndicate in the famous Jack Hilton era.

Roger had dropped out of carp fishing for a while but had come back with a vengeance, joining the Savay syndicate and catching some great carp, so I was a little taken aback to find him on my turf, but I guess that word had got out after all.

With Roger Smith was Bob Jones and Roger introduced him squeakily, "Not the famous Bob Jones (a reference to another very famous carp angler) but the other one."

The other one? Who? I decided not to ask. Bob was a rod-builder – I say 'was' because sadly, a few years later, he was to succumb to the bottle. After the introductions, Roger said,

"Well, I've heard of you." he said. "You're ever so, ever so famous!"

Until you get to know Roger, you're never quite sure how much is a piss-take.

"Come and sit down and have a cupper tea."

This particular style of a 'cupper tea' was a new experience for me, or rather the process of making it.

Roger took the lid off his kettle, poured some water in, and then chucked in half a dozen tea bags. Once boiled, the liquid that spewed from the spout was as black as ebony and so stewed and acidic that I had indigestion for the rest of the day. I did eventually learn to drink Roger's tea, and in fact, ended up making tea in the same fashion. To this day I still have a kettle like Roger's.

Roger has been a good friend ever since and has influenced me in many ways; from tackle design right through to strangely, even philosophy. He is certainly unique and one of carp fishing's true characters.

Roger, Bob and I really hit it off. It was late afternoon before I dragged myself away and remembered that I was meant to be here to start fishing. With Roger and Bob in my favourite swim, I chose the next best – the Plateau – and baited with chick peas along the bottom of the shelf. These were flavoured with a new flavour, I'd obtained – hazelnut.

I had tracked down and gone back to the source of the company who produced the maple flavour, working on the same logic that if the maple was that good, then some of the other flavours they had could be, too. The trouble was that this company only provided in bulk to other businesses, which would then bottle up their flavours and sell on under their own name. They had a couple that I really loved the smell of, one of which was the hazelnut. It was edgy and reminded me in a small way of the maple. The minimum order was 25 litres, which I could never use up. It was not only excessive for my own use but also expensive. I got round this later, by adding a selection of the flavours to my Happy Hooker range.

The first night passed quietly for all of us. It was a cold and rainy start and that may have had something to do with it. It is a fact that I've noted on numerous occasions, that carp in Essex don't like rain. You'll catch them before and after, but rarely during steady and persistent rain.

At lunchtime, when I was debating my culinary choices of delight, a small tin of macaroni cheese or a large tin of macaroni cheese, Roger and Bob came round.

"Are you coming up the pub?" Roger asked.

I was completely taken aback by this because I was fishing and, never before had I left the lake to go anywhere other than maybe to shoot into a newsagent to stock up with fags and lemonade.

"Go to the pub?" I said. "What? I might miss the opportunity of catching a carp!"

"It won't count, anyway," said Roger. "That's cheating."

I couldn't get my head around this until he explained.

"Me and Bob are going up the pub, so if we're not here, we won't be able to stop you catching fish that we might have caught instead, so it doesn't count, does it?"

"Er…" I was still trying to work it out.

"It's a bit like going out on the football pitch," Roger went on, "and kicking a ball into goal while the goalkeeper and team are in the changing room."

My head was spinning over that one and I knew I would need time to grasp it.

"What about our gear, though?" I said "Someone might nick it."

"Well, if they do, we'll have to get some more, won't we." Roger wanted to get to the pub. "Come on. Are you coming up the pub, or not?"

It was a little wobbly me who arrived back on the lake two hours, and two pints, later. I wasn't a great drinker then anyway, but lunchtime drinking was something else. I'm sure it was only the shepherds pie and chips that saved me from being pissed.

I was converted by the end of the week and since, if I've been on a water and there's a nearby pub that sells food, I will pull off for a break, if it's safe to leave the gear and someone's around to look after it, and I know there are those reading this who won't condemn me for it. 'Break' is the key word. I've been on sessions when I've been completely demoralised, my confidence shot to bits and not knowing where to turn next, only to go to a pub with mates and, two hours later, arrive back on the lake refreshed as bright as a daisy, with a new plan and the confidence back up where it should be.

Apart from that, it's a way to get a meal down you. I really do hate cooking on the bank so pubs are great, for the informed. There's nothing like an hour or two in the pub to get your head straight, a couple of lunchtime pints, the day's food down your neck and have a wash and scrub up in the toilets.

Roger was to do much more, though, than introduce me to a carp fishing ethos. He was also responsible for what could be deemed my biggest selling, or I'll put that another way, the carp world's most profitable product ever – the rod holdall to accommodate tackled-up rods.

One morning, we were chatting in his swim while drinking tea when Roger said,

"You should look at the rod holdall that my old dad made for me, and make them yourself."

He pulled out a roll-up holdall, which is what we all used in those days. Along its width were three, square pouches so you could place a tackled up rod on a sheet of canvas. The rod was secured into a pocket on the bottom, the reel dropped into a pouch, and a tie secured the two joints at the top. After fitting all three rods, the canvas could be rolled up and fastened with buckles.

I was immediately struck by the enormity of this simple and yet ingenious idea. Until then, we'd been carrying our rods around in our hands, in a bundle, tackled up. This was a pain because sometimes a hook might fly off and inevitably, it would snag in something such as a car seat, or there was always a risk of the main line inadvertently being damaged. So, a rod holdall that could accommodate our laziness of leaving our rods tackled up, as well as completely protect rod, reel, line and prevent hooks from detaching themselves from the butt ring and snagging, was a revelation.

Roger kindly and generously loaned me his rod holdall to show to my girlfriend, who could make me a pattern and we did make one up, but it was virtually impossible to sew. The problem was the large, thick piece of canvas which had to be forced under the machine's small throat, in order to sew all around the pouches. Then I had an idea. Instead of rolling up the canvas, if I sewed three pockets side by side on one half of it, I could then lay the other half on top of the three rods, and secure with a zip along the top and side. This way, it would be much easier to machine stitch.

The Hooker rod holdall was born. It proved to be a resounding success and looking back, it is without doubt the product that really brought me to the attention of the angling world. It was a unique innovation, but 100% practical and a big step forward in rod holdall design.

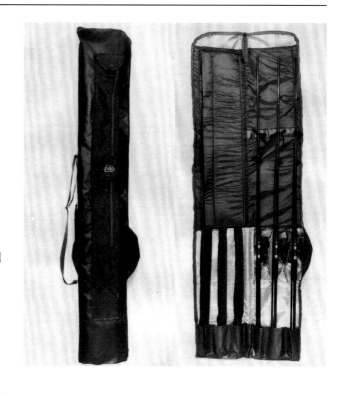

ABOVE
The original Happy Hooker holdall. Hundreds of thousands have been sold since - shame they weren't all sold by me!

I told Cliff Kemp, the then owner of Essex Tackle in Leigh, that I'd come up with an awesome idea. He said I should get it patented and introduced me to a friend of his who was a patent lawyer. He took pity on me, an inexperienced kid with little money, and wrote and filed my patent at no cost. I didn't realise at the time that there was no way I would have been able to afford his huge fees.

However, despite the protection of my patent, it was no safeguard against competition because I was completely naïve in business and the complex world of intellectual property protection. It wasn't very long after when the Hooker holdall was first copied by a company called Stevens. I got a local lawyer to write to them. Stevens' lawyers, knowing the game, wrote back forcefully and because of my greenness and my lawyer's advice, I backed off. I think it's fair to point out that there has not been millions of pounds-worth of my design of holdall made, but tens of millions, possibly more than a hundred million. There is not a company in the world with a range of carp luggage without a holdall based on my original design.

If only, I'd been more streetwise. That one product could have been all I needed. Imagine if I'd had the sole rights to making holdalls to accommodate tackled up rods for 20 years! It was a lesson I was to learn, time after time, as my ideas were ripped off by others with more financial backing and business experience.

The modern carp scene was invented and developed by passionate carp anglers, and the tackle and baits that emerged came from them. Some of we ordinary guys found our way into business almost by accident and a lot of graft went on in those pioneering days. A few of us would travel all around the country doing talks on carp fishing and selling our wares, which would barely cover the price of petrol; it was a real grassroots sport. Then, as it mushroomed, the 'businessmen' arrived, and took advantage of the financial opportunities that we carp anglers had developed and, in effect, given them on a plate. It's a sad fact that the people most passionate about the sport, the ones who have made this modern carp scene, have had so much taken away from them by the big tackle companies as well as certain businessmen who moved into it purely for gain.

The second night of the season, at just after midnight, I was awoken to a bright moon, and a bright LED as my bite alarm signalled something was occurring. After a short fight, I slipped the net under a heavy carp that turned out to be Stardust, down on her previous weight this time at 19½lbs, and that was

BELOW
Silver End's Stardust.

the only carp caught during that opening week; that was possibly an omen of which I should have taken note.

Certainly, my ability to catch the Silver End carp with any regularity was fading. I only notched up another two mid-doubles in the next month and the only comfort I could take from this was that I must be doing something exceptional because Roger and Bob continued to blank.

I'd had no choice but to restrict myself to just a Tuesday overnighter and a Thursday overnighter, packing up on the Friday evening, because of the ever-increasing demand for my small range of Happy Hooker gear. My reduced fishing time wasn't helping the matter but my old stroke of disappearing when the season opened wasn't tolerated any more by the likes of Jack Simpson. He gave me an ultimatum, 'supply me with your tackle when our customers want to buy it, or don't call again.' So, it was a real juggling act, holding down the engineering job and working into the night with Happy Hooker, going fishing and at weekends, working on Happy Hooker and trying to keep the girlfriend sweet.

As if that wasn't enough, I started holding parties at my house/factory/office, and not your normal parties with birds, booze and music, but carp parties. I would invite friends down on a Friday evening for a few beers and to talk carp. After meeting Roger Smith, he came along to one of these events and thereafter the parties were named 10 and 41. We always used to ring out for a Chinese takeaway on these Fridays; 10 was special rice, and 41 was sweet and sour pork balls. Roger said, "You should call your parties '10 and 41 nights'" and so the name stuck. Many of the foremost Essex carp anglers came to my 10 and 41 parties; Bill Lovett, Micky Lindsell, Zenon Bjoko, Stuart Demon, Brad, Paul Gower, Freddie Gibbs, Phil Harper, Geoff Kemp... to name just a few.

The BCSG had folded by this time and so the 10 and 41 parties became the not to be missed carp meeting. It was quite amazing how the grapevine spread about when I had a party coming up. One particular Friday afternoon, I had a phone call from a guy right down in Hampshire who'd heard about them, and asked if he could come along. I even had a couple from Liverpool once. The parties were a hot-bed of carp knowledge and many ideas were conceived at the 10 and 41s, including items of tackle that are still used to this day, like anti-tangle tubing and the first purpose-made bolt bead that I was later to produce.

The Happy Hookers were also born out of these meetings. They were a team of top carpers to whom I gave samples of my new tackle ideas for them to test and give me feedback. The parties became so popular and involved so many thinking carpers that they started dragging on a bit. I remember on one particular Saturday morning, Zen opened the curtains and said, "Bloody hell! It's daylight." Later, the parties went from Friday night through to Sunday, with carpers talking solidly and animatedly the whole time. Shining times, indeed.

It was one hot Friday afternoon when I found the big mirror, up by the car park in a bed of potomegeton. I nearly missed her, too. It was only because I was convinced that there must be carp up in the shallows on this hot day that my persistence kept me looking. It was the slightest movement that turned out to be the lobe of her tail poking out from the water, not more than one-eighth of an inch between two potomegeton leaves, that caught my attention. I didn't know what it was, but I knew it was something. I kept staring at that spot, my eyes moved around and away from it and after a while, I realised that I was looking at glimpses of a carp body between the gaps in the leaves. It was like a jigsaw, with just a few pieces scattered on a table, but by looking at it hard enough, I could make out a picture.

I went and got my gear and moved into the rushes on the bank below the car park. As it was warm, and presentation was everything, I stripped off my jeans and waded out at the slowest, stealthiest pace I could, trying to avoid even a ripple, then I stretched my arms out as far as I could with the rod and lowered the bait on the edge of the bed of potomegeton. I couldn't see her head, but by the piece of dorsal I could see I figured out that the bait was about two feet from her mouth. Slowly, I backed out from the shallows being careful to lay my line down between the weed so that it didn't snag, made my way back to the bank and placed the rod in the rest.

As I had this rod on the button, I saw no point in putting other lines out, which would be difficult to conceal and could possibly spook her as she swam out of the bed that she was lying in. So, thinking, one rod on the spot is worth a hundred cast to nowhere, I settled down with great anticipation as the sun began to set.

The next morning, with no action, as the sun got up in the sky, helping me to see into the water, I climbed up the steep bank to see if there was any sign of carp. Immediately, I spotted her, seemingly, exactly in the position she had been the day

before. If she'd moved at all, I would guess it was only about six inches to the right. I couldn't believe it. Talk about having a lie in!

That evening, I wound the bait in and went home. It was probably the most boring session I'd ever had. It had been like watching a statue all day. She laid there for hours, inert, then a ripple or two would come out from the potomegeton leaves and my hopes would get up that she was on the move, but no, she wasn't. She would settle down again. She hadn't moved more than three inches, left or right, front or back, all day. This was the first encounter of what was probably the most frustrating six weeks I'd experienced in carp angling until this point. I'd go back, time after time, and find her in the shallows, lying under the bed of potomegeton that she favoured. I think the greatest change of position I ever saw was around three feet.

Until then, I hadn't realised that carp are capable of long periods of virtual inactivity. I'm sure that the carp didn't move out at night and was just lying in the same spot 24/7, or if she did move out at night she repositioned herself to within an inch the next day. Equally, I'm sure that she didn't feed. I never saw her once tip up or show any signs of feeding activity. I saw similar behaviour later on at the Snake Pit when in one long, hot period the big common was holed up in the snags. I can't be as certain if she stayed in there at night, but I have a feeling that she did. I could guarantee that I'd see her any time in the daylight hours, in a pool, motionless. She would occasionally reposition but never really seemed to move out of an area more than six feet square.

I was to see this behaviour several times over the years. It almost became an indication of your chances. If you arrived at the Snake Pit, went directly to the snags and could see fish there that appeared torpid and lazy, it was odds on that you would have a blank session. I'm sure they just lazed around in the snags, not feeding and never moving out from their protection. Conversely, if the carp were active and swimming around in the snags, you knew that you had a greater chance of catching out in the lake, because they would move out from their woody haven at some time and be catchable.

I had six weeks of this, trying everything. I even hooked maggots over a potomegton leaf to dangle in front of her nose. I'm sure it wouldn't have been more than six inches away, but I never got the slightest sniff of interest. As I was pulling off, one morning, Andy Kellock, another Essex carper who had become a good friend, was moving on for a long session. I told him the score and my experiences of the moribund mirror, so he elected to go right up the other end and not waste his time trying to catch it.

I decided to have a break that weekend. I'd had enough and needed a tactical rethink, but before I could come up with a plan, the heat wave broke, she swam out from the potomegeton and up to the other end where Andy caught her under the oak tree.

This finished me off. I really was pissed with her. The effort I'd put in over those six weeks, just for her to play that game on me – it really was as if she was tormenting me. I remember waking from a bad dream in the middle of the night, drenched in sweat and cold. I could still see her eye searing into my brain on that foggy morning and the pain was like the worst migraine. I had a carp that clearly was possessed by the devil; a good mate of mine had been an absolute bastard and nicked her from under me, the girlfriend was playing up because I was seeing her so rarely, and the tackle shops were doing my head with the pressure of wanting to buy more and more. I had a break from the Pit and before I knew it, winter was upon me. All thoughts of going back would have to wait until the next season.

Chapter Sixteen

Silver End: Bill's Triumph

Bill was coming on board fully, as opposed to – as I would put it – dabbling at Silver End. I was chuffed. I always enjoyed fishing with Bill Lovett and it was never as regular as I would have wished. Bill was quite literally a 'one-nighter to the next afternoon' once a week, carper, with a few days off as holiday at the start of the season. Jill Lovett, bless her, maintained an iron grip!

So we made plans for a close season baiting campaign. Our hope was to wean the Silver End fish on to boilies. Until then, the particles had been far more productive, but it wasn't only Uncooked who had sussed what I was doing, other locals were chancing it on the pit with particles, so now I needed the confidence of a bait that was all mine – and, of course, Bill's.

Bill had yet to catch a carp from Silver End so he was well up for it, and even volunteered to do the baiting, which from my point of view was a right result because the business had really taken off and I was struggling to keep up with the orders, let alone hold down a day job and see my bird – and on top of that, to drive an hour each way a few times a week to bait up.

Bill popped round at the beginning of June and got some bait ingredients off me. We decided on a high protein, liver-based boilie. I got the base mix from Rod Hutchinson; Catchum's protein mix with a few little additions of my own, for good luck and confidence, and the liver source was courtesy of Geoff Kemp who had an awesome liver powder. As soon as we tasted it, we just knew the carp would love it and that it would be a wicked bait. Bill went home and got straight into rolling, bless him, and then the baiting up began.

He concentrated on two areas; a swim that was just down from the shallows where I'd seen the big mirror spend so much time the season before, and a plateau area in the centre of the pit from where I had caught the majority of my carp the previous year. He didn't bait much in my old favourite spot below the Oak Tree because it had become the hot swim, increasingly occupied with a growing number of carpers moving on to the pit.

I got up there myself a few days later on a lovely, sunny afternoon. I stepped out of my car, walked over to the edge of the steep bank and looked down. I couldn't believe it; there was the big mirror, back in the shallows, just like she had been the last time I'd made that concerted six-week effort to no avail. This time, though, she wasn't stuck moribund in a potomegeton bed. To the contrary, she was actively cruising around.

She swam past me, going left, and I waited a second then lobbed out a boilie, which I'd hastily squeezed flat so that it would not only make as little disturbance as possible when it hit the water, but also flutter down. It landed four feet behind the mirror and I was amazed. It seemed almost before the bait broke the surface that the big fish had spun round and gulped it down. I repeated the process with the same result. As soon as my flattened boilies landed, she was on them and I just couldn't believe this frantic feeding reaction. Clearly, Bill's baiting had worked and the mirror loved our protein liver bait. You can imagine my confidence. This carp was now going to be so easy to catch and I couldn't wait to get home and ring Bill to tell him the news.

The next day, I was back up and again, the mirror was in the shallows and exactly the same feeding response ensued. Baiting sorted, I just needed to set up my swim now. It seemed that the warm weather would continue into the season so I chose to fish in the shallows. There wasn't really a swim as such, just a boggy bit of ground and I felt sure that it wouldn't be a favoured spot at the start, but I wasn't going to take any chances. I had to make sure that I procured this swim and caught the big mirror.

My predicament was that I knew the lake would be rammed and the season opened on a Wednesday night, so when would a 'keeny' turn up? Would it be the Tuesday? Or as there was only Monday after the weekend, would people have the week off and turn up on Sunday? Such was my paranoia, or commitment – you make the call – I chose not to take any chances and turned up early on the Sunday morning, four days before the start, to guarantee absolutely that I'd get my swim, or so I hoped.

I arrived to find every single swim taken. I am joking. There was not another angler in sight and there I camped, feeling at times a bit stupid as I had no rods out for four days. The weather was gorgeous, though, and what's more, I sat on the high bank every day, flicking flattened pieces of paste to the big mirror. Her reaction was ridiculous, really. As I write this, I can't think of any time when I had a carp so hooked on a bait; I bet I could have had her feeding out of my hand if I'd tried. I'm sure her reaction was down to the fact that this was the first time she'd properly recognised boilies as a food source, and now she had, did she love them!

I hadn't seen Bill for a couple of days because he'd been away on a business trip, but he turned up at around 11pm on the 14th with an old chair to bag himself a spot in the back of the shallows in the reeds. Then he was away again, muttering that he had to see Jill, roll some bait and go into the office the next day. He told me that he'd be back in the evening, though, and asked me to guard his spot. Like me, he thought the shallows were the place, but I had the main area tied up so he ended up in the middle of a reedy swamp – better there, than where there was no carp, I guess.

I got up on the morning of the 15th to a different day. All week, in fact for several weeks, a light, warm breeze had been pushing up into the shallows, but today, it was going the other way, toward the bottom end and the Oak Tree. What's more, the mirror didn't come into the shallows at all that morning and I was beginning to get desperate by mid-afternoon, especially as a couple of other anglers had turned up and I knew that within hours the lake would be packed. I couldn't believe my situation. I had a 'pet' carp, just waiting to be caught but it seemed that after waiting to be caught for five days, she'd got bored and had gone elsewhere in the lake.

I knew that I had to find her. Never was location more important. I felt that the first angler's boilie she came across, she was going to eat and I had to make sure that angler was me! I went for a walk around the pit and, sure enough, she was on the wind, mooching around just off the bank in the potomegeton bed under the oak. In fact, she was more around the corner from the oak in a spot that I'd never seen a carp before. I jumped into my car and shot up to the phone box to get the weather report. I was informed that the wind would remain in its present direction for the next two days, so there was no choice. I have to say, though, I felt a bit of a nod, after camping out on the lake for three days to grab my swim before the start of the season, only to move swims just hours before the start.

I wasn't happy at all, especially when Bill turned up, the last angler to settle in for the start. He couldn't believe his luck! The swim I'd been in, I wasn't in any more and neither had anyone else moved there. He didn't need telling twice. He popped round to see me, and I just felt so tense and arsey. I had a premonition that this was all going to go so badly wrong for me. The baits were out for midnight and I jumped into the bag, tossing and turning restlessly; all I could see was that demon eye.

The next thing I remembered was opening my eyes and a sickening feeling. What was it? Then I realised. I'd fallen asleep with the gentle breeze kissing my face and I'd woken up to still air. The wind had turned and was pushing into the shallows. At that moment, if the lovely-spoken lady on the end of the telephone for the Met Office had walked by, I would have dismembered her piece by piece.

Bill's story:

'I cast out exactly on the stroke of midnight. Rod number one was margin-fished peanuts to the right of the swim; number two, peanuts at around 10 yards in the centre, and number 3 with the boiled bait to the left.

Dawn showed tench bubbles over the baits but there were no signs of carp. However, a couple of hours later, a carp bow-waved across the swim from right to left, and a light breeze started from the south-west, directly into the shallow bay.

At 8.30, the buzzer sounded and there was a very fast take on the middle rod. I clicked over the bail arm, and the rod slammed round as the fish shot out of the bay into deeper water, taking 20 yards of line in a very powerful run. Kevin, who by this time had moved back into the shallows, appeared on time to slip the net under a well-conditioned mirror, which weighed in at 20lbs 12oz, and proved to be a fish he had caught two years previously and named Stardust. The carp was quickly photographed and returned, and baits repositioned as before.

As the day wore on, the breeze grew stronger, still pushing nicely into the bay, but no further carp were seen. Around 4 o'clock, I decided to try a different part of the swim with the boilie rod, casting 4-5 yards further out on to the edge of the slope. As this area seemed to contain more weed, I moved the anchoring and shot further from the hook to allow the bait to rise three to four inches from the bottom. A combination of warm sun and contentment in the shape of an opening day 20 made me feel particularly tired and I soon dropped off to sleep.

An hour later, the buzzer of the boilie rod woke me – another fast take – and another powerful fish moving very quickly out of the shallows on an unstoppable run, taking seemingly yards and yards of line.

"That's going well – must be a good fish?" said Kevin from the high bank behind me. "I don't know, it feels too fast to be very big. Probably an upper double," I said.

Kevin didn't seem convinced.

I gained line slowly, and got the fish back into the shallows. The immediate danger was the snags to the left, and the fish appeared to be going that way. I applied more pressure, confident in the 12lb Maxima, the carp turned, coming away from the snags and toward us. Kevin got a good sight of the fish.

"It's a 30," he said.

My knees turned to jelly, and severe panic set in, as I saw the carp. He wasn't joking.

The carp must have sensed my change in attitude, and made a desperate attempt to reach the sanctuary of the snags. I had to give line as the fish moved into the first reed stems, and turned behind a large floating log. I knew this had to stop or the fish was lost, so I applied maximum pressure, which to my surprise turned the fish over and freed the line.

The carp now swam directly towards us and over the arms of the landing net. Kevin, quite correctly, (despite Anglo-Saxon encouragement from me,) didn't try to net it as it wasn't ready, and the fish once more made a bid to reach the snags. This time, I managed to turn it quite easily and brought the fish slowly back over the net. Kevin lifted the fish out, congratulating me on having caught a '30' at last.'

ABOVE
Bill with the big girl.
A great result mate!

It is only true carping friends who can rejoice in their mates' captures, but this one was a little tough, I confess. I had no envy of Bill's result. In fact, it was amazing and he got quite emotional, which made the importance of the event come home to me. There were not many carpers in the country who'd caught a mid-30 and this fish was the pinnacle of any carper's career at 35lbs 4oz.

My emotions were mostly of anger toward the Meteorological Office. I felt that I didn't deserve the outcome because I'd done everything right. I'd put the work into the lake, identified the carp's whereabouts and habits, got her on the bait and most of all, I hadn't taken any chances. I'd sat on the lake, camping out for four days for the start, only to get a bum steer from Mrs Weather-Lady – the bitch!

I was really feeling sorry for myself. In fact, I was beginning to have weird thoughts about being cursed and occasionally, the nightmare of the carp's demon eye would haunt my dreams. Whatever...I had a point. I had caught all but three of the pit's residents which were; a common that looked to be in the low doubles, which I'd never seen feeding and I felt sure that I'd never hooked; the long, dark mirror that I estimated around 26lbs that spent a lot of its time with the big mirror, and used her to test baits. This carp had never been landed and I believe that was because for 99% of the time, she fed with the big mirror, using the bigger fish almost as a shield to ensure that it was safe to feed. I had hooked her in the shallows on float-fished chick peas one day when I found her on her own, only to lose her when my main line parted. I'd just bought that line; it was rated 12lb BS but when I tested it, it broke at only 4lbs. I was gutted, as normally I was so careful checking my tackle, but I had been in such a rush to spool up with new line and get fishing that I'd overlooked it. It was a hard lesson, but from that day I've always checked all my tackle carefully before chucking out. The third fish still to be caught was, of course, the big mirror, the one I was after which I'd come so close to slipping over the landing net on that fateful, foggy, October morning.

The rest of this season, and even the next, I feel are not worth documenting. This was a period when my carp fishing became fractured. I've always said that to catch regularly, you need to fish regularly, for me – that's the only way it works. I have to focus on one water at a time and most importantly, keep in touch with it by fishing it at least weekly, and/or using the eyes and ears of others to know what's going on in my absence. In between fishing, the best situation is when I can snatch the odd hour or two to visit the lake, to bait and to keep an eye on the fish.

None of this was now possible, though, because Happy Hooker was really an Unhappy Hooker. My customers were increasing in numbers and becoming more and more impatient at having to wait for me to fulfil my orders, and I was under immense pressure to juggle the balls every which way from everyone around me.

I could barely cope and when I look back at my life at this time, I realise now that it was no wonder the fishing had taken a back seat. I had a full-time engineering job, albeit four days but I still had to work a minimum of 40 hours to keep my boss happy, necessary as I had a mortgage to pay and all on my own, at that, so this is how my working day would go:

I'd be in work at 7.30am.

At 10am, we had a 15-minute tea break. I lived a few minutes down the road, so I'd shoot home, grab the post and be back by the end of tea break. If I was even a minute late, I'd be docked 15 minutes pay.

Between 10.15am and lunchtime, I would open the post while the guv'nors had their backs turned. The orders went in one pile and the cheques were entered into my bank paying-in book.

At 1pm – lunchtime – I had just 30 minutes to go to the post office and deal with my parcels which had been made up the previous night. I'd weigh them, buy the necessary stamps, go through the complicated process of remembering which purchased stamps needed to go on to which parcel, stick them on and hastily give them to the post office clerk. Then I'd rush to the bank to pay in the cheques and be back in work by 1.30pm.

At 6pm, I'd leave work after a 10-hour working day and go home.

On the doorstep of my 'house' which had turned into a small factory, there would be half a dozen schoolkids, waiting to be let in to pack the orders that I had in my hand. They spent the evening doing this and then let themselves out while I was in the garage cutting up the materials for making carp sacks, slings, side-wraps and what was becoming my star product – the Happy Hooker rod holdall to accommodate tackled-up rods. The cutting procedure would, on average, take me to 10pm, or so, when I would start my outdoor round, dropping off the work and collecting the finished articles from the homes of my machinists. I'd usually be back before midnight and then clear up after the kids, do the necessary paperwork and address all the parcels ready for the next day.

By the time all this was done, it would probably be between two and three in the morning and I was really past eating much by then, let alone cooking, so I'd grab a few biscuits and stumble off to bed. I am going to shock the carp world now, by talking frankly about my years of addiction, and let this be a warning to all young carpers.

As I mentioned, a couple of years earlier Nigel Dennis had moved in with me when I bought a house that I couldn't afford and so took in lodgers to help with the bills. Nigel Dennis was a McVities biscuit salesman. Every week, a lorry would pull up and drop off 12 cases of McVities digestive biscuits, as 'sweeteners' for him

to give out to customers. He told me that they always delivered far more than he could ever reasonably give out and I should help myself, so I did. In fact, at one point, with a surfeit of McVities digestives in the house, I even crumbled them up and added them to my bait, but it became too easy to grab a packet of biscuits instead of cooking. There were 48 packs in a case and I was on 3-4 cases a week – almost mainlining digestives. I became addicted and even when Nigel was no longer living with me, the eating biscuits habit had continued.

If all this wasn't enough, I'd parted from the girl from Chigwell the year before, who rather unreasonably, I thought, suggested that carp fishing and Happy Hooker seemed to be more important than her and there comes a time with women when you have to realise that it's not worth arguing. I have to confess that while I could be accused of being a bit chauvinistic in thinking that women are another species, and generally raving mad, I love them to bits. I find them much more interesting to talk to than hairy-arsed blokes in the pub whose depth of subject matter starts with football and ends up with sex. So, as if I didn't have enough on my plate, the Chigwell girl had really dropped me in it because now I also had to go out on the pull, and if I told some of the stories about some of the birds I met and the close shaves I had, that would be a book in itself.

I began to see two girls on a somewhat casual basis and one was okay but it was never going to be serious; I'll just say that we had a good time together. Prior to her, I'd ditched a girl who was a university student and I can't recall exactly what she was studying but I'll take a stab at it being 'how to be a feminine psychopath'. After seeing her several times, I started getting flashbacks of 'Play Misty for Me' - an epic Clint Eastwood film where he played the part of a DJ who is stalked by a lady psychopathic listener. The novelty of her intensity, especially in the bed, on the bed, the banister, stairs, landing, porch, garage, back and front gardens and even in the road if she got caught short, was beginning to wear off, so I attempted to distance myself from her – a gesture she didn't understand or appreciate. I tried being a little less subtle but she didn't get "sod off" either. I was being stalked.

So, there I was with one bird who was good company and fulfilled the needs while I shopped around for a better model, but I also had to watch my back for the raving nutter who would have had me for breakfast had she got the slightest inkling that I was seeing someone else and, trust me, I wouldn't have got much past the 'toast' stage.

One night, I went clubbing just to meet up with a few mates for a drink. I had no desire to meet a girl. In fact, birds were positively off the agenda, mainly because I was still in a twitchy state as I relived the night before when I'd left work, looked in my rear-view mirror, and found that I was being tailed by guess who? I had to drive for half an hour before I shook her off, and even then I parked up in the adjacent close before going home.

Anyway, without boring you with events, I got pulled by a lovely young lady who I decided was worth seeing again so a date was made, which only left me needing to ditch the 'on and off' current bird before I went on my first proper date. It had been arranged for the girlfriend to come round the following week so I left the plan intact, deciding to break the news like a man, face to face, rather than like wimps, over the phone, or through their mums.

Well, it didn't quite work to plan and she took a bit of convincing. In the meantime, though, she wanted to prove to me the folly of my decision so we were upstairs in bed when the doorbell started ringing with some urgency. Clearly, someone on the other side was desperate to contact me and, without thinking, I slipped my trousers on, shot downstairs and opened the door. There stood the stalker wearing a long coat which she opened up to reveal the fact that she was stark naked. "Come and have a piece of this, boy," she said as I slammed the door shut. I leaned against it as she hammered with her fists and feet on the other side, venting her anger and frustration at my rejection.

Meanwhile, the girl upstairs was saying, "What's all that row?" but for some bizarre reason, my mind had completely cut off from it all as I realised that I'd got my nights wrong, and I was supposed to be taking my new girlfriend to the pictures on our first date. It was at that point that I knew I had to sort my life out so I left the stalker hammering on the door, while I went upstairs and told the other one that it was over. That just left me with how to explain to my potential new love why I'd stood her up on our first date. Luckily, she accepted my explanation - which I'm sure bore no resemblance to the actual event - and we began dating seriously. I say 'dating' but I was seriously struggling time-wise.

As I mentioned, I'd done a deal with my boss to cram all my hours into a four-day week, hence the 10-hour days, but the Friday (as well as the Saturday and Sunday, in fact) was increasingly being taken up with my attempts to satisfy the demand for Happy Hooker gear, so there was hardly time to see my new girlfriend, let alone get into regular carp fishing. Something had to be sacrificed and that was my fishing and the obsession with catching the Silver End mirror. It was a tough time for me, especially after having seen Bill catch her. Equally, I didn't have the commitment. When people say they haven't got time, my mind always thinks, 'that's bollocks' because if you really want to go carping and catch them, you make the time. There have been many points in my life when I've had to create time. Sometimes, the only physical hours available would be those spent sleeping and you can't catch them when you're at home in bed, but you just might if you're kipping behind rods.

That has always been my philosophy and I've always believed that the key, single reason behind success in carp fishing is energy, but for the first time in my life, I didn't seem to have that energy. Even when I wasn't working, I just felt so tired. My girlfriend was beginning to complain that I was hardly worth seeing because I was always semi-comatose and not my normal life and soul of the party (read hell-raiser).

By the spring of '84 I felt positively ill, completely drained and at times, especially when I got up too quickly, light-headed and dizzy. I've never been in any way a hypochondriac. If anything I've tolerated ailments and suffered unnecessary pain until they went away because I didn't want to bother a doctor when I should have done, but this time I was getting worried and wondered what I had. Was it the first symptoms of Weil's disease, cancer, a brain tumour or worse, syphilis; would my knob fall off?

After a weigh-in and a short examination, the doctor declared that I was only seven and a half stone and he asked me what I'd been doing. I explained my work and life patterns and was somewhat shocked by his abrupt diagnosis. Basically, he told me that it wasn't any of my feared complaints, which was a relief, especially with regard to the last one – how on earth would I break that news to my now fiancée? My 'illness', he said, was total fatigue, the result of too many hours working compounded by an excessively poor body condition due to minimal sleep and a poor diet.

"So, Doctor, in your opinion, McVities Digestives are not a balanced food source?" While I felt relieved, that there was nothing immediately life-threatening, or worse still, venereal, I did feel rather stupid when I left the surgery, after having a consultation for an illness which was so obviously self-inflicted.

I had a dilemma. What could I do about the orders? It was May, repeat purchasing time as anglers got ready for the new opening of the season, so I couldn't slow down and lose my customers and there was my full-time job to worry about. For several years, I'd been telling mates at work that I was going to chuck it in and concentrate on Happy Hooker full time, and I'd got the retorts: "Yeah, right! We'll be dead before you do that." Like many, we all hated our jobs and just wished to escape. I guess that's why the football pools, and now the lottery, were always well patronised. Everyone has that dream to escape from the mundane life and grind.

The fact was that I wasn't earning enough from Happy Hooker to pay the bills. The business was growing but there were not enough hours in the day to make it pay and further, I didn't know if there would be enough demand to make it work. The risk seemed too great and if it didn't work, I could lose my house, but the situation couldn't carry on; I had to decide between the day job, or Happy Hooker. So, I decided on a plan to make the call and this was to go off sick.

I've already mentioned that shortly after firstly going on to Silver End I had an accident that kept me off work for ten weeks. When I was machining a large casting on a lathe, my white coat got caught in what's referred to as 'the lead screw' which is a permanently revolving thread that carries the length of a lathe bed. The lead screw grabbed my white coat and was dragging me in toward the revolving casting. The lever that was used to switch the machine on or off was embedded in my stomach, so I couldn't switch it off. Just before what could have been at the least a very serious injury, or even certain death, I made a desperate attempt to escape by flexing my arms and body against the bed of the machine to fight the force of the lead screw pulling both coat and me into the casting.

I braced myself and screamed with the effort as the white coat parted on the seam, tore all the way up my back and was pulled off me harmlessly to wrap around the lead screw. My life was saved but I did suffer cracked ribs and severe bruising, and had to have ten weeks off work. Luckily, this was just when I started fishing Silver End - what a result!

So, I made up a plan to fake the same accident. It was deceitful, I'll admit, but sometimes needs must and I was not cheating my bosses out of wages, or any other such thing involved because I was a self-employed engineer. In those days, you could decide either to be in the PAYE system or to opt out and work for yourself. There were tax benefits for the latter option, but the downside was no sick pay. It was the only way, though. If I'd asked my boss for six weeks off, because the company was so busy he would have said no, so I went ahead with the plan. I thought I'd made a pretty good job of it, actually, and even considered momentarily that perhaps my true vocation was the stage.

A week later, I felt compelled to phone in to work and I felt sure that my boss was suspicious. He probably wasn't, but that's what guilt does to you and I really was concerned that he had sussed I wasn't really off sick and was doing something else. I feared for the sack so I went to the bait cupboard, made up a potion of black bait dye and another of yellow and painted my chest and ribs. Then, that next

Friday, I went into work. Rick, one of the guv'nors, inquired, rather sceptically it seemed, how I was doing so I lifted my T-shirt and showed him the 'bruising'. There was a look of absolute horror on his face and I knew I was believed. It's amazing what you can do with a bit of bait dye!

Two weeks later, I was overwhelmed with orders so I jacked my job in. I hadn't realised that until you make something you can't sell it, so by making a limited amount, you reduce the potential and it's a case of 'the more you make, the more you sell.' I probably could have jacked in the engineering job a year or two before, but you don't know until you try, do you? So, with my new venture off the ground, I had to go for it. There were bills to be paid and I had to make sure that I could set myself up to make a living.

I completely missed that year at the pit. I did have a go at the start for a few nights, but really, I was just going through the motions. I heard that the famous Ritchie MacDonald had moved on to Silver End, and if he was prepared to trek up from the carp Mecca of the Colne Valley then I guess that really was a reflection of this carp's position in the 'most desirable' league table.

The arrival of Ritchie was significant because he was the first to apply boilies heavily on the pit. He was one of the first blanket baiters and it was clear why he was having such a run of success on other waters. When carp are first baited heavily, the results can be spectacular, but it wasn't to be the case for Ritchie on the pit. To the best of my knowledge, he never landed one carp from the water.

That winter, Phil Harper and Paul Gower, a BSCG member I knew from old, had moved on to Silver End, and late one cold, winter night my phone rang. It was Paul to tell me that Phil had just caught the Silver End mirror, but it wasn't that news which shook me, it was the weight. She weighed an incredible 40lbs exactly, no doubt thanks to a huge winter feed up, courtesy of Ritchie MacDonald. Essex now had a 40!

When I put that phone down, my mind was made up. The mirror was now one of the largest carp in the UK and I was going to stop messing about. I vowed to maximise my efforts that following season and catch the damned thing.

Chapter Seventeen

Silver End: The Pot of Gold

Happy Hooker was really kicking off and finally, I was out of the daily grind of the engineering workshop. It was great. I had to work longer days than I had in engineering, but it was different; I enjoyed it and more importantly, I could relate to it. I was making carp gear, talking to customers about all things carp and with a bit of ducking and diving I had my time back to concentrate on Silver End. That was a real bonus, and what's more, the time was flexible because I was my own boss and could choose when to work. So, if it was a nice, sunny day I'd venture up to the pit to go fish spotting, and then work through the night to catch up on my orders.

I've already mentioned that I'd started to sell my own flavour range which I named Carp Krave, and to procure the maple flavour, I had to buy in bulk. The company didn't insist that I bought just maple. It was more about a minimum order value and they let me order less of the maple, providing I ordered sufficient of the other flavourings to make up the order, so that's what I did, and that's how I hit on a couple of their other flavours that turned out to be epic fish catchers, like the hazelnut. This led to me deciding to bring out a range of flavours of my own.

By this time, Rod Hutchinson had also set up his business selling carp tackle and baits, and he started treading on my toes by having sacks and slings made up locally to his Lincolnshire premises. One night on the phone, the subject of competition came up and a solution was agreed. We decided to carve up the market, just like the Stones and the Beatles had when they agreed not to release singles at the same time. This way, each band got to number one in the charts and maximised their sales. In a way, Rod and I did a similar thing and dominated the market in our specific areas. He pulled out of tackle and from then on, bought from me and I pulled out of bait and bought from him.

With the warmer weather emerging, around the middle of April, I set about my baiting campaign. I chose to stick with Rod Hutchinson's protein mix as it had proved so successful with the Liver, for Bill anyway, but I dropped the liver and this time flavoured with Rod's Pukka Salmon, a flavour that he'd brought out the previous year that had proven to be devastating. I popped over to the pit three times a week for the following two weeks, putting 50% of my boilies into fancied spots in front of the oak tree and along the bank to the right. The other 50% were scattered around the rest of the pit in any area that I knew the carp frequented. I had to go away for a few days on the third week of my baiting campaign, but didn't want to break the rhythm so I explained my predicament to Bill on the phone one night, and kind person that he is, he volunteered to bait for me.

BELOW
The Oak Tree swim.

On my return, the news he gave me made my blood run cold. He'd got to the pit mid-afternoon in warm early-May weather, climbed up the oak tree, and soon spotted a couple of carp sun-bathing on the edge of the potomegeton. He flattened the boilies and flicked one out in front of a mid-double, which promptly gulped it down. He had three carp ravenously feeding and then the big mirror swam in. As he flicked a bait in front of her, she became agitated, her dorsal shot up, her pecs went rigid and straight, as if she were in abject fear, and she promptly spun on her tail and bolted out of the swim.

Bill was amazed at her reaction and didn't believe that it had anything to do with him throwing the bait near her, because the others were feeding confidently and were not frightened at all. It seemed that as soon as she smelt it, it scared the shit out of her. I was gutted and felt that there was no way I could continue baiting with the Pukka Salmon because my confidence was destroyed.

Quite why the big mirror was so frightened will doubtless be a mystery that I'm unlikely to solve. I haven't seen Ritchie McDonald for many years but I hope that we'll meet up again one day, because he may have the answer. Ritchie was very close with Rod at this time and I wonder if Ritchie had conducted his blanket baiting with Rod's Pukka Salmon. While I know that he never landed a carp from Silver End, I don't know if he hooked and lost any. It could be that Ritchie had lost the big girl on Pukka Salmon, and that would explain her dramatic reaction.

For the rest of that evening, I was at a complete loss as to what to use. As I rifled through my bait cupboard, my hand rested on my number one fishing edge, a flavour that I'd never used on a baiting campaign. Instead, I kept it for when I knew I'd be fishing waters on a one-off or infrequent basis, because it was so unbelievably instant.

It was a strawberry flavour and that might sound a bit unexciting but this one was different. In fact, you wouldn't have said it smelled of strawberries at all. It was difficult to put your finger on it; strawberry maybe, but there were other smells. It was pungent and mysterious. I am not clear about the source of that strawberry attract flavour and I wish I was because it was one of the best bait edges I ever had. When Nigel Dennis stopped lodging with me, he effectively gave up carp fishing and a growing interest in photography became an obsession. So, as a goodbye present he left me his bait cupboard which contained a significant array of goodies, including a Ribena bottle full of this strawberry flavouring. I asked him if he'd tried it.

"No, I haven't," he said.

"It does smell good," I said. "Where did it come from?"

"Len Bunn, I think," Nigel told me. "If I remember rightly, he got it from

Rowntree and it was the strawberry flavour used in their strawberry fruit gums."

Now, there's a thing, I thought. I don't know about the reader but when I used to eat fruit gums, I'd offer them around, being the generous person that I am, but I'd make sure that I was only offering the green and yellow ones and would grab the strawberry one for myself. No wonder the carp went mad for it.

The first time I tried this flavour was after a certain Mr Fox had turned up on my doorstep one day while I was Regional Organiser for the Carp Anglers' Association. Fox was just dipping his toe into carp fishing and so came round to my house, networking and hoping to gain information.

Later on that year, in early winter, he invited me to go fishing with him. He'd been trying to get round me and tap me up for all the latest carp-catching stuff, but for some reason, instinctively, I held back on some of my best edges and I think he knew that, so it may be that he saw a fishing session as a chance to learn more.

I wouldn't have agreed to this if he hadn't got into a water that I'd long wanted to fish, called The Grove. Effectively, it was a closed shop for any known carp angler, unless he'd got in before the carp boom had started, but it was known to be alive with carp – and carp to over 20lbs, at that.

When I turned up, Fox had been on a five-day session and rather excitedly, he told me that he'd caught one, which was his first carp from the Grove. He then went home, said he'd be back later and asked if I could I watch his gear.

Light was fading rapidly as he drove off, and as I got my gear out of the car I thought that I'd better get going. I'd never even seen the lake before so I had no idea what it looked like, or where its features or the best areas were. With about 15 minutes to go before darkness, I didn't have much chance to find out. I walked down to the water's edge and as I looked out I noticed that there was a promontory jutting out, halfway along the bank to my right. This commanded a magnificent view over most of the lake and I felt sure that it was *the* swim, but unfortunately for me, that's where Fox had his bivvy set up. I stood surveying the water as the light faded; the trees were bare and the whole lake appeared to be lifeless and shrouded in the depressing dampness of a winter's eve. What to do?

With nothing to go at, I made up my mind where to fish and settled on where I was standing, the swim next to the car park. As I said before, the swim nearest to a lake's car park can be the most productive because it's where most anglers fish when they're too lazy to walk to more distant spots, so it goes without saying that it's the area that receives the most bait. Sure enough, my confidence went up a notch when, as I pushed my bank sticks into the soft ground, I saw a carp roll not 20 yards away.

The rods were out so I jumped straight into my sleeping bag; it was so damp and chilly cold that was the best place to be. Three or so hours later, Fox came back and round to the front of my brolly where he could see me tucked up in bed.

"Nothing doing?" he enquired.

"Oh, I wouldn't say that," I replied.

"What? You caught one?" he said, in a somewhat stunned and unhappy tone.

"No, I haven't caught *one*," I said. "I've caught four."

The look on his face was one of disbelief and there was not a hint of congratulation. He just turned on his feet and said he'd better get back to his bivvy.

I heard his boots thumping on the bank as I had my fifth run of the night. There was no way that he didn't hear the alarm, but he didn't come back to offer assistance. All this went into the Nash mental notebook. It was an amazing night of action, the likes of which I had never before experienced. I ended up with 17 carp that night and didn't get a wink of sleep. It wasn't so much the case that I was always playing carp, but rather I had to work at it. It was like being back on Layer when you would get takes but then they'd dry up, but you could get them going again by adjusting your rig.

After that fifth fish, I started to experience some twitches so I wound all the rods in and varied the length of each hook link. I found a new going length that would work for a take or two, and then it'd be back to twitches until I changed something else.

It was the quality of the fishing that was amazing to me at the time. I had 17 carp, 14 of which were good doubles to just over 20lbs. I used every sack I had but if I caught a bigger carp than one that was sacked, I'd put that one back and replace it with the larger fish. Rigs were flying out everywhere, rods were striking, sacks were being lifted in and out of the water; it was hectic! Somewhere, there is a photo of me in the morning with a dozen, or so, carp around me, but that was in those days. With better understanding of carp welfare, now I wouldn't even take a brace shot.

I could have caught more but most of the carp I saw roll up until midnight were 30 yards in front of Mr Fox. It wasn't until 1am, after half an hour of no activity for me and with fish still constantly rolling in front of him, that I crept around to his bivvy to have a chat, as you do. As I stealthily approached the back of his bivvy, I could hear him snoring his head off. Pukka! I tippy-toed away for about ten yards because I didn't want to disturb him, and then virtually ran back to my swim in my haste to recast my rods out in front of him. From then on, it was action all the way.

When I got back home, I rang Bill and told him the story. We laughed for ages. So, it was with some surprise that even after hammering him, I received an offer of another guest session from Fox. It was just after Christmas, freezing cold and if it had been any other lake I may well have said 'no'. The weatherman had predicted one of the coldest nights of the winter and I'd have a probable blank on the cards, but the previous red-letter session had me champing at the bit. I was well ahead of these Grove carp with my rigs and what I considered to be a significant edge – the strawberry flavour from Rowntree.

I rang Bill and told him that I had another guest ticket on the Grove, and knowing that there were no ardent carp anglers in the club who would be likely to fish in such severe conditions, other than Fox, of course, I suggested he come over, too. Bill did and to his utter delight, he had two takes; one he lost and the other was Bill's first 20lb-plus common, a PB of 20lb 8oz. Commons of that size were as rare as rocking horse poo in those days, probably comparable with a 50-pounder today, so as you can imagine, Bill was well chuffed.

Just like Bill, I also had two takes, but I was fortunate enough to land both of mine. I was well satisfied – what a result, on a night of such bitter cold and with the lake freezing as dawn broke! To my mind, though, the amazing element of the story is that Bill then suggested that we try to join the club. I just laughed at him.

"Bill, you know the mentality of the committee! They're never going to let 'names' like us in!"

Bill has a stubborn streak, though, and nothing will budge him once he's made his mind up, regardless of a possible fruitless outcome. He put both of us down for application but I was turned down without any explanation, whereas - bizarre as it seemed at the time - Bill was invited to appear in front of the committee.

Straightaway, one of the committee members steamed into Bill.

"We know you poached the Grove," he said.

Bill immediately realised that he'd been found out and the game was up, with the obvious conclusion. He thought he had no chance of getting into the club so he was a little bemused when the committee man then said,

"We've discussed your case and decided that the best way to stop you from poaching The Grove is to invite you to become a member."

When Bill told me this, I thought, 'Well, bugger me! I had a legitimate guest ticket and I get blown out, and he poaches and gets in!'

Sometimes, it's a funny old world. Bill is still a member to this day and now the carp are over 40lbs. It's just struck me, perhaps I should go and poach it, and then they might let me in at last!

I've gone a bit off track here, but the whole point is that Rowntree strawberry flavouring proved itself exceptional at the Grove and several other waters, without any pre-baiting. I was desperate to finish the Silver End saga, so with a little reluctance, I decided to use up my remaining super-attractor, but I hadn't figured on how much I would need. With only two weeks left for baiting, I was down to just a quarter of a bottle. I was so desperate, that I rang a couple of carp friends in Norfolk and obtained Len Bunn's phone number.

Len was surprised to hear me on the other end of his phone but we had a nice chat. I love talking to anglers who have been legends and I take part in such conversations almost with reverence. Eventually, we got round to the point of my call and Len told me that he thought he remembered the strawberry but had never used it himself. It was just one of a batch of flavours that he'd accumulated from here and there and had given to Nigel. I'd reached a dead end. In fact, my situation was to become critical when I rolled my bait for the opening night session and I only had 30ml of the magic strawberry left. If I didn't catch her in a session or two, I'd have blown it.

After a week of baiting with the strawberry, I'd gone up to the pit mid-afternoon on a hot, sunny day with the hope of finding her and, just like Bill, I climbed the oak and soon had three carp fighting over my flattened boilies; a mid-double mirror, the leather I'd caught on my first night, and Stardust. The baits would waft down no more than 12 inches before one of these three carp got in first and sucked it in. Then, the big girl arrived. I held my breath. I was as nervous as hell, and sweat broke out on my forehead as I flattened a boilie and flicked it out in front of her. Stardust saw it, and roared over to eat it, but the big mirror was having none of it and barged her out of the way. With no hesitation, she took it. I let out a sigh of sheer relief and continued to flick the flattened boilies in her direction. Watching her greedily gulping down every one of these baits had my confidence sky-high.

As the close season seemingly dragged on endlessly, I continued to visit the pit whenever it was good fish-spotting weather. On each occasion, I had the big mirror avidly gulping down the strawberry boilies. In fact, she was just as enthusiastic for these tasty morsels as she had been for the liver bait that Bill and I had used when he'd caught her two seasons before.

By this time, Roger Smith and Bob Jones had gone to pastures new, Uncooked had moved off, doubtless lying under a car somewhere in deepest Essex, and apart from a couple of the local youngsters, everyone else had given up because the pit had become rock hard, so I had no problem procuring my favourite area, the Oak Tree, for the start of the season.

Bang on midnight, I cast out and was so excited that rather than get my head down, I sat on the bank. The landscape drenched in moonlight reminded me of my first session so long ago. I relived the sheer power of that first fish as it had lunged away from the shallows toward the centre of the lake; the very first carp that I'd caught from the pit. Now, as I cast out on the stroke of midnight, I felt sure that soon I would be leaving my memories behind, I felt so confident that the mirror would be mine. As I settled into my bag, in my mind's eye, I saw her gulping down my baits with relish and although I don't remember, I must have stopped my reminiscing at some point and gone to sleep.

At 5am that morning, I had a screaming take. I hit it, but unfortunately the rod was locked solid after a carp had taken my bait and gained sanctuary in a snag. I was gutted. After some time, it became obvious that if the carp was still on, which I doubted, I wasn't going to get it out, so I pulled for a break. As I did so, the other rod roared off straight into the same snag with the same predictable outcome. I had fished this swim on dozens of occasions and had never encountered any unmovable snag. To this day, I don't know where that snag came from or what it could have been. It was so heavy and solid that I don't believe someone could have thrown it in. It's just one of those mysteries that make carp fishing so interesting, I guess, but at the time, I was beside myself. It could be that I'd blown it, and lost the big girl.

I had no other action during the day, but I spent a lot of time up in the oak tree and I'd noticed carp drifting into the potomegeton bed, eventually emerging from it to my right, close to the bank in only 18 inches of water. Clearly, this was a regular patrol route so I moved the rod down the bank to cover it.

A storm broke the next morning and just as the rain stopped, the rod I had positioned where I'd seen the carp emerging from the potomegeton, was away. In fact, the take was so fast that it was a one-toner. I picked up the rod and it hooped over into a satisfying, hefty curve and I thought, 'this is a good fish' – just as the hook pulled. I guess we have all been there; sometimes it just isn't our day!

A day later, I packed up, with two big issues and not in the best frame of mind, it has to be said. I'd had the opportunity to land three carp on my opening session and I'd lost the lot, but the real uneasiness for me was that one of those fish could have been the big girl, and now she would be scared of my bait. What do you do? What you do is put it all behind you and forge on. You must believe and keep your confidence but it's difficult to do that with no bait, and I was quite literally, one mix away from that. My precious strawberry flavour was a mere dribble in the bottom of the Ribena bottle. What a situation to be in! I couldn't just pop into a tackle shop and pick up another bag of boilies, like you can today.

Nonetheless, I was buzzing when I arrived back at the pit six days later and conditions, to my mind, were perfect. I'd left home on a hot, humid, damp morning; one of those summer days when you look at the trees and swear that you can see them growing. The air is just so fertile that it reeks of abundance and you know that nature's flora and fauna are having it off. There was the faintest drizzle as I drove up the A12, which added to the hothouse steaminess. To heighten my optimism, two magpies flew across the dual carriageway and I showed them respect by bidding them, 'Good morning, my fine feathered friends'. Perfect carp-munching weather and the sighting of two magpies for luck – I was going to ravage this pit!

If the magpies weren't enough to boost my confidence even higher, my swim was primed and waiting for me. Two of the lads from the village had popped round to see me just as I was packing up on my opening session. They were great boys and I trusted them, so I asked if they would trickle some bait in for me and they'd agreed so I felt sure that they had. Then I drove into the car park and my heart sank. There was a bivvy underneath the oak tree.

I stood there in disbelief. What was it about this pit? Was I cursed? It certainly seemed that the carp gods had an issue with me, but I told myself to get on with it and figured that if I couldn't get underneath the oak, I could at least cover part of the area by fishing further down the bank to the right. This would allow me to have at least one rod on a known productive spot, the one where I'd watched the carp exit from the potomegeton and lost the fish on my second morning. Ironically, I was in exactly the same spot as on the night of the demon eye, when I'd lost the big girl on that fateful foggy morning.

I dropped my gear in the swim and decided to acquaint myself with the owner of the bivvy; I wanted to kill him, and so with machete and AK47 in hand I made my way along the path. There was no obvious sign of any inhabitant so I peered into it and after my eyes had adjusted to the gloom, I spotted a bedchair in the distant corner. This was the biggest bivvy I'd ever seen in my life. I guess it would be considered small these days, but I was amazed. You could almost have parked a car in it!

Soon, I found myself talking to George. I'd never met George before, but he lived in the area and had decided to have a go on the pit. This was fine by me, providing he didn't fish it when I wanted to! Seriously, though, he was a likeable guy and my initial hostility waned when, like all proper carpers should, he offered me a cuppa. As we settled down, mugs in hand, he explained that he'd been fishing for two days without a bite and he didn't reckon his chances now because at some time under the cover of darkness someone had filled the lake in. I expressed my disgust at this and joined him in decrying this lack of angling etiquette, while secretly sending myself a mental memorandum to give Nige and his mate a drink for their creativity and effort.

Then, a carp rolled to our right.

"That's where they baited!" George said. "I've seen a carp roll several times on that spot."

"Same fish?"

"Yeah, it's got a light belly."

'Indeed it has!' I thought. The big mirror was the only carp in the lake with a really light belly. My heart sank, as I realised that George would have a bait on it, but I glanced at his rods and none of the lines were angled to the right, covering the spot.

"You haven't got a rod over there then?" I asked him.

"No," he replied. "I'm happy where I've got mine."

"Would you mind if I moved in next door to you, mate?"

"No," said George, "be my guest."

Needless to say, I couldn't believe my luck. Some people just give it to you on a plate.

Just after I'd cast out, the big mirror rolled right over my middle rod. The expression is, 'you have your heart in your mouth' but this felt more like

my rucksack. I was so on edge
– any second now, surely?

The atmosphere was electric with
the faintest hint of rain in the air. It
was so fine that I wasn't sure if I was
imagining it. Were they droplets of
rain kissing the surface of the lake, or
was it an insect hatch? It was only by
stretching out my hand that I could
feel a suggestion of drizzle on the back
of it.

The lake was steaming, like a
giant cooking pot, and faint wisps
of mist diffused into the air. I was
wearing an unlined, lightweight
waterproof jacket over a T-shirt, but I
needn't have bothered I might as well
have been standing out there stark
naked. I was drenched through with
sweat. The humidity was more akin to
a rain forest and I wouldn't have been
at all surprised to see a little, short-
arsed bloke walk past with naff all on,
holding a blow-pipe.

ABOVE
*I didn't feel that
my 'pot of gold' was
at the end of it.*

The mirror rolled again, but this time it was more to my left and now my
heart was sinking. It was only a few yards from George's right-hand bait. We sat
there drinking tea and the conversation slowed into silence, whenever she rolled.
We entered into our own separate world of thoughts as we visualised one of our
rods roaring off with this monster carp attached. She rolled again in front of me,
right over the middle rod, and tiny bubbles broke the surface, indicating that she
was foraging on the bottom. The line flicked off the rod tip where it entered the
water. It just had to go. George and I had been sitting on the boundary of our
two swims so we could chat, so I got up and walked the yards down the bank so
I could be by my rod. There was another eruption of bubbles as hundreds of tiny
orbs of gas rose to the surface, bursting with a misty vapour as they atomised.

There was a single bleep, again from my middle rod and as I looked up, the
line that had momentarily tightened, dropped back. It was going to go, I knew
it. Then she rolled again, but further out this time, a good three/four yards and I

thought, 'Where you going, darlin'? Please come back.'

The sky was clearing and patches of blue were breaking through the cloud as the sun's rays penetrated the mist. I looked up and there was a rainbow arching across the sky from behind me and seemingly disappearing into the distant shallows of the lake, but I didn't feel that my pot of gold was waiting at the end of it. The whole lake had changed and now appeared totally dead of all life; the broodingly expectant atmosphere had gone.

Early evening, in a somewhat dejected frame of mind, I had decided to try to improve my mood by keeping busy, so I brought my rods in to redo my rigs. My old friend, Phil Harper, came over to see me and as we waited for the kettle to boil, we soon got talking. We devoted the allotted five minutes to women, and then got down to the serious, carpy stuff. Phil explained that he was running out of ideas on the particular ball-breaker of a water that he was fishing at the time and had popped over for inspiration. We chatted about his lake and how hard it was and how much pressure the carp were under because every carp angler of repute in the county was on there, or so it seemed to Phil.

Then it struck me. I remembered the dental floss and how its exquisite subtleness had given me an edge when I most needed it at Braxted Res, so I told Phil the story. Until this time he'd never seen dental floss and he was well impressed when I held a length of it under the surface and he watched it virtually disappear as the gossamer threads separated. Then he pulled it out and laid it on his hand.

"It feels just like silkweed, Kev," he said. "I've got to give it a try."

He went away with half my dental floss wrapped around a stick and left me thinking. I'd seen these Silver End carp develop their awareness and avoidance skills of my rigs. In essence, I had been training them for what to look for and avoid, but one school lesson I'd never given them, was dental floss, so I changed all my rigs to the stuff and put them back out on the spots. One went to the left, at the entrance point of the potomegeton, and my middle and right-hand rods out 20 yards in front, over the area which Nigel had baited and where I'd seen the big mirror feed earlier that day.

I popped up to George, told him that I was shortly going to get my head down and wished him good luck while thinking, 'I really mean that, George. You can catch all the carp in the lake, but just make sure you don't get the big mirror!'

I went back, made a brew and then sat on my bedchair and stared out into the inky darkness, feeling dejected and with little confidence. I slipped my boots off, lined them up next to my bed and got into my sleeping bag.

I'd only been asleep for about an hour when the alarm on the middle rod screamed. I ripped the bag open, the zip protesting at my forcefulness, put my right foot over the side, straight into gloopy mud and sank up to my ankle. In my rude awakening, I'd forgotten the muddy puddle that had collected under and in front of my bed. One foot down, but I was determined to preserve the other so I leaned forward, picked up my middle rod, engaged the bail arm and pulled into the fish. This time I was in!

The rod took on a satisfying curve as something on the other end seemed hell bent on reaching the far side of the pit. It was a really fast run and I thought it must be one of the long, lean, mirrors, or more likely a mid-double. The speed of those fish was quite amazing, more akin to tope than carp, and this one caught me out. I was so focused on getting my left welly on without a muddy sock, that before I knew it the carp was in the potomegeton, directly in front of George. I laid the pressure on and the rod took on a healthy curve. Then the tip slowly and steadily eased back as she came free of the potomegeton, only to dive into the bed nearest me to my left. I had to stop her. This was where the snag was that had proved to be so disastrous in the opening week.

I piled on the pressure as much as I dared, just as George arrive on the scene.

"Christ!" he said. "You're going to break that rod!"

The carbon had taken on its maximum battle curve and I could feel the cork handle creaking under my hand. There was no more power to exert but I knew I was losing the fight and I could feel this lunatic carp burrowing into the potomegeton. It may not have been very big, but damn it, this was my first carp of the season. I'd already lost three and I was determined not to lose this one. With the rod bent alarmingly, I walked back several paces and the water erupted as I quite literally turned the fish over on its back. It was thrashing and lunging as if its life depended upon it, and leaves of potomegeton and water showered down.

"You're a raving nutter!" George said.

"I've got her out, haven't I?" I said as the carp bored out into open water.

George was keen to know about the events that had occurred before he arrived so I filled him in and lost concentration, to be honest. I'd allowed the fish to come in to my right under a willow, and felt a jarring sensation through the rod.

"Shit!" I said "I've let the thing get into the roots."

I applied maximum pressure but nothing was giving. There wasn't the faintest indication of that subtle easing of the tip that you feel through the rod when you're winning. This carp seemed chained to a tower block.

"How sloppy was that?" I said. "I had it all under control and then, talking to you, I let it get in the snag."

I eased off the pressure and was a little taken aback when the carp immediately swam out. A few turns of the reel later, with the rod over to the left and parallel with the surface, and the carp was out in front of me, completely safe and near to being ready to net.

"Shall I do the honours?" George said.

"Yeah, mate, that'd be good." I replied.

Really, I don't like strangers netting my carp for me, I've seen some right cock-ups with noddies lunging at carp like demented fly swatters but George had seen a glimpse of the fish in the darkness as I turned it over on its back in the potomegeton bed and had estimated it at around 15lbs, so I let him do it.

The carp surfaced directly in front of me, George slipped the net under it and I took a step back with a big sigh of relief. Thank Christ for that! Finally, I'd broken my duck with my first carp of the season.

Then George said, "This carp is a bit bigger than you think, my son."

I'll remember those words until the day I die. I felt the hairs go up on the back of my neck and in that second, I knew, I just knew. I rushed forward, parted

BELOW
..."This carp is a bit bigger than you think, my son."

the mesh and saw the immense pale belly of the big girl. I let out a whoop and gave George a big hug and a snog. God knows what he thought, but it might explain why I've never seen him since. Some guys just don't like French kissing, do they?

With the carp in a sling, I lifted up the scales while trying to concentrate on keeping my hands as steady as I could. That's quite challenging when your hands are attached to arms and a body about as motionless as a pneumatic drill on speed. Eventually, the needle settled and George called it at 41½lbs. I couldn't believe it.

"Are you sure, George?" I said.

I checked the scales myself and sure enough it was true. I'd caught the Essex record and it was only the second 40 ever to be caught in the county. My mind immediately flashed back to Phil, the previous captor, and the first angler to break the 40lb barrier in Essex, and it seemed relevant somehow that he'd been over to see me the day before. It was as if he'd passed on the baton for me to take up the race and win.

ABOVE
...as she faded into the deep.

I slipped her into the sack and waded out to make sure she was comfortable and safely positioned, then sat on the bank just staring at the bankstick and the draw cord where it entered the water. I sat there until dawn in a state of disbelief and it was almost as if it was a dream. I felt trapped in a time warp as I relived the years of effort and anguish and then I saw her eye as it had stared at me all those years before when I'd lost her, on that foggy morning. That demon eye searing into my brain and then the 'smile' or so I imagined as she faded into the deep. It was the smile of the carp gods. I'd been tested and I'd felt betrayed by them because my carping ethos was based on the simple belief that if you fished well and worked hard, and paid the lake with pieces of silver – in this day and age, pound coins - to appease the gods, then the lake would always pay you back. You'd get what you deserved and catch your carp.

I considered that I had more than paid my dues and so had been let down by the gods but now I understood; that look and the smile was the carp gods all-knowing. I just needed to be tested to see if I would keep my faith. If I'd landed the big carp on that foggy morning five years before, I would never have returned to the pit. Likewise, when I was so cruelly deceived by the weather girl, when Bill caught her; if I had caught her then, she would have been a 30 and not the ultimate destiny that had been planned for me - the Essex record.

Chapter Eighteen

Snake Pit: The Ultimate Challenge

When I was fishing Layer Pits in the 70s, there was a guy on there whose name escapes me now, but his job was in vermin control for Essex Council, and he used to travel all over the county dealing with infestations of rats, mice and whatever. At this time, we believed the biggest carp in Essex to be in Layer Pits, but this guy always reckoned that he'd seen bigger fish in two other lakes. I followed up one of those lakes and visited two or three times, but all I ever saw were small carp, so I just thought he was one of those who either didn't know what he was talking about, or was trying to impress us. That lake was Silver End and later, after I'd caught the Essex record there, I thought back to my rat-catcher friend, decided that maybe I should have given him a bit more respect and turned my attention to the other lake he'd mentioned, Doneylands in Colchester.

I spent some time in the next close season walking around spotting carp; well, I say spotting, but I never did see one. In fact, I didn't see much of anything. Doneylands seemed pretty devoid of any fish life, so eventually, I chose to fish elsewhere. The same thing happened, more or less, the following season, and this time Bill Lovett and I really did spend weeks looking around, but still never saw a thing.

After three years of looking at Doneylands, I made up my mind for the 1988 season to have a go. I had nothing to lose. Really, catching the Silver End mirror

THE SNAKE PIT

had changed me forever. Until that time, I'd been happy to catch above average-sized carp, which in those days would be 20s, the equivalent of a 40 now, but after Silver End, only one size of carp lit my fire, and that was the very biggest. The very biggest Essex carp could possibly be in Doneylands, if I listened to the rat-catcher who had proved to be so right before, so I adopted a banker plan. Just a couple of miles down the road was another lake, the Garrison, which was quite an unusual pool, a sand pit with very steep, wooded sides with about I'd say an acre and a half, max, of crystal clear, weedy water.

This lake had a good track record, being one of the few Essex lakes to produce a 30. I decided to bait it and have a go, but really, it was a water that I was just dropping in on, because it made the long drive to Colchester worthwhile. My plan was to bait Doneylands on the way to fishing the Garrison, and every two weeks, I'd drop in until I either saw a carp or caught one, in which case I'd then switch all my attention to Doneylands. The sighting, or the capture of one carp, no matter how small, would convince me that the rat catcher was right. Alternatively, after a season of baiting and blanks, I would let it go and give up.

I knew that the Garrison would be busy at the opening because there was a young Colchester crew of budding carp anglers fishing it, so I chose to fish elsewhere with Bill Lovett for the opening night, at another gravel pit which turned out to be a complete disaster. We caught nothing and got totally wound up by a psychopathic swan, but that's another story.

Two days later, I drove up the A12 to Colchester, dropped into Doneylands to bait and as I walked round, I was surprised to see a bivvy set up in one of the three spots I'd been baiting. There was a guy standing outside it and as I approached him he went inside his bivvy and zipped up the door, but I still asked him if he'd caught anything. There was no reply, though, so I figured his bivvy had been soundproofed, áThen I went to the Garrison and was greeted with, "Have you heard the news?"

"No," I said. "What news?"

"Doneylands has done a 40lb common."

I couldn't believe it. The lad I'd seen standing outside his bivvy had decided to do the start of the season in one of the spots that I'd baited, and he'd had a mind-blowing hit of carp; four or five, including a 40½lb common, only the second carp in Essex to achieve the magic weight. This was the only session he fished and tragically, he committed suicide soon after, but that wasn't to be the only death associated with Doneylands.

I'd heard all I needed to hear; not only did Doneylands contain carp, but also, as the rat-catcher had believed, they were monsters. I put my gear in the car and turned my back on the Garrison, never to return.

BELOW
...then I went to the Garrison "Have you heard the news?"...

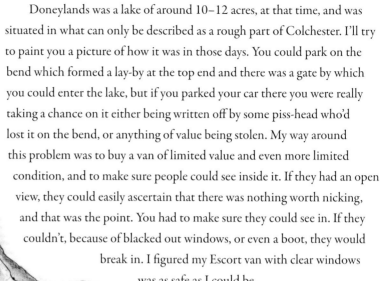

Doneylands was a lake of around 10–12 acres, at that time, and was situated in what can only be described as a rough part of Colchester. I'll try to paint you a picture of how it was in those days. You could park on the bend which formed a lay-by at the top end and there was a gate by which you could enter the lake, but if you parked your car there you were really taking a chance on it either being written off by some piss-head who'd lost it on the bend, or anything of value being stolen. My way around this problem was to buy a van of limited value and even more limited condition, and to make sure people could see inside it. If they had an open view, they could easily ascertain that there was nothing worth nicking, and that was the point. You had to make sure they could see in. If they couldn't, because of blacked out windows, or even a boot, they would break in. I figured my Escort van with clear windows was as safe as I could be.

I always left one item in the back of the Escort, an old, lidded emulsion bucket covered in dried paint. I kept my spare leads in it so I could always go back to the car to collect some, rather than lug unnecessary weight round the lake. Also in the bucket was a grand's worth of camera equipment, but I guess the low-life figured that the old paint bucket wasn't worth the effort. The milkman who fished the lake wasn't so lucky. He had his wellington, (yes, I did mean singular) with a hole in it stolen from his Caravanette. You may say, no great loss – or you could question what he was doing with a wellington with a hole in it, anyway. If you'd known the milkman, you wouldn't have asked; by the time he'd explained, you'd have lost the will to live. The whole point is not what was nicked, but the damage and cost caused by the smashing of his Caravanette window.

If you walked in the gate, you could look out across the lake to a vista of submerged, bush-covered islands, and a high percentage of the open water between the islands was bottom to top with weed. Clearly, once upon a time, the lake had been a lot shallower. It had also been a lot bigger but it had been back-filled, which raised the level and was how the bush and tree-covered islands ended up being submerged. I always reckoned that Doneylands was 30% submerged trees and 70% weed – with just a handful of carp living in it that could have all fitted in a bath. It was no wonder that on my previous close season visits, I never spotted them.

The gate end of the lake was used by the locals to dump their garden rubbish and oversized items that wouldn't fit into their dustbins, such as sofas, mattresses, old cookers etc. Adjacent to the top end of the lake on the left bank was an old Victorian house which was a home for wayward kids, and there was a hole in the fence. It was worth watching your gear in that swim! I named it the 'Hole in the Wall'.

Behind the right bank of the lake was a footpath with gaps among the trees where the public could walk through, so it was wise to keep an eye on your gear here, too. You had to watch this bank because all sorts of outcasts, tramps, nutters and thugs would use it, especially throughout the hours of darkness. I used to hear the crew with their dogs and lamps going along it on their badger hunts, for badger-baiting purposes. Some nights there might be screams from a woman who'd got into something she was regretting and I even heard a rustle one evening, and looked round only to have a 12-bore pointing at me from a mere three feet away. It turned out to be a local who had befriended me and thought it would be amusing to creep up with a loaded 12-bore. You can imagine, I was ecstatic!

At the far end of this 'scenic' venue, was a tip. A local builder owned the lake; he was back-filling it and couldn't lose, really. Instead of having to pay to have his building debris carted away and tipped, he'd bought a disused gravel pit instead, so that once he'd filled it in, he had a piece of land to develop. It seemed that he was halfway there.

So, every day, a stream of tipping lorries would be going backwards and forwards, and if the wind was in the wrong direction, the dust would end up covering you, as well as rods, reels and bivvy. When I first moved on to Doneylands, the traffic was excessive. Lorry after lorry would come in, dumping loads of mainly broken breezeblocks, and someone told me that the builder was demolishing an old supermarket and building a new one on the same site. It was this tipping that attracted the locals like flies. You'd be fishing and a constant stream of assorted characters would be going to and fro behind you, their supermarket trolleys full up with broken breezeblocks. Clearly, these locals didn't work for a living, so I was amazed by the effort and time they would invest, spending hours rooting through the rubble for perhaps a virtually whole breezeblock, or the pot of gold, a short piece of copper pipe.

I stood on top of the bank one day, trying to get a higher vantage point, wishfully thinking that I might be lucky enough to spot a carp, and watched the constant stream of supermarket trolleys going past me. One guy seemed particularly industrious and I'd seen him make several trips. Clearly, he was on a major building project and was collecting a significant number of broken breezeblocks, so I asked him what he was building. His reply was, 'Oi'm buildin' a rabbit 'utch'.

I was quite taken aback by this, either he had one enormous rabbit or a lot of 'em!

Anyway, now my interest was up and I asked the next two guys who came along what they were building. They were building rabbit hutches, too. It seemed that every nutter in Colchester had rabbits!

I couldn't believe the number of weirdos that frequented this one lake. In fact, it was a mystery for several years, but then I found out the reason. In Colchester, there was a mental hospital called Severalls and they had a halfway house, the purpose of which was to rehabilitate people back into society. These mental patients all lived in a house near the lake. A couple of weeks after the 'county rabbit hutch building programme', I saw Phil Harper at the lake and he told me a story with a somewhat bemused look on his face.

He'd been over the weekend before when I couldn't make it. A guy had come up to him, they'd got talking and Phil asked him about the history of the water. The guy obliged and Phil was really interested. You've got to understand that out of nowhere there comes this 40lb common, the first time the lake was fished by a carp angler, and the big question now was, 'what else could be in it?' Anyway, Phil asked if the guy had seen any big fish in the lake.

"Oo ar," he confirmed. "There's these big black an' whoite fish, six feet larng, and crocodoiles, too!"

We'd been on Doneylands for a few weeks and the old problem was beginning to rear its head; the old cloth-capped fishing club versus the carp angler feud. Suddenly, we were receiving regular visits from club officials clearly trying to catch us out with three rods, or other hanging offences. It was a real pain, because at this time, the water authorities had, in their wisdom, cut the three-rod limit down to two rods. If you'd been brought up fishing three rods, to be told you could only use two was like having your arm cut off, let alone being on this ball breaker where if we'd had 20 rods, we'd still struggle. It was a rule that we broke all the time if we could get away with it, but after managing to get your bait out on a very rare clear spot, the last thing you needed was to be frantically winding it in and stashing the rod before the poxy bailiff caught you.

One day, I'd got a bailiff in my swim and he hadn't noticed my third rod, which I'd just had enough time to stash in a reed bed. I'd passed the health check, but then he hung around talking and I really wanted him to piss off so I could get the third rod out before dark, which was rapidly approaching. He was moaning, mostly about the fact that he was on a rota and had to check regularly on this new lake they'd just got – Doneylands. He thought it was completely pointless because there were only half a dozen nutter carp anglers fishing it anyway, and every bailiff had confirmed it was the same six people, and they were all paid-up members, so what was the point?

I came up with, dare I say, an inspirational idea. I would volunteer to be a bailiff. As I was up there fishing it all the time, and was such an upstanding citizen, they could rely on me (scouts' honour) to keep an eye on the water, and especially those naughty carpers. I found out that they had a committee meeting once a month at a 'sports club' so I went down there to offer my services. I had the devil of a job finding it and kept walking around a tatty old football pitch in the dark, sure that if there *was* a sports and social club there I would find it. On the second lap round, I heard voices coming from, quite literally, the garden shed. I pushed the door and squeezed through the four guys who just about fitted in there, sitting at a table. I put my case to them in my most sincere manner and was awarded the distinction of bailiff. Clearly, to them, it was a position of such honour that it was almost like receiving a knighthood. We all got quite emotional.

Now we could really rock and roll. My merry band of carp anglers and me were all of a similar mind. We were the young guns, the Jack the lads of Essex, proper blokes. I was fishing alongside Zenon Bojko and, trust me, Zen was more of a lad then than he is now, if that's possible, and in tow, was his boy. At around 10 years old, Rael was an utterly horrible brat and to make matters worse, he was his dad's lackey and spy. Zen would send Rael round and coincidentally, his visits were always at recasting time, so a game would commence. Rael would stand there making childish conversation, while hoping to get a glimpse of my bait or rig so that he could report back to his dad. He had no chance. I should mention here that later on Zen and I became close friends and shared all our fishing information. Zen is one of the biggest wind-up merchants I've ever had the pleasure to meet, your classic Essex boy, and that's a compliment. Zen was a good-looking lad who dressed well and had style. He had a cocky grin and constantly pitched himself with the wind-ups at whomever he met.

Then there was Phil Harper, who I've mentioned before. He was the first 'proper' carp angler I met, outside of Rayleigh Angling Club, when I fished a lake called the Railway Pond in Maldon, as a teenager. Along comes this kid on a bike, a proper greaser with long hair, tight jeans, and a biker's black, tasselled leather jacket; shame was on a pushbike. I often wished that I had a photo of him taken then; I could have used it so many times in future years when he was chatting up birds in pubs. Phil and I became firm friends and often ended up fishing on the same waters, as well as keeping in touch on the phone. We spent quite a bit of time together in the 70s on Layer Pits when he had a fiancée, but that relationship apparently ended in the years when I didn't see him because I was at Braxted.

Anyway, at this time Phil was footloose and fancy-free. He was the pretty boy of carp fishing, really. Girls swarmed around him like bees around a honey pot. Zen and I reckoned he was too pretty to be a bloke and should have been a bird and in one of his many wind-ups on one particularly long session, Zen suggested that Phil could be our bivvy bitch. He never took us up on that offer, I hasten to add, but it stuck and we always took the piss out of him as will be revealed as you read on.

So, now I was a bailiff and we hoped we'd be left in peace, but as a bailiff I needed to have respect so we all settled on a proper set of rules. My mates promised faithfully that they would keep to them and not give me any trouble. I was sceptical with such stroke pullers as they were, but we'd agreed and I was determined that the following rules would be upheld:

1. You could only fish with a minimum of three rods and four would be looked upon positively.

2. Whoever was pitched up in the swim nearest the gate was responsible for organising the takeaway, and as this was the biggest swim, for sweeping an area to make a dance floor.

3. We particularly spent some time deciding on rules for Phil and decided that at all times he should wear stockings, suspenders, and stilettos of at least eight inches. Actually, he kicked off about this. He said it would be dangerous what with the uneven paths, and all, so with me having in mind my responsibilities to the club and health and safety and all that, we settled on six.

4. For Phil, lipstick and make up were obligatory. After all, this water was an absolute ball breaker and we didn't know how long it'd be before we next saw a bird.

5. Should it be deemed that Rael was becoming particularly irritating, any of us could kick him hard without fear of any retribution from his dad.

We were sorted. All we had to do now was deal with one small detail; catching a carp.

I turned up one Saturday morning to find the lake almost deserted, except for an angler who I spied at a distance. He was on the back bank, and sitting on a box, float fishing. I couldn't believe it. In the couple of months that we'd been on the lake, I'd yet to see a fish other than the four different carp that we'd identified when they visited the snags. Certainly, this wasn't a hectic match venue!

I nearly left the guy alone. I wanted to fish just inside the gate in the first swim, you know, the one with the dance floor. I didn't want to trudge all the way around to the other end, but then I figured that this guy was so out of place, he could be a spy sent by the committee to check that the lake was being properly bailiffed, so I walked round to investigate. Sure enough, he was float fishing, had been since dawn and five hours later he was still fishless. No surprise there, then.

I chatted in a friendly way with him and planned to go back and set up in a couple of minutes, when we were joined by a distinguished looking gentleman dressed in tweeds and plus-fours, and we soon got talking about the lake. It transpired that he'd lived in the area all his life and what he didn't know about Doneylands wasn't worth knowing. This, to me, was an incredibly lucky break. He told me when the lake was dug, pointed behind us and I was amazed to hear that it had once gone back to a far hedgerow, so it had been more than twice its current size. Now I understood why all the islands were submerged. It had been back filled

BELOW
...it was likely that they'd walked within feet of the Doneylands common, which used to love sunbathing tight to the bank in bushes just inside the gate...

significantly, which had raised the water level.

I steered the conversation toward the subject of carp and immediately, he said, "Oh yes, I remember when it was stocked 12 years ago."

"Really?" I said, keen to know. "Can you remember how many?"

"Yes, 24," he said.

Now this really did my head. We'd only seen four, possibly five different fish that regularly visited a set of snags, ironically right next to the gate. I was often amused by the number of anglers who had heard about the big common and so had come over to check out Doneylands. They'd walk round, searching every nook and cranny for carp, eventually giving up and deciding that this water wasn't for them. The few raving nutters who were fishing this weed-filled, submerged forest of trees for the odd carp, could keep it, but it was likely that they'd walked within feet of the Doneylands common, which used to love sunbathing tight to the bank in bushes just inside the gate.

Like I said, we'd only seen four or five carp, though, so where were the remainder? I remember thinking, 'Wow – what is the potential of this lake?' and then the guy said,

"...and there's great big, six-foot, black and whoite fish and crocodoiles..." Talk about get taken in!

As if the nutters weren't enough to contend with, there were also the snakes. I first became aware of the snake element when I was fishing with a mate, Mark. We were both fishing along the right-hand side and I was in my customary position, sitting up on the high bank above the swim, scanning the lake for signs of life. I saw him emerge from his cut-out some 50 yards away, and climb up the bank to have a pee, but he was there for ages and I was thinking, 'Bluddy 'ell Mark! How long do you pee for?' Well, it was getting ridiculous and after what seemed half an hour, I wandered down to witness this interesting occurrence.

As I got nearer, I called out to him and I could see him trying to reply; his lips were moving, but there was no sound. I couldn't figure out what Mark was doing, holding his knob and whispering, but as I approached I could see that a few feet away in front of him, where he'd gone to have a pee, was a bloody great adder sunbathing in the grass. I dragged him back, and he was in a terrible state. It turned out that he suffered from ophidiophobia – an irrational fear of snakes. He'd been so frozen to the spot that he couldn't even let go of his knob which was, by this time, very much shrivelled up. I do wonder if he could have been there until nightfall if I hadn't gone to his aid.

At this time, I was writing a weekly column in Angling Times with Rod Hutchinson – Nashy and Hutch – a somewhat cringe-worthy title, pinched from the American cop series Starsky and Hutch. It was *not* fortunate that as I signed up for this series Doneylands came up, because when you write a weekly column, the reader does expect you to catch fish. In fact, a few years later, a youngster who is now a big name on the scene came up to me and said he was a great fan of mine. He referenced Nashy and Hutch and said that he loved my articles but he couldn't believe how I could go fishing so often and blank!

To disguise the name of the lake in my weekly writing, Doneylands became the Snake Pit, which it's still known as today. It's a worthy name. The place was infested with adders and before or since, I've never seen a lake with so many of them. I remember writing of one incident that happened when I was fishing a swim along the top bank that was cut into the Snake Pit's steep sides. It was a really hot August day and trying to shelter from the worst of the sun under my umbrella,

I'd dozed off in the afternoon heat. I remember being startled awake by a thud of something hitting my umbrella, but this was a regular occurrence as stones and pieces of dried clay slid down the bank, so I took no notice and dozed off again.

When I opened my eyes, my head on the pillow, and looked down at my Coleman stove that was positioned next to my bedchair, I nearly hit the roof of my brolly. Coiled around the stove, presumably because the sun had heated the metal, was an enormous adder and when I moved, it started hissing at me. It must have fallen down the bank and while I'd thought a rock had thumped against my brolly, it was really Hissing Sid!

It could be positively dangerous over there. A couple of us were fishing in cut-outs along the right bank when

someone set fire to the bank between the lake path and the public footpath. Snakes were swarming out of the bank to get away from the fire and the only way they could go was toward us at the lakeside – luckily, Mark wasn't there that day! The only place we could go to get away from them was into the lake. So, you can see that it was an interesting first summer on the Snake Pit, only lacking in one small detail – carp!

Brian Ash had moved on and he was the first to catch, underneath a marginal bush, from one of the two swims on the top bank, the one adjacent to the main snags which we named the Snags. He caught a really fat, dumpy 22lb common, but this seemed a one-off capture and to the best of my knowledge that spot under the bush in the snags swim never produced another take. Apart from the 22lb common, we indentified the 40lb common; there was also a double-figure mirror, a low-20 mirror, a mirror definitely in the 30s, and some claimed to have spotted a 40-plus leather, but I was never convinced. One day I was watching a big fish lying deep in the water in the snags and I was really excited, because it seemed that at last I was watching this mythical leather, and then she blew her tanks and rose to the surface; it was the big common.

I don't believe there ever was a big leather, but we will never know because in that first year, a couple of fish were lost and at least one of them was tethered and died. For a long time afterwards, there was an oil slick kicking up from where the fish had been lost in a row of submerged bushes. The 30lb mirror that was regularly spotted disappeared, so I assumed, somewhat sadly, that this fish died, and may have been the one that was tethered.

The summer months were passing rapidly and autumn was upon us, yet we were all still blanking big time. We only saw carp in two places; the snags in the left corner next to the gate, and the main snags in the right corner of the top bank. Both these areas were jungles of submerged trees and so were considered to be unfishable and it would have been unethical to attempt to pull a carp out from there. We hadn't seen one carpy occurrence anywhere else in the lake to give us a clue where the carp might go to feed and so couldn't identify a spot where they fed regularly.

One weekend, Bill Lovett came over and fished his regular Friday night slot.

As I've mentioned, Bill had been a fishing companion for a long time but he could never get into lakes like I did. He has never spoken about it but I know that it must have really done his head as he saw his mates putting in the hours to catch a carp, when all he could do was his regular weekly Friday night sessions, because of family commitments. Ironically, it may well be why he is still as keen as mustard today, because he never got too much of it and burned out.

Anyway, as Bill packed up on the Saturday afternoon from the Dance Floor swim, he spotted a big carp roll some 70 yards out. That was a real revelation; the first time a carp had actually been spotted out in the lake, and a rolling fish, too, that could be feeding. The next thing he did left me scratching my head. When you bear in mind how limited his fishing time was, you'd think, wouldn't you, that he'd want to keep this sighting secret so he could milk it? Not, as he did, tell what he'd seen to Zen when he walked past ten minutes later - but then I guess that's Bill for you. A more lovely and generous guy you'll never meet. Can I just say, though, if you're reading this, Bill, I would have much preferred it had you told your old mate, Kev, rather than Zen!

Zen is as sharp as a razor and doesn't need a second hint. Immediately, on Bill's withdrawal, he moved into the swim with Rael and it became his 'property'. Back then, there was still a semblance of etiquette left over from the good old days, so as Zen made it clear that he was going to be baiting this swim regularly, he was as good as saying 'keep out and don't jump in my swim', so the rest of us had to sit on our hands and watch events unfold. Zen had another advantage, which remains a key element of success at the Snake Pit to this day. When you look at the list of anglers who have caught the biggest residents over the years, the original big common, Dippy and the current Snake Pit Common Mark2, the captures mainly fall to locals or full-timers. Quite simply, unless you are a full-timer, or live close enough to pop in regularly and keep in touch with the water, the odds of any consistent success are against you.

So Zen was popping down and baiting his swim every day and on a harvest moon he got his result, or some may suggest that Rael did... whatever, the reader can decide. This particular night, Zen had gone round to the other side of the lake to have a social with Phil Harper who was fishing the Hole in the Wall, when Zen had a take. Luckily, he'd left Rael to guard the rods in the Dance swim, so the boy hooked the fish and played it until his dad could make his way back. I got a phone call on the Sunday morning, as I couldn't fish that weekend, and went up to do the photos of Zen and the Snake Pit common. I remember thinking, 'what an amazing carp'. It was stunning; a perfectly formed woodcarving, and when Zen caught her she weighed 40lbs 8oz.

Zen and Rael effectively emptied the lake over the following weeks from that one baited area, catching all the remaining surviving fish that we'd seen going into the snags. Their next biggest was an upper-20 mirror, which became known as Rael's Fish. Clearly, with Bill's sighting, Zen had optimised on the pit's autumn feeding ground. I remember being in Zen's swim one day when he wound a rod in and there were several bloodworm caught in the rig. That area must have been heaving with grub.

The lake shut down as winter approached and it was clear that there was no point in staying at the Snake to hit our heads against a brick wall, so we made our plans for a June 16th start the following year. The events that followed were mind-blowing. Some time after, I was asked by the Carp Society if I would contribute to their magazine, 'Carp Fisher' so I wrote an article with a humorous slant about an underlying, potentially dangerous situation that we found ourselves in.

Previously published in Carp Fisher, Summer 1991

15th June 1989

The scene: Basically, a square lake of some 10 – 12 acres; not the prettiest of places. At the road end, the lake is used as a tip by local residents. Every kind of household debris you can imagine finds its way into the water, from cookers and sofas to dustbin liners full of grass cuttings.

The opposite end is used by a contractor to dump waste from his building projects. Sadly, he is now beginning to make progress into the remaining lake, which will soon be gone. These tipping operations attract myriad bounty hunters, a motley assortment of characters from the local council estate, who travel constantly from their homes to the tip with various forms of carts, wheelbarrows and supermarket trolleys in which to carry their booty of timber, bricks or – prize of prizes – a piece of steel or aluminium back to their homes to do goodness knows what with. Often they stop to enquire about our fishing fortunes. Some have become well known to us; a few definitely have various screws loose. Still, it all adds to the interest of the place.

The lake banks are heavily populated with adders and at times great caution needs to be exercised. It was because of this wildlife that I named the lake the Snake Pit, while writing for the Angling Times. The name has made the lake famous, one of its four carp inhabitants being the magnificent Snake Pit common.

There can't be many lakes that are more of a ball breaker than the Snake Pit. Strangely, the pit is a water very close to my heart. Perhaps it's because of the excitement that first season, when a new water was discovered of seemingly enormous potential, or more likely, it was the bond developed between the water and the small band of anglers who 'had a crack'.

Zen and I were both set up and I had walked round to his swim where we sat in the morning sun, chatting excitedly about future prospects while drinking tea. The sun was really bright, reflecting off Zen's designer shirt, which he proudly modelled for Rael and me. To celebrate the start of every season, Zen buys a 'fishing shirt'. This one had obviously been designed by John Travolta while he was at a disco drinking the juice, I would imagine.

The metallic ring of high heels on gravel signalled the arrival of Phil Harper, cursing wildly as apparently he had smudged his lipstick on his Stalker sling strap. Zen, Rael and I tried to hide, but Phil knew where Zen would be fishing, so we had no choice but to help him round to my swim, which Phil was to share with me. Baulking at the task, we got stuck in – after all, what are friends for? Rael carried the mirror, Zen and I took an end each of the dressing table, leaving Phil to struggle with his two rucksacks of various toiletries essential to his posing – oops, I mean fishing.

The JCB was called over and in a jiffy the site was cleared for Phil's four-bedroom detached oval bivvy. It always amazes me how he gets his wardrobes and dressing table through the comparatively small door. Still, he does, and in next to no time it was gleaming and all the work was done. It was time to relax, do the wind-ups and steal Rael's sweets.

Just down the road from the Snake Pit is the Garrison Lake. Damien and his mates were dug in ready to go, as well as a new guy, Graham, who popped over to see us, spending the afternoon tapping us up on rigs and bait, and drinking our tea.

The light was failing and it was almost time to chuck the leads out. We were excited, savouring the expectations of another season. Graham left for the Garrison and we called after him wishing him luck. Few lakes can build up the giddy feeling of certain expectations as the Snake Pit does to me, and no lake can dash my confidence as much, plummeting me almost to the depths of despair. However, at the start of a new season only optimism prevails. Leads away! Which take tonight is going to be the common and to whom? Zen, Phil, or me? Probably Rael.

The faint light over the trees signalled another perfect dawn. Not a bleep all night. I put it down to Phil's perfume, the thick, heady odour tainting the baits. Zen's lack of action was obviously Rael's fault, it always is, which explained why Rael was looking sheepish and limping badly. The Garrison lads had fared no better apparently, as Graham reported when he popped over first thing in the morning to see what had occurred.

Later, we all had the hump with Graham, when Damien came over and reported a fish had indeed been caught – and by Graham! Why tap us up for rig and bait info, accept our hospitality, and tea - and then lie to us? Obviously, he wasn't aware that there were no secrets between what was happening on the Snake and the Garrison and that we would find out as soon as we saw Damien and his crew. We thought it was pretty poor behaviour.

"Caught anything?" came the enquiry.

"No," was my reply, as the afternoon sun beat down unrelenting.

It was one of those situations which I'm sure we have all experienced, when an enquiry after our fishing fortunes is from a non-angler who proceeds to just stand there. No conversation, just staring. After three hours, Phil and I were really wishing he would piss off. However, he hadn't lost his voice after all, the conversation went something like this.

"I went to the barracks but the sergeant wasn't there."

"Oh, yeah," was our reply. The non-committal tone a hint that we really didn't wish to get dragged into this conversation.

"His corporals were there, though. They said I would have to come back."

"Oh, yeah?" we replied.

"The time's not right."

"Oh, yeah," I replied. Phil had by this time given up acknowledging him.

"But I went to Hereford and saw Captain Peters."

"What?" I said. A fatal mistake; I shouldn't have said that.

Phil looked at me with real despair, wishing I hadn't said it, now we would never get rid of him. Obviously, we had found the Snake Pit's newest *arrival from the nut house, but the relevance of Hereford, to me, was that it's the HQ of the SAS.*

"Captain Peters said the time wasn't right, but when it was he would see me."

I could contain myself no longer and risking being impaled on Phil's six-inch stilettos, I had to ask the question.

"Why wasn't the time right?"

"Suzy says."

"I see," I replied.

Frankly, 'I see' was just a reply which bore no resemblance to my understanding of the conversation, which I didn't see at all, if you see what I mean.

"The problem is, I'm only using one lung, at the moment." He paused and then carried on the next snippet, almost as a casual afterthought. "I can only run 50 miles non-stop at 100mph."

"I see," I replied.

Our friend continued. "When my other lung is operational, I'll be able to run 100 miles non-stop."

"What, at 100mph?" I questioned, with some sarcasm.

"Oh no, 200mph," he replied.

"I see, then I suppose the time will be right?" I suggested, feeling quite smug with myself for sussing the reason why the time wasn't right. 'Ave a word with yourself, I thought.

Evening was drawing in; it had been a tiring day in our exposed swim, unable to retreat from the sun. Five hours of our new-found friend was more than enough. So, I gave Khan a kick and received the growling response I was after, suggesting to our friend that he'd better go or my Doberman would eat him if he showed his face after dark. He got really stroppy at being told to go, but after several threats and snarls from Khan, as I discreetly pulled his ear, (Khan's ear, that is), thankfully, he did, and retreated into the bushes, hopefully into a nest of adders.

Arrangements were made for the evening meal and refreshments - wine, curries, tikka masalas and a bag of sweets for Rael. Zen's swim was the chosen restaurant. Simple, because he had dug it out and it would easily accommodate the dining table, dance floor and disco – and of course, the powder room for Phil.

On our way round to Zen's swim, I noticed our friend hiding, peering through the bushes at us. This creep was beginning to get on my nerves! Good grub, good company, we all sat in Zen's swim, sated and relaxed, enjoying the warmth of the evening. The wine had gone to our heads and we giggled like children as Phil and I conveyed our conversation with the nutter to Zen. Then, a figure loomed out of the darkness and walked straight into the middle of our gathering. The nutter was back!

It was obvious that our only chance of getting rid of him was not to lead him on, but just keep quiet as he prattled trying to induce a response. Those who know Zen will be aware of the wicked sense of humour he has, never missing an opportunity to wind up his mates. Oh what a heaven-sent opportunity for Zen this was!

"Suzy says the time isn't right."

"Who's Suzy?" said Zen.

"Suzy's my nurse."

"Oh," said Zen.

"Wendy says the time isn't right"

"Who's Wendy?"

"She's Suzy's friend, my other nurse."

This conversation went on for another hour, as Zen gleefully kept asking questions, knowing that he was winding us up, more and more as we saw our relaxing evening fast disappearing. After all, we'd put up with this head-case all day and had come round to Zen's for an evening's respite. It was the same old stuff about Captain Peters, the barracks, sergeant, his lungs, heart etc., and even Zen was getting bored with the repetition, when he had a stroke of inspiration. The enquiry as to whether the nutter would like to meet a colonel in the army, met with an excited response, so Zen gave him the directions, and off he ran – to the Garrison Lake down the road, to see Graham, who was about to find out he was a colonel in the army. We giggled at the cleverness of getting our own back on dear Graham. Even Phil was happy again, his stilettos repaired; rig glue came to the rescue again.

I was awoken some time later by an almighty row coming from Zen's swim. From what I could gather, someone was going to shoot him. Still Zen had Rael to protect him. He couldn't rely on us; both Khan and I had drunk too much lager, and Phil could be heard next door, snoring loudly, so naturally I went back to sleep.

In the morning, we asked Zen what had occurred during the night and his reply was difficult to understand on account of him laughing hysterically as he tried to relate the story. Apparently, Mr Nutter had indeed visited Graham's swim, creeping up silently from the bushes behind him in the middle of the night, and Graham took it so well he jumped in the lake in fright. Graham eventually put together what had gone down and managed, after several hours, to persuade Mr Nutter that it was a case of mistaken identity and he wasn't, in fact, a colonel. Graham then rampaged over to the Snake Pit, threatening all sorts of violence on Zen, and what's more, his six brothers were on their way to systematically take Zen apart. All of them, apparently, of Graham's build, some 15 stone, I'd say.

Zen was doubled-up and rolling on the floor with laughter as he pictured the scene of our friend creeping up on Graham in the dark and scaring the hell out of him, and that wasn't helping Graham's temper. Eventually, with more threats to Zen, he went back to his own lake, apparently, we later heard from Damien, tripping over the nutter who was curled up asleep on the path.

Day two of the season had started with much excitement and laughter. Shame about the fishing, though. Finding the four Snake Pit carp in 12 acres or so of weedbed and snags was proving impossible in the sweltering summer heat of 1989.

It was midday, the sun beating down and Phil and I were getting a little despondent, especially as the nutter was back discussing the usual topics to which we kept completely silent. Suddenly, he started jerking his head violently and my concern for him overcame my irritation, after all he seemed harmless enough.

"What's the matter?" I enquired.

"They're talking to me," he replied.

"What? Who's talking to you" I asked, in complete bewilderment.

"My nurses," he said. "Suzy and Wendy."

"What do you mean? Suzy and Wendy are talking to you?" I exclaimed.

He jerked his head upward violently, looking to the sky.

"Voices in my head. Suzy says the time isn't right."

This nutter really was on one! I cracked up. I lost control. I threw him out of the swim telling him to clear off and to stay away, otherwise the dog would eat him. He got really angry, but I was past caring and all attempts at politeness had failed me.

With the nutter on his way round to see Zen, I thought about the situation. What we had here was someone fantasising about being in the army; indeed, by the references to Hereford, the SAS! He was obviously under, or had been under, medical supervision, hence the references to Suzy and Wendy, and was hearing voices in his head. Christ, the possible implications were sinking in. You see these kinds of people on News at Ten. It was only two years before when the country had been left reeling when a guy dressed up in army fatigues, commanded by voices in his head, had gunned down 31 people, killing 16, in the Berkshire town of Hungerford. Instinctively, something told me that we could be in danger and I had a bad feeling that it might not have been wise to lose my temper and make an enemy of this guy. Considering all this, I came to the conclusion that the fishing was impossible. The Snake Pit rarely is possible but in this heat it really was impossible. I think, in honesty, that the uneasy feelings were the real reason, the poor fishing merely an excuse. We packed up, moving on to the hopefully more productive fishing at Harefield, and sane people – or so I thought. I met Essex John!

One evening, a month later, Zen was on the phone. Nothing unusual about that, we seemed to report to each other weekly on our few successes and many failures, and the carp vine gossip.

"You ain't gonna believe this," Zen said, and over the phone he read to me the headline of his local paper. 'Murder victim hidden under bed' and the sub-heading, 'Son murders mother and hides her under bed for two months until she was discovered.'

Our nutter friend had murdered his mum and hidden her under his bed for two months. While we were over the Snake Pit with him, his mum was lying very dead under his bed! Later, I found out that his mum's name was Wendy.'

Chapter Nineteen

Harefield: Induction

I turned up at the Snake Pit one weekend and found a new guy fishing there, so I went to have a chat with him. As I walked into his swim, I remember thinking that he had no chance. He was sitting there on a chair reading a book instead of applying watercraft; his eyes should have been glued on the lake, looking for the few carp that the Snake Pit held. It was no surprise when he blanked, and I never saw him again, but he was a nice enough guy and I ended up chatting to him for a couple of hours. He told me that he'd been fishing Harefield in the Colne Valley, and he showed me some photos. I was quite taken aback. He had a thick pile of pictures of 20s up to 30, and some of them were stunning fish. He said the fishing was so easy that he could just drop his baits in the margins where the workings were, and along would come a carp while he read a book! So, I checked the water out and saw a photo of a carp that took my breath away, the biggest fully-scaled in the UK at the time, at around 32lbs. I gazed at that immense carp and its incredible scales, and made up my mind that one day I would go after it.

All of this went in the Nash computer bank. I told Zenon and Phil, and we all got tickets. We had a rule in those days; if we got to hear of an up-and-coming water, we'd grab a ticket. Even if we weren't going to fish it in the near future, we'd grab the ticket anyway because we might not have been able to get in later. This has happened on so many waters, especially down in the Colne Valley, where in the early days you could walk in straightaway; waters such as Harrow and Cons,

for example. If only we'd jumped on the tickets at the time - they're now closed shops. Once it was realised what was in the lakes, and they started being fished hard, the door was slammed firmly shut. Anyway, my Harefield ticket duly arrived in the post and went into my membership wallet, ready for the day when I moved off the Snake Pit.

That day came rather prematurely as I pulled off the Snake Pit in the virtually impossible conditions of unseasonably high temperatures, not to mention, of course, the murderer! I never intended to do more than fish the rest of the opening week at Harefield because my plans were definitely set on sticking it out on the Snake Pit until I caught the common, but then Harefield got to me and the party started.

When I did get to Harefield, the water had certainly changed from the picture painted by the guy I met at the Snake Pit, of having the place to himself with naïve carp jumping on the bank. The water was hot news and had attracted a number of the very best young guns, the ambitious carpers who really wanted to be over the road on Savay, *the* water at the time. Savay was a difficult water to get into and because of this, many chose the next best option, which was Harefield.

I stood on the causeway bank of Harefield. It's high above water level and I could see anglers' lines in the swims along it, stretching out into the distance, bowstring tight. With my soft to medium action rods, I had no chance of getting out that far, and I walked around aimlessly, trying to find an area with fish in, but there were no fish to be seen anywhere. I tried to find a swim I fancied, but I didn't fancy any that were vacant. The majority of the swims at Harefield involved fishing at range, out into open water, which was in contrast to the smaller Essex lakes that I was generally used to.

These Essex lakes were more 'up close and personal', allowing us to hunt the fish at close-ish range, or to features like islands or near to far bank margins. Harefield was mainly about casting to distant gullies between the gravel bars, and what bars! The only bars I'd found in Essex sold lager, but not at Harefield. Here, they ran almost the length of the lake and the tops were covered in sharp flints and mussels.

It was a dangerous place to have a line fishing over the top and the loss rate was immense. If you got out over the first bar, which depending on where you fished would be about 50 yards out, you'd lose three out of ten carp hooked, on average. The second bar, seven out of ten, and the third bar; nine out of ten, at best. That's an horrendous failure rate, but one that the anglers accepted at the time. Well, maybe not accepted, but put up with, because everything they could think of to stop their line being cut through had been tried. I even heard that steel trace wire had been used for leaders. To this day, I haven't heard of any water where the

BELOW
...Harefield was mainly about casting to distant gullies between the gravel bars...

bars were anywhere near the problem that they were at Harefield. In later years, after I'd left, the tops of the bars were skimmed off, but when I was there, it was an absolute nightmare.

On this first session, I ended up in one of the first swims along the causeway. This was because I had found a big fish in a silty bay at the top of the lake, where the workings were. It turned out that it was from this workings side that the guy I had met at the Snake Pit had caught his fish. Now it was all silted up from the sand filtered out of the gravel washing plant, so this was up close and personal, exactly my kind of fishing.

I spent a couple of days stalking this bay without success, and I came to the conclusion that the carp wasn't happy being in there. It seemed to be in distress trying to find a way through one of the shallow channels, and spent a lot of time with its back out of the water attempting to push itself over a shallow bar, like a stranded whale. There was another guy having a go for it, and he was from Essex, too. I guess, like me, he was trying to get Harefield to become an Essex pool. His name was Jon Watson, and we became great friends; somehow, he became 'Essex Jon', a name that has stuck to this day.

I had one day and night left of my first session, so I chose to move to the other end of the causeway and rather than follow the crowd, who were trying to get out over the second and third bars to where, apparently, all the carp were, I fished short, over the foremost bar. Firstly, because of the rod and reels I had, I would be pushing it to the limits to get over the second bar, and secondly, at the range of 50 or so yards that I was fishing, I was in my comfort zone. I was doing what I do best, baiting really tight and accurately, and watching the water for the slightest movement or sign of bubbles.

As the evening drew in, I did see some bubbles and it was lucky really because, with the angle of the dropping sun, I saw them glisten and burst on the surface on the extreme left-hand side of my swim, just over the first bar. I wound a rod in and put it over the bubbler, not with any confidence, I have to say. In fact, my confidence was at rock bottom. I didn't feel that my style of fishing and Harefield would get on and I was having second thoughts about the place. Then, in the middle of the night, all of that changed.

I had a screamer! I was up and into it, the rod took on a healthy curve as an obviously big and powerful carp plodded off and then everything went slack. I wound in and the line hanging limp from my rod tip told the awful truth, I had been cut off. I was so gutted and to this day, losing that first carp at Harefield is one that I've felt most. Nonetheless, it gave me the resolve to want to beat the place and I had proved to myself that I could catch them... well, hook them, anyway. I've

ABOVE
*The helicopter rig became
the vogue at Harefield.*

always said that the first take on a new lake is the most difficult, and you really need it to get belief in yourself and your confidence going; after that, the rest is easy.

Harefield was going to prove that it was never going to be easy, though, and I never had the opportunity to make hay there. It was partly my own fault because I got into the social scene and you can judge me if you like as this story unfolds, but that first year at Harefield holds more happy memories than any other season's fishing, for me.

It was a unique year with a unique syndicate, an absolute bunch of characters all on one lake so at times, fishing Harefield was as mad as a box of frogs. Some of the goings on are definitely not for printing, but the comradeship was amazing and many of us became really close friends. There wasn't any jealousy if one of your mates was having it off while you were sitting there on your hands. Quite the reverse, in fact, we would will each other on, and become 'the wife', by keeping the lucky angler topped up with cuppas and bacon sarnies. How different carp fishing is today when there's little etiquette or comradeship. I haven't included my time at Harefield just to tell you about the partying though, rather, to record the significance of Harefield and its relevance in carp fishing history. The place was a hotbed of innovation for me, and was responsible for some of today's tackle developments and trends.

As I drove home after that first session, I was already planning the next weekend. Because of that one lost carp, I just couldn't wait to get back and I got really busy in the week, dusting down my long-range kit and changing my gear to the distance approach of helicopter rigs. I'm not sure where the helicopter rig came from, but I think Mick Lindsell and Zenon Bjoko had a lot to do with it at Layer and I picked it up from Zen at the Snake Pit.

The helicopter rig is certainly the best, non-tangle, long-range rig and it became the vogue at Harefield. I used to fish it with 8-10 inches of Tricklink braid, and a size 6 Owner hook. The hair was still pinned with tubing to the back of the shank opposite the point, fished either with a bottom bait, pop-up, or critically balanced presentation, but this was also an era when other thinking anglers were really beginning to get into rigs.

At this time I got friendly with Rob Maylin and his friends, the famous five. There was a lot of great stuff coming out of their camp - most notably the swimmer rig; a pop-up rig with a bait very tight to the shank, and the bent hook

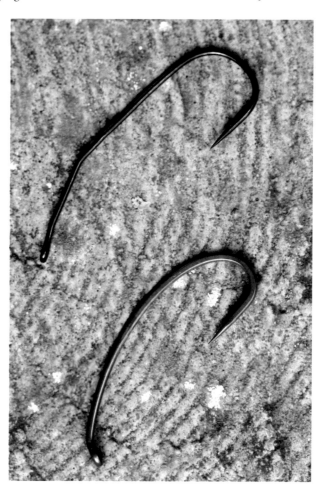

BELOW
The original bent hook, made by bending a fly lure hook and an equally dangerous modern equivalent.

rig. The bent hook rig was *the* rig to use for a time, but then I became very uncomfortable with the hook holds.

For readers who may not know what the bent hook is, basically you took a double-length shank hook, what we refer to as a long shank hook, which was then cranked over at a severe angle about halfway up its length. It was a great hooker, but the problem is the mechanics of the cranking, and the extra length of the shank, made the hook have a tendency to work deeper into the carps' flesh while you played them. Often the hook would work through, and come back out of the flesh causing unacceptable damage, or, the worst situation of all, double hooking, as the now exposed point and bend would take hold again. I even heard stories of top and bottom lips being pinned together! So eventually we stopped using it, and in fact I wrote articles condemning its use.

There was a lot of debate and controversy. Some anglers were saying that there was no problem with the bent hook rig and more ludicrously still, one suggested that there could be an issue with small carp, but it was okay for large carp with big mouths! Quite how anyone can fish a rig and prevent small-mouthed carp from taking it, I was at a loss to understand, but eventually, common sense prevailed and the bent hook rig became a no go. However, I will note that from time to time, companies and anglers start pushing long shank hooks with an emphasised curved shank. These hooks act in exactly the same lethal manner as I have described above, and should not be used in any circumstance, in my opinion.

I mention all this because I think it's worth noting that the carp world was really beginning to wake up to the importance of rigs, and that bait alone would not necessarily bring success. It was, if you like, the true beginning of the rig revolution. I have to smile when I think back to a vigorous debate I had with a young, strong-minded carp angler, who had just started a lead business, on a ferry to a tackle show in Holland. My point of the debate was that rigs were just as important as bait, while he wouldn't have it, arguing that rigs didn't matter at all, and it was all about bait. This certain individual now has a company selling one of the biggest terminal tackle ranges around.

Chapter Twenty

Harefield: All's Fair In Love and War

I t was an unusually hot summer, so by the time I got out of my van after being stuck in a traffic jam on the M25 for two and a half hours, I was wringing. In those days, we didn't have barrows and I certainly didn't fancy the long trek with a weekend's worth of gear. The lake was so big and it took the better part of an hour to walk around, so I'd stripped my gear out as best I could, and I'd been in training. One of my mates was going for selection in the SAS, so I'd been running with him, with a heavy Burgen rucksack on my back, to build up my stamina. All this was so that I could walk to my swim in one trip, and not waste too much time having to go back to the car park for more kit. It was really hard work, especially with the weight of the weekend's water supply, leads and bait, and the sweat was pouring into my eyes as I traipsed down the causeway, trying to find a vacant swim. Every one of the lads I passed said, "You coming up the pub tonight?" and to every one I replied, "No mate, I'm fishing." I was so determined to get my own back on the Harefield carp, and bank one this weekend.

All the swims were taken along the causeway, and I ended up right round on the unfavoured back bank. As I dropped my gear down, exhausted and parched, my resolve dissipated and I thought, 'Sod it, I'm going up the pub' - a big mistake. Many may suggest that the location of Harefield is perfect. There's the big pit of around 47 acres that we called Harefield, on one side of the road, while on the other is Savay. Next to Savay, and opposite Harefield, was the famous Horse and Barge pub, which was run by its equally famous landlady, Shirley.

As I walked along the causeway, I couldn't believe it. The lake was empty; where the hell had everyone gone? I went through the gate at Harefield, across the road, into the Horse and Barge and found out where everyone was, as was generally the case, I discovered later. The only two anglers left on the lake were Carebear and Frogger - aka Chris Ladds and Simon Lavin; everyone else was in the pub. Immediately, I felt a tension from the right side of the pub, where some of the Savay clique were drinking, and as I glanced across at a guy I vaguely knew, he quickly turned his back. I knew exactly what this was about.

Rod Hutchinson and I had a very public fall out when originally he asked me to take a stake in his company, Catchum, as it was in financial difficulty. We fell out when he couldn't deal with the financial measures that I had to put in place to save the business, and eventually the company was split up. Tim Paisley, editor of Carpworld, idolised Rod and allowed him to print a letter in Carpworld, which stated a number of opinions that were quite simply untrue, so I had no option but to reply and that's how our dirty laundry got washed in public. Rod had previously been at Savay when the syndicate started and rightly, there was a great deal of affection for him around Savay and the Colne Valley. In fact, it is worth getting a hold of a copy of Rod's book, 'The Carp Strikes Back', which tells about that first season when Savay was opened up to carp anglers. It's a great read.

Anyway, I went up to the bar and there was definitely a chilly feeling in the air, with all the Savay lot glancing over at me, glaring away and generally letting me know that I wasn't welcome in the Valley. Then one of the guys walked over and introduced himself.

BELOW
*...as evening drew in...
I was having second
thoughts about the place.*

ABOVE
*Shirley, (second from
the left) with her
team of barmaids.*

"Hi Kev," he said. "I'm Dougal, welcome to the Valley."

With that one gesture, everything changed and I was accepted. It was the immense Dougal Grey who had come over and shaken my hand. In the valley and beyond, Dougal was a legend, and indeed, I still consider him a legend today, back then, though, it was because of his build. Imagine the upper body of a gorilla welded to another one and you'll get the gist. That was Dougal. You just didn't mess with this guy. The stories about people who had taken him on were well known. Dougal had done time for violence, and now he wanted a straight life and to avoid trouble, but he was a bit like a sheriff in the Wild West; gunslingers who fancied their chances would seek him out for a fight.

One night in the Horse and Barge, on a quiet, midweek evening, Essex Jon, Dougal and me were leaning against the bar, just having a nice, chilled evening, when this guy came in. He walked up to the bar, then over to us.

He said to Dougal, "I think you're ugly, and you've got the biggest fucking nose I've ever seen."

I was completely taken aback. What was this bloke on? Didn't he know whom he was messing with? On quick appraisal, perhaps he did. He was clearly tasty, nowhere near the build of Dougal, but a good foot taller and with the build of a heavyweight boxer.

Dougal kept really calm and said to the guy, "Leave it out, mate. I don't want trouble. I'm just having a quiet drink."

"Fair enough," the bloke said, and walked away.

We all breathed a sigh of relief and then he turned around and came back.

"You've still got the biggest fucking nose I've ever seen, you ugly ****."

Dougal tried yet again to defuse the situation, but this bloke wasn't having it, and threatened to rip the big nose off Dougal's face, there and then. Mindful of Shirley and the nice pub, Dougal offered the guy 'outside', and so they did. That was the first time I saw Dougal in a fight and it was an awesome spectacle. It turned out that the bloke was an ex-pro boxer, and had been led on by some carp anglers on another water, who thought they were Jack-the-lads, so they set this guy up, thinking he would demolish Dougal. 'Demolished' is the best word to describe events after Dougal had finished with him.

Anyway, back to my first experience at the Horse and Barge. Dougal stayed drinking with Essex Jon and me all evening, I guess because the Savay boys were lightweights. There were tales of the heavy-drinking Savay boys at the Horse and Barge, when Rod was on there, but those days had long gone. This Savay syndicate should have been mostly tucked up in bed with a cup of cocoa by 10pm, except for Rob Maylin and the famous five, one of whom was my dear mate, Phil Harper, who were on there, making some waves, I can tell you. I was certain Rob wouldn't last in the Savay regime, and that was soon to be proven.

As Shirley called time, my mind had turned back to fishing and getting the rods out before bed, when Dougal said, "Are you coming to the Indian?"

It did seem a great idea. I had the munchies after the lager, and so off we went to the Indian. We left there after 2am, very much the worse for wear, and I don't remember much else, just waking up in the morning to find that all three rods were fishing somewhere out in the lake.

At nine o'clock, the next morning, Dougal walked round and asked me if I was coming to the Harefield café. Well, I didn't want to offend Dougal, did I? So I wound the rods in and went with him. Just like the Horse and Barge, it was *the* café in the Valley and packed with carpers; we were lucky to get a table.

There was so much banter going on, mainly because the very funny Albert

Romp was giving an audience, that we didn't leave the café until nearly 11am, and then Dougal said, "Are you coming for a drink?" 'Christ', I thought, 'am I ever going to go fishing?' So off we went to the Horse and Barge and only left there when Shirley called time at 3pm! I got the baits out by four.

It was Saturday afternoon, and everyone was going up for a pint at 7pm. I was told by the other lads that it would have been impolite not to go, and I couldn't believe my eyes as we walked across the road on that steaming Saturday evening. The Horse and Barge was absolutely mobbed. There must have been two to three hundred carp anglers standing outside and it was like the 'Who's Who' of the carp world; Roger Smith was there, with Kerry. Lockey and some mates were there; Rob Maylin, Alcot, Harper and the rest of the five, and they all welcomed me as we walked across the road. It was amazing.

There was no place like the Horse and Barge and the carp community that it attracted, and I doubt there ever will be again. When the pub closed we were all the worse for wear, but trooped up to the Indian and I don't know what time we got back but I didn't trust myself to be able to cast out, so I got my head down. I woke with a searing hangover to Dougal saying, "Come on Kev, we're all up the café". I was groggy and couldn't understand what he was saying. As I understood it, the Harefield café didn't open on Sundays. That was correct, apparently, and that's why, on a Sunday, everyone drove over to Farlows for breakfast in the café on the lake.

After Sunday breakfast there, it was back to Harefield to pack up, drop in the Horse and Barge for a lunch time pint, bid farewell to the other syndicate members, and then set off for the long drive home. I'd had baits in the water for less than eight hours that weekend. I could hardly say I was fishing, and that was really how it was for most of that exceptionally hot summer, a season of just one big party with the biggest collection of carping lunatics I have ever seen in one place. Like I said, it could hardly be termed fishing, and I admit to that, but it was one of the most memorable summers I have ever had – great friends and great fun, and I have no regrets.

By now, Essex Jon had become a good friend, and I got to know him well. For Jon, it was about the craic, and pushing yourself and everyone else to the limits, and if Mad Alan was around, we are talking some limit here; raving nutters, the pair of them. Essex turned up one weekend, limping.

"What's happened to you, mate?" I asked.

"I shot myself in the foot with a nail gun."

"How the hell did you do that?" I said. "That was a bit careless, wasn't it?"

It turned out that he hadn't been careless at all. He'd done it deliberately and when I asked, in utter amazement, why on earth he'd want to shoot himself through the foot with a four-inch nail, his reply was, "I wanted to see how much it'd hurt." Like I said, a nutcase.

Mad Alan was exactly as his name suggests. He was utterly over the top. Before arriving at Harefield, he'd been in the Foreign Legion and had joined up because he wanted to know what it was like to kill somebody. You can't get a much harder outfit than the Legion, and Alan's greatest claim to fame was the fact that not even the Legion could tame him, and he was chucked out. There was no form of discipline they could lay on him that would keep him in line. They would put him into solitary for some misdemeanour or other, and beat the hell out of him, but he would never submit to authority and when he blew up the Colonel's flagpole, they'd had enough, surrendered, and discharged him! I wasn't there, but one weekend when Harefield was frozen over, the lads were camping on the banks for the nightlife, despite the conditions. Alan had an idea to prevent him and Jon from getting bored during the day; they would jump off the high causeway bank into the frozen lake, for a dare, and they did.

With the likes of Essex and Dougal around, whatever happened would get out of control. We had a firework party in the car park one night, and a local complained about the noise so two police cars turned up and everyone scattered. Mad Alan however, closed and locked the gate and the coppers had to radio in for help, a bit sheepishly, because they'd got themselves locked in a car park. I have to smile when I think of the things Alan used to do, and the fact that he discovered religion and now spends his time helping others. Mad, or what.

BELOW
Frogger with Harefield's magnificent fully-scaled, at 33lbs.

Actually, unless your name was Carebear and Frogger, it was a ball breaker of a year at Harefield. Because of the heatwave, the carp didn't really get their heads down, and there was just the odd take at night or early morning. They lived in the middle, in a big weed bed, but every few weeks for some reason they'd go for a lap of the lake, and this is when Carebear and Frogger would get on them. They were short-range experts, and they'd have a hit while we were all in the pub, and then the carp would go and sit out in the middle again.

Any member who caught five carp that summer was a top rod; Carebear and Frogger caught many more, but we all agreed that most of theirs didn't count, as they cheated and fished when the lake was 'closed'. After all, Harefield was going to be easy, if you had the lake to yourself, so you had to be cheating if you were catching carp while everyone else was having a 'Harefield meeting' in the pub!

Many attempts were made to get Carebear and Frogger to see the light and join us in the pub, and eventually Frogger was renamed Delkim because he was converted to the lager; this being a reference to the original Delkims which were conversions from the Optonic bite alarms. That was one

of the greatest achievements of the syndicate, and to this day, you will see Simon Lavin clutching a beer glass at carp shows. I'm very proud of that!

Carebear, though, was a different story. After relentless pressure, Essex and me were chuffed with ourselves when we got him to come and have a drink one lunchtime. We were on our second drink, but Carebear was still on his first and I was trying to get him to drink it quicker so I could get another one, but he kept looking at his watch.

"Why do you keep looking at your watch?" I said and he replied that he only had 55 minutes left. I couldn't understand what he meant; the pub was open for at least another two hours. He explained. He'd set himself a target of catching one carp every 24 hours; or if he couldn't achieve that, the equivalent for a session. So if he fished for three days, he had to catch at least three carp.

I was gobsmacked; 95% of the syndicate had caught zilch, 4.999% were the top rods with five carp and there was this guy stressing because he'd only got 50-odd minutes left to catch one, otherwise he's been a bad boy and not caught one today. I remember thinking at the time, 'with that sort of obsessive behaviour, you're going to burn out, mate' and it was true. Carebear did burn out and gave up carp fishing, altogether. He got back into it recently, though, and does the odd session. I know that because some ten years later, he rang me. I knew he was in banking while we were on Harefield, but he'd risen up the ladder to become a big shot, with the brief to find clients wherever he wanted in the country. It's crazy to think that I ended up, for a while, with a bank manager who is called Carebear!

I have to add here that Carebear is one of those unknown anglers who never sought publicity, but could fish the arse off most. I remember one day we

TOP
The formidable Chris Ladds with Harefield's Tattoo, at 33lbs 13ozs.

ABOVE
If you ever want to pull the birds, just get yourself a big dog.

had a 'banking' meeting just after he'd returned to carp fishing. He joined Yateley's Car Park Lake, you know the one, where anglers sit, year in, year out, proud of their ability to blank. (cough). Anyway, Carebear promptly caught one of the stars of the Car Park on his first overnighter. I guess his self-imposed 24-hour rule still applied!

It was around this time that I bought myself a Doberman, Kahn, who I used to take up to Harefield. He wouldn't be left out; he had become a proper carp dog, and as soon as he saw the rods coming out and me loading the motor he would jump in as if to say, 'You ain't leaving me behind!' Kahn was making quite a name for himself and was the only dog member of the Carp Society. I took him into the Horse and Barge and realised what an asset he was; if you ever want to pull the birds, just get yourself a big dog! The lovely barmaids were round in a minute, coo'ing and aww'ing.

Kahn loved the attention and had a wicked party trick. I would order two pints of lager and two packets of crisps, and then I'd drop one bag of crisps on the floor, Kahn would go up to it and stamp on the bag with his size 10 paws and there'd be a big 'pop'. People who hadn't seen this trick would look round and go, 'Wow! Look at that dog. He opens his own bag of crisps.' Then I'd get one of the large bar-top ashtrays, pour a pint of lager into it, and put that down next to him to hear people say, 'Oh my God! He drinks lager, too.' In fact, Kahn became pretty adept at drinking lager, and certainly could have done all the Savay syndicate, except Rob and the famous five, of course.

Kahn knew how to play up to the girls, too and had an embarrassing habit of whacking his wet nose up ladies' skirts. They'd all scream with shock...or was it joy?

Shirley absolutely adored Kahn, and every time I took him in the pub, she would be over to see him and chat to me. I thought the attraction was Kahn.

An old family gravel company called Boyer Leisure owned Harefield as well as Rodney Meadows and Farlows. Their fisheries were managed by a guy called John Stent, who oversaw the bar, café and tackle shop at Farlows, and I was in regular contact with him because he would order gear from me for his shop. I was talking to him on the phone one day when he bemoaned the aggravation he was getting at Farlows. It was in a dodgy area, the fence was always being vandalised, and all sorts of iffy characters were getting on the lake, either fishing or looking for gear to nick. It was hardly your idyllic carp pool.

If having a pub and a café on the lake wasn't bad enough, some of the types attracted to the lake were, shall we say, unsavoury. I heard of one guy fishing there who was a paedophile, allegedly, and he had interfered with another angler's child. Well, one winter's night, the father and a couple of his mates went round to see this guy, who was asleep in his bivvy. They 'visited' him, with lumps of two-by-four, and gave him a good going over before, would you believe, putting him on a pushbike (he was already dead) and then pushing him down to the canal where they chucked him in. Then the canal froze, so his body wasn't found for some time. You get the picture of Farlows.

Dougal was scratching for work at the time, so I suggested to John Stent that he took Dougal on, to sort Farlows out. So that's what John did and as a result of that, Dougal also became head bailiff of Harefield. This was not one of my better ideas. The power went to Dougal's head (Dougal, I hope you will forgive me for saying it as I saw it). All might have been great if Dougal hadn't got himself a girlfriend, a youngster who just appeared at a barbecue on the lake with another carper one day; she had come up from the South coast somewhere. Dougal obviously fancied her, and quite simply nicked her off the bloke. That was it, no argument. I was impressed! I didn't like her, though, because she was very gobby, and it was her mouth, really, that was the beginning of the reckoning for the Harefield syndicate.

One day in the Horse and Barge and in front of Shirley, this girl said that she was 17 and that put Shirley in an impossible situation, because now she and her barmaids knew that she was aware of someone underage drinking in her pub. She had to take action; otherwise she could have lost her licence. She told Dougal's girlfriend that she would have to stay out of the pub until she could produce a birth certificate proving that she was 18. Dougal only saw it one way, did his nut, and walked out.

Dougal then announced that he was moving pubs and that he would now drink in a pub in Harefield village. In other words, 'That's where I am drinking, and I expect you lot to join me.' We were all really pissed off and a bit concerned because no one wanted to troop off to Harefield village and drink in this other pub, which was nowhere near as big as our beloved Horse and Barge. It didn't have the atmosphere and it was too far to walk so there was a drink-drive concern, but most importantly, Shirley wasn't the landlady.

The lads were worried that they would take the brunt of Dougal's displeasure. I found myself being the focal point of all of this, and to this day, I still don't understand why, but somehow I became the spokesman without wishing to be or even knowing that this was my role. All the members kept coming up and asking me for my views, and when I expressed one, it somehow became everyone's opinion. I think some of these 'opinions' got back to Dougal, and sadly, things became a bit frosty between us. I thought we'd cracked it when someone said they could get hold of a fake birth certificate for £200; after all, that's all Shirley wanted to see. Thinking that was quite a result, I went to tell Dougal that for £200 he could get back into the Horse and Barge. He flipped and made it quite clear that he wasn't forking out the money to get into a pub. Oh well, it had seemed like a good plan.

The nightmare was drawing to a head, and the event that was to wreck everything was a Colne Valley reunion. This was a yearly event when anglers, past and present, met at the Horse and Barge for a weekend reunion/social. Dougal had made Harefield an open lake for the weekend; in other words, you didn't have to worry about drinking and driving, or finding a place to stay because you could bivvy up on Harefield. The reunion was all set up and Shirley planned a big spread of food - all free, bless her – and then Dougal announced that he was moving the reunion to the pub in Harefield village.

You can imagine the chaos that caused. Frankly, the syndicate was rattled and some members were absolutely shitting themselves. There was no way they wanted to go to the other pub for the reunion. Shirley heard about it and asked me what was going on, and whether she should cancel the food because she didn't want it wasted. So I told her that I was going to compromise. I would go and have a drink with Dougal in the Harefield village pub, and then I would come down to support her and the efforts she was making for all us carp anglers.

When others asked me what I was going to do, I told them my plan, and that's exactly what I did. I walked into to the pub in Harefield village early on the Saturday night and couldn't believe it. The pub was smaller then I'd thought and I couldn't move, in fact, I could barely get in the door. It was completely rammed with the Harefield syndicate. I couldn't even get to Dougal to say 'hi', as he was at the other end of the pub behind an impenetrable mass of people. I got a drink, not enjoying myself at all, and when I'd finished it, I sneaked out.

I'd parked my car a away from the pub and by the time I'd found it and driven to the Horse and Barge, I walked in to find it mobbed with all the guys I'd just seen in the pub in Harefield. Apparently, I'd been seen leaving and that was the signal for all of them to leave. One of the lads told me that the whole pub had emptied out, except for Dougal and two of his bailiffs.

I never gave it any thought; it was just nice to be in the Barge for the reunion and it was filling up fast with loads of the old faces and names. I was having a great chat with Rob Maylin and Phil Harper when suddenly, the doors of the Barge crashed open, we all looked round, and Dougal walked in. He looked like the Incredible Hulk. I've never seen anything like it, his whole neck and forehead was throbbing; it was an awesome sight. Dougal was more than pissed off. He thought that he'd been stitched up when everyone emptied out of the pub and left him there on his own.

"Right you lot," he shouted out. "Get out and get your gear off my lake."

That was telling everyone to break their bivvies down on Harefield and the whole pub went dead silent. I went over to him to try to make him see reason, but Rob pulled me back. He knew Dougal better than me.

"Leave it, mate," he said. "You'll get badly injured."

Unbelievably, the whole pub just emptied and everyone walked out sheepishly, collected their gear from Harefield and left, leaving just me, Maylin and Essex Jon at the reunion.

While these sagas were going on with Dougal, there was a whole lot of other stuff happening to me. Sadly, my secondly marriage to the lovely Carol was effectively over and at this time on Harefield, I had a girlfriend who used to come down to join me at weekends. Does fishing get any better? - a lake next to a pub, with a café and an Indian up the road, and a bird to join you, to keep you cosy at night. Essex Jon also had a girlfriend and we both became famous for playing carp while not having any clothes on.

One mad night, John Stent had given me permission to fish on the workings, which normally wasn't allowed because they were concerned over the health and safety issues with the machinery. I got back from the pub on a steaming hot Saturday night and shortly after, this music started; it sounded like someone had put a couple of 500-watt speakers behind my bivvy, it was that loud. I found out from the newspapers on the Monday that it was the first rave held in the UK. It was close to Harefield hospital and it caused mayhem there, with four patients having heart attacks and half a dozen pregnant mums giving birth prematurely as a result of the loud music – and the hospital was over a mile and a half away from

the lake! I had never heard anything like it, and it was impossible to sleep through it so I ended up dancing in the moonlight on the workings. After all, the music was cool. I remember looking across to the Hump, the first swim down the causeway, and there in the bright moonlight was Essex doing the same.

OPPOSITE PAGE
*Rave night
Harefield carp.*

In the early hours of daylight, I had a take and shot out of the bivvy, stark bollock naked, as my girlfriend and me had been doing what boyfriend and girlfriends do, and hooked into a carp. I hadn't understood how shallow the water was in front of the workings, because it was silted up from the washing plant and although I got the carp within 20 yards of the bank, I couldn't get it any nearer because it was effectively floundering in the mud. I waded out up to my thighs, netted it, and there I was, stuck. I just couldn't move in the mud. I was standing in the middle of Harefield, starkers, stuck in the mud, with a public footpath only 50 yards away. I was lucky that it was 5am on a Sunday morning. The answer was Essex. I shouted across to him, but he was completely out of it after the heavy night at the Barge and our late night dance party, so I remained in that predicament until 7 o'clock when one of the other members spotted me and came around. With a lot of messing about, eventually I got out...with the carp as well, I might add.

It was coming up to Guy Fawkes Night, when the Barge was to host a fireworks party. I'd gone into the Barge one night a few weeks before and Essex was already in there, earnestly talking with one of the barmaids, Mandy. I left them to it and went to talk to Phil Harper, who was sitting further down the bar. Essex and Mandy kept glancing at me and smirking. I took it in, but wasn't going to let them have the satisfaction of being the brunt of their joke, whatever it was. Later that night, though, when I saw Essex on his own, I pulled him.

"What was that about, mate?" I asked him.

He was bursting to tell me but wouldn't - he just kept winding me up. Eventually, he cracked and dropped the bombshell.

"Shirley really fancies you, mate, and she's hoping that you're going to the Guy Fawkes party."

I was completely bowled over by this news, and it explained why I had been getting funny looks from everyone in the Barge for the last few days.

You have to understand Shirley's status. As I said, she is part of carp fishing folklore and maybe that first came about because of Rod's writings in his book, but it's more likely to be because the Horse and Barge became the carp pub in the Colne Valley, all due to the splendid atmosphere and feeling of welcome created by Shirley. It was the magnet for the Who's Who of carp fishing, and has its rightful place in carp fishing folklore.

There was a night when Martin Locke, of Solar fame, was nearly killed, for

example, when a car full of drunkards came roaring down the road, lost control and ploughed toward the crowd of carpers who were enjoying a pint outside on a summer evening. Everyone dived for cover, but poor Lockey didn't make it. He was catapulted through the air for some distance, apparently, and was lucky to live. The joke has always been that Lockey is truly Mr Stainless because not only does he make pukka banksticks, but also half his bones are fixed together with stainless screws.

I think it's fair to say that Shirley loved running the Horse and Barge, in fact it was her life until sadly, she lost the pub, but that's another story. I always felt that her favourite customers were the carp anglers.

I can still hear her call in my ears, "Come on you carpers, drink up!" and then, "That's it, time to go." No one ever argued or gave Shirley any grief and she was protected by us all. If you upset Shirley, then you would have upset half the carp anglers in the Colne Valley. We loved her with great affection; and talking of love, we all fancied the hell out of her. I guess Shirley would have been about fifteen years or so older than us lot, but as a mature woman in her prime, she had everything, that indefinable sex appeal that can't be achieved by design. You can't create it with the clothes you wear or the hair-do. A woman has just got it - and this lady had it in oodles. What helped her iconic status was the legend (and I am sure it is just a legend) that once upon a time, she had fancied another carp angler who had fished Harefield, and they'd had a relationship for a while. The story goes she would be seen taking a tray, with a beer and his dinner on it, to his swim. Could it get any better than that?

So, this is where I was at. I'd got a girlfriend who I wasn't sure about because she seemed a bit nutty, and picked fights for no reason on an increasingly regular basis. On the other hand, apparently, the Colne Valley goddess fancied me. Well, I wasn't quite sure where that would go, but I was up for the adventure. I just had the little problem of juggling the girlfriend and getting her out of the way.

As it got nearer and nearer to Guy Fawkes Night, the atmosphere was electric. All the syndicate knew what was going on, and most of them, like blokes do, were egging me on. Of course, there was a bit of envy, but the syndicate were so tight and so unique that in love and war it was the same; you weren't jealous of what your mate caught, carp or the top lady. The weekend was upon me. I don't know whether it was guilt or because of my inherent honesty or what, but the previous week I'd had had a big row with my girlfriend and told her I wanted a break. So, the scene was set.

Essex and I went in the pub at lunchtime on the Saturday and Jon was called over by Mandy. She told Jon that Shirley was really going for it and was so hot for me that she'd made a real effort, and had bought a new, sexy outfit, including a skin-tight leather skirt. She did have some form, Shirley, I can tell you. I can hear Jon down at the end of the bar going "Naaaw!" as he shared Mandy's indiscretions. He came up and told me of the treat in store. Was I buzzing, or what!

That evening, I walked into the pub and the power could have been off but still every light bulb would have been kicking out the watts, the air was that electric. Straight in front of me, behind the bar as I walked in was Shirley. She looked so gorgeous, so sexy - she was drop dead. She had the slightest smile, and a kind of knowing look as if to say, "You're mine, boy." Well, I can tell you, I was ready to surrender and submit completely.

It was still early and with not many customers in, so Shirley came round to my side of the bar to where I was sitting with Phil Harper, for a chat, or more likely to show off her kit. Now, Phil was the pretty boy of carp fishing and the girls loved him. He always was a real ladies' man. There was Shirley, getting as close as she could to me (and believe me, I am being discreet here) and on seeing this, Phil turned to her and said, "Shirley, what's Kevin got that I haven't?" He'd always fancied her.

Straight away, she said, "You started at the bottom boy."

I didn't understand what she meant, but Phil was totally deflated and gutted. I found out later that he'd had a fling with one of the barmaids, so what Shirley was saying was, 'You may have had a chance, but not after you went out with one of my staff'.

The pub was filling up and time was getting on. Another couple of hours and it would be 'drink up' and the fireworks would start - quite literally, I hoped. I can still see Shirley in my mind's eye, as I write this. She was right in front of me behind the bar, chatting away animatedly, when a black shadow seemed to pass over her. Suddenly, she had a face like thunder as she looked over my shoulder. I looked round and there was my girlfriend. I was bollocksed. I knew how violent my girlfriend could be, and if she'd known what was going on with Shirley and me, it would have really kicked off. That was it, blown it.

With cooler, or more to the point, more comfortable weather upon us, I felt that I'd had enough partying, and Shirley had gone somewhat tepid on me so the Barge didn't seem so welcoming. The long, hot summer party was over, as was my love affair. It was time to get carping.

Chapter Twenty-One

Harefield:
The Tackle Revolution

I had realised that getting takes at Harefield was not the big issue, helped to a great degree by a rig edge that Carebear had shown me. Until then, we were still fishing the hair pinned to the back of the shank with tubing, opposite the point, with the main line tied to the hook via a palomar, or grinner knot. This was before the 'discovery' of the knotless knot, so the hook link projected straight off of the eye, as opposed to the hooklink passing through the eye and kicking out at an angle. Carebear had realised that if you could angle the hook link, down off the eye, the hook flipped over and dug into the carp's mouth easier and so you got more takes. He used to file a flat on the hook eye so that when you tied your knot, it pointed downward and would hold there because of the flat - helped with a bit of Superglue. Unbeknown to us at the time, this subtle rig change was heading in the direction of the line aligner.

Actually, the Harefield carp were pretty easy to hook, certainly a lot easier than the finicky Essex carp that I was used to, where locating and fishing accurately on feeding spots was essential. If you were off by a foot, it might as well be no-man's-land. Harefield was different. All you had to do really was be in the right gully between the bars.

The carp decided which gully they wanted to be in on the day, and then patrolled up and down it so the whole bar, which could be made up of several hundred yards, became a feeding spot. My method was to put a rod in each of the three gullies, and then, should I get a take, I'd pile all three rods into that gully. It often amazed me how a guy could be fishing and be having action over one of the three bars, and not pile all of his rods into it. Doing what I did gave me the big opportunities and big hits, if I could land them. That was the problem, though, landing them.

I had seen how successful Carebear and Frogger were. Carebear had figured out that Harefield was an averages game and rather than lose most over the bars, Carebear and Frogger were fishing inside the first bar. Maybe, at times, they were fishing *over* the first bar, but they couldn't have got much further out because they were using heavy-duty sea line, that if I recall was between 40lb and 60lb breaking strain to combat the horrendous swan mussels and flints.

However, Carebear and Frogger were blanking because the carp had moved out into the middle of the lake, and increasingly, as the weather got colder, they stayed out in the middle so I needed to find a way of putting the odds in my favour. At the time, everyone was going down to 8lb main line to get the distance and that's why the leaders, even the extreme steel trace wire, didn't really help. The issue was all of the main line back from the leader to the rod going over the sharp bars, i.e. you were getting cut off maybe as far as 100 yards back from your bait and lead.

I had to find a way of fishing at range with a sensible breaking strain, or more to the point, thickness of line to improve my abrasion resistance. There is a simple logic you can apply - the thicker the line, the greater the abrasion resistance. So, I

BELOW
A more intimate part of Harefield.

turned to sea reels. Shimano had just
brought out a huge new surfcasting,
fixed-spool reel called the Biomaster
and Gary Bayes had ordered the largest
size for the Catchum shop. When Rod
Hutchinson and I broke up Catchum
88, Nash retained the retail side of the
business for a time. Immediately, I saw
the potential of this huge bucket spool.
It was massive in comparison to the
carp reels we were using at the time,
so I bought three and took them to
Harefield.

There were a lot of very surprised
carp anglers about when I started using
the reels, I can tell you. The lads would
walk past my set-up, stop dead in their
tracks, and say things like, "What are
those reels? They aren't carp reels,
they're like buckets!" The lads thought
I was being extreme, and believed that
I had gone way over the top with the
massive spool sea reels to cast further
than them, but it was never about that.
My reason for the massive reels was
to be able to fish a decent thickness of
line over the second and third bars, and
it certainly worked. I could get well
over 120 metres with 15lb main line,

so had significantly more abrasion resistance than the others using thin 8lb lines
which were necessary for them to achieve the distance with their small spool reels.
This was the start of the so-called 'big pit reel' trend that we have today, or more
accurately, the start of long-range carp fishing with sensible tackle.

That spring, I was offered a carp consultancy with Daiwa and as Nash didn't
make rods at the time I didn't see any conflict of interest, and apart from that,
there was a lot of dough at stake, so I agreed. I had big issues with the Shimano
Biomasters. I don't know whether they've been improved today, but the originals
I used were a nightmare for line going behind the spool. I was forever taking the

TOP
..."*They aren't carp reels,
they're like buckets.*"...

ABOVE
*The first SS3000s
imported to the UK.*

spools off and trying to untangle the line that was wrapped around the spindle, so one of the first things I did when I joined Daiwa was to look at the range of reels they had. There was nothing with the mega-sized, tapered spools that the Japanese were using for tournament and surf casting in the English catalogue, so I asked the sales director, John Middleton, if he could get me a Japanese catalogue, which he did. In this catalogue was a cool-looking surfcasting reel, with a huge tapered spool, called the SS3000, so I asked John if he could import three for me to check out.

When they arrived, I was immediately impressed. I thought they were great reels and what's more, they had an ingenious system to prevent line getting behind the spool. So the legend of the SS3000s was born and I am still using mine today as I write this; the original three imported from Japan. The only change I made is a swap of the spools and handles, to the Tacklebox conversion, and they look really cool, all in black.

Rods were the other area I looked at. I'd been in rod design for most of my life and felt it had to be possible to improve a carp rod. This was my main focus on joining Daiwa, to see what was possible, because at this time I believed Daiwa rod technology to be the best in the world and I began to understand why. A Japanese guy, called Nobou Nodera worked in their Scottish factory and he was really unusual in that he had broken the regimental way the Japanese worked. Daiwa Japan used to send their technicians over to Scotland for a few years, for the experience and to get a feel for the European market. They would then be summoned back to Japan to be 're-Japan-ised'.

Nobou turned out to be a rod design genius and his talents were so invaluable that Scotland persuaded Japan to let them keep him. He well overstayed his time in Europe, and as a result became the most experienced man on the planet in rod design. We became great friends, and Nobou quite literally designed thousands of different rods for the European market over his time spent at Daiwa Scotland. Eventually, he was summoned back, which was the beginning of the end for me as well at Daiwa because not only had I lost a friend, but Daiwa had also lost an irreplaceable talent, and his replacement was just not up to scratch. I had difficulty working with him.

After I'd left, and Nobou was back in Japan, interestingly, he couldn't hack it and conform to the Japanese regimentation so he left Daiwa too. Later, we joined forces and designed the Nash Xtreme Pursuits.

You may be wondering why I didn't bring out my own

KEVIN NASH
HAPPY HOOKER TACKLE

5 SILVERDALE, RAYLEIGH, ESSEX, ENGLAND
TELEPHONE: 0268 770238

range of rods earlier, and the answer is simple – I couldn't afford it. Since my first catalogue in 1984, of just 29 products, my range had multiplied massively. The carp market had rocketed and the ideas had accelerated dramatically and so had my product range. I was struggling to keep up with demand and the necessary level of cash required to hold such a large range of stock. I was, more or less, supplying the whole carp community on my own because, at the time, I was the only main player.

Now, just five years later while on Harefield, I started working on an ambitious project of a tackle annual; a massive tome of 120 pages that listed my entire range, as well as a number of articles. To understand the huge increase in tackle innovation, in such a short time and the role that I played in it, I will reproduce an article from the 'Kevin Nash Tackle Annual'. The article below was written by Rob Maylin as an amusing piss-take of my range of tackle, but it does make the point of how I produced everything that a carp angler could need.

ABOVE
The carp world's first tackle annual.

'An article to promote Kevin Nash Tackle, by Rob Maylin, author of 'Fox Pool and 'Tiger Bay'.
First published in Kevin Nash Tackle Annual 1990

Towards the end of the 1988-89 season, Kevin Nash approached me with a proposition. 'Write me a brief article for my new catalogue and I'll give you loads of free tackle'.
It took me a full second to make my mind up. I sat down with pen and paper; it seemed an easy request, write an account of an angling trip and carefully hide a few mentions of his tackle. Keep it well disguised; you

know, subtle, drop a few hints...

Dawn broke and the sky remained obscured by a blanket of heavy cloud. The wind had dropped right off, conditions looked perfect, overcast and flat calm. I knew now what I had to do to be sure of action. I unzipped the top flap of my Kevin Nash rucksack and pulled out my tackle box. Right, I thought, now all I need is a Kevin Nash Hair Bead, my Kevin Nash Stiff Boom Tube, and inch of Kevin Nash Rig Tube, 50 Polypops (Kevin Nash, of course), and a three-foot square of Rig Foam, made by Kevin Nash. I sat on the rig foam; it was a bit uncomfortable so I searched the Kevin Nash Jumbo Carryall that I had in the back of my Kevin Nash Brollywrap. I found a bag of what looked more comfortable; what did the label say? 'Kevin Nash Butt Foam'. I should have known that Kevin Nash would think of everything.

Pulling out my Kevin Nash Rig Book, I searched its well-thumbed pages; where did I see that rig? It must have been in the Kevin Nash Advanced Rig Book, so I pulled it from under my Kevin Nash Hooker Holdall and eventually found just the rig. Incidentally, talking of the Kevin Nash Hooker Holdall, did you know he also does a Deluxe Roll Up, a Hooker Holdall 'S', Fisher Holdall, a Specialist Matchmen Holdall and a Matchmen Roll Up? Amazing, eh!

Well, back to the rig. According to the drawing, I also needed a Kevin Nash Swivel Bead, two Kevin Nash Swivels, 25 Kevin Nash Carp Beads and a Kevin Nash Boom; it was 7.20am. As soon as I had tied up the rig I would cast out, ready for the early morning feeding spell. 'Thread up the Kevin Nash Silicone Tube and tie on a Kevin Nash Outpoint Hook, size 6'. Okay, that's all done, now all I need is a Kevin Nash Hair Rig, a 2oz Kevin Nash Cruise Lead, and two Carp Controllers (just in case it starts misbehaving).

Kevin Nash Boilie Baiting Needles, a Kevin Nash Boilie Hair Stop, two Boilie Hair Needles and Beads and a Floater Riser. Christ, this was taking longer than I thought it was. Nine o'clock now; I'd have to get my finger out or I'd miss the early feeding spell. I decided to replace the lead with a Cruise Quick Change Lead, made by Kevin Nash, just to save time. The only other question was, should I use a Kevin Nash Snag Hook, or would a Kevin Nash Specialist Carp Hook be all right? I settled for the Snag Hook, just to be safe.

I tied on the Kevin Nash Bolt Rig, replacing the Kevin Nash particle Bait Rig I had been using last time out. Great, now all I need is bait. Bait! Oh shit, I've left it at home in the fridge. I'd spent so much time loading all this bloody lot in the car, I'd forgotten the bait. I looked at my watch, 3.00pm. Oh well, I'd missed the early morning feeding spell anyway, having taken so long with all this lot. Looks like I won't get a chance to use my Kevin Nash 56lb scales, Kevin Nash Camera Monopod, Deluxe Kevin Nash Stalker Sling, or my Kevin Nash Carp Sack fitted with Kevin Nash Sack Clip and Kevin Nash Extension Cord. I threw the whole mess into my Kevin Nash Carryall and began to pack away, neatly folding the Kevin Nash Groundsheet and pulling out my Kevin Nash Strong Bivvy Pegs with my Kevin Nash Bivvy Peg Extractor; it seemed only five minutes ago I was bashing them in with my Kevin Nash Bivvy Mallet, but it had been nearly a week, a week which had passed so quickly.

I remember, Monday was spent carrying my gear from my car to my swim; so was most of Tuesday, for that matter, but after 28 trips I'd got it all round. I spent Wednesday choosing which bivvy to use, not an easy choice with a dozen to choose from; I'd settled for the Kevin Nash Oval Bivvy, which unfortunately meant a drive of 80 miles home as I'd forgotten my Oval Umbrella and it looked bloody stupid flapping about on my other umbrella, so that was Wednesday gone. Thursday was spent arranging my Kevin Nash Rod Mat and positioning my Kevin Nash Storm Rods, fitted with Kevin Nash Storm Caps. The Kevin Nash Sleeping Bag Cover was stretched out over my Kevin Nash Bedchair Mattress cover and I looked forward to my first sleep for five days, having worked solidly since I arrived Sunday night, getting my swim perfect for the week ahead.

Saturday had been on me before I knew it and I was almost ready to get the rods out of my Kevin Nash Holdall when I felt a spot of rain, and decided to spend the rest of Saturday proofing my Oval Bivvy with Kevin Nash Proofing Agent, just in case it rained, which, of course, it hadn't, as is Sod's law; every time you spend a day proofing the bivvy it doesn't rain, and you end up having to do it the next time you go out.

Sunday morning, is where I began this story; I felt so confident, only to be beaten at the last hurdle by one small mistake. I'd forgotten the

> boilies. So I loaded my car and its trailer, and placed my umbrella in my
> Kevin Nash Umbrella/Net Bag, and my holdall in my Kevin Nash Clean
> Holdall Sleeve next to my accessory bag containing my spare Opti Pouch,
> Kevin Nash Carp Ears (for the hard of hearing), Kevin Nash Speaker
> Covers, Kevin Nash OptiPolos, Kevin Nash Large Bore Rig Beads, Kevin
> Nash Weighted Anti-tangle Tube and, of course, my Kevin Nash Pulley
> for loading and unloading the car.
>
> So ended another enjoyable session. If only I could figure out why I
> keep blanking.'

Nobou and I had a long day's meeting so that he could understand what
I required in my carp rod range, but firstly it was made clear that I needed to
conform to what Daiwa wanted. He presented me with a list of different lengths
and test curves, and the various kinds of action, none of which were particularly
ground-breaking. None of them stimulated me, but I went along with it, and
helped him to design the range. I think the biggest thing I brought to the party
immediately, was sorting out the test curves. When I joined the company, a
Daiwa Whisker 2¾lb TC was more like a pound and a half, so I beefed up all
their rods, and then told Nobou about my dream.

At this time, we either used rods to fish at short to medium range, or long
range. There was no one rod that could do the lot. It was really frustrating to have
to carry two sets of rods around, or maybe miss out while fishing because you'd
taken your medium range rods and the carp were out of range. I felt convinced
that it must be possible to build a rod that would cast extreme distances, but
would still be a pleasure to play carp on; and more importantly, not suffer hook
pulls as you played them in the margins. This was one of the problems with the
long range broomsticks at that time.

As Nobou and I worked through the carp rod range, he kept saying,
"No problem, no problem…" until it got to my rod, when he said "Ahh! Big
problem, Kevin."

I was devastated. "What do you mean, Nobou, impossible?" I said.

He paused, and said in his typical Japanese inimitable way, "Big problem,
but maybe not impossible."

This gave me a bit of heart, but I wasn't convinced.

Just a week later, a big box arrived in the post. In under a week, Nobou had
turned around the rod designs. I was amazed. I went through them and they were

exactly as I'd suggested. I can tell you, such was the genius of Nobou that not one rod was changed in the slightest from those first prototypes; he had translated my designs perfectly. As I got to the end of the box I realised that one was missing, my design baby. I spoke to Nobou on the phone and he explained that he was working on it, but 'big problem' – he was struggling.

Two months later, after I had almost given up, another box arrived; it was the first Amorphous Infinity. It was to be the carp rod that changed everything, a rod that would reach extreme distances and a fishing rod to boot. I am very proud that my design became the most successful carp rod ever sold in the 90s, and most long-range rods are still based on the original Amorphous Infinity design.

So now, with three of the revolutionary Amorphous Infinities, and my SS3000 sea reels, I could reach way out into Harefield with a respectable line, and I hoped for some decent winter action. The trouble was that after the hot summer, Harefield was in a bit of a state from low water levels and the bars were out of the water in places, or dangerously close to the surface. One day I had a take that just stopped and as I picked up the rod I saw a carp swirl, but the line was solid in front of it. With a heave, suddenly I gained contact with the carp, but it really felt weird and it was because I had a dirty great six-inch swan mussel clamped onto the line. It was incredible, and I certainly would have lost that fish if it hadn't been for the big-spooled reels and being able to use a more sensible main line. I will pause for a minute to explain that.

High abrasion resistance in monofilament is achieved in two ways; firstly, by the chemical make-up of the line, and secondly, by the diameter. It is quite simple. A line of 8lb breaking strain will have less than half the abrasion resistance of a line of 16lbs because it's a lower diameter. That is why I wanted to use 15lb line to reach the middle, rather than 8lb, the norm at the time. In fact, my 15lb line was understated and broke around 18lb, so I had well over twice the abrasion resistance edge above other anglers.

One weekend in early December, I turned up to fish Lofter's Row, a swim along the causeway, out at range to the middle. I'd only been there an hour when the alarm kicked off. My monkey climber shot up, cracked the butt, and promptly hit the floor again - some drop back. I grabbed the rod, frantically winding up the slack and that kept going until the line came through the rod tip. I'd been cut off before I'd even picked up my rod. I was gutted. As I was retackling this rod, the middle one went off, with the monkey rattling away. I picked it up, it arched over and then the tip sprang back, and to my disbelief, everything went slack. I wound in and, again, the line was cut. I stood there, seriously pissed off. How often do you get the chance of two big Harefield carp in five minutes in winter? Then the third rod kicked off and once more, the monkey cracked against the butt and dropped back. I'd been cut through. I was totally gutted, but also realised that this was ridiculous; this swim with the exposed bars was now just too dangerous to fish. I've always believed that it is senseless to fish swims in which you can't land the carp safely, and Lofter's Row was proving impossible with the low water levels.

I moved round to the Road Bank to join Essex Jon and incredibly, within half an hour I had a screamer. On this side, the bar problem was not as bad, so I was delighted to find myself playing a carp without my line being cut off, but after half a minute, all went slack so I wound in and found that my bloody hook had snapped in half. Some days, it's just not meant to happen.

As Jon and I sat there talking about things that men do, the big subject of how to land a sensible ratio of these Harefield carp was the topic of the afternoon. Jon related a discussion he'd had with Dougal some weeks before when Dougal had said he was thinking of PVA'ing his leads onto the hooklink swivel. The theory was that after he had cast out, the PVA would melt and the lead would come off, leaving one fewer item to catch on the flints and swan mussels. I knew this wouldn't work. Because of the undertow on Harefield it would be impossible. Without the lead, this would be, in effect, a free-line rig at distances well in excess of 100 yards, which would be dragged for miles by the undertow. However, what Essex had told me got me thinking; it reminded me of a product that Nash Tackle were selling for pike angling.

The Dead Bait Casting Clip was designed to enable the user to cast soft, dead baits long distances, without the hooks tearing out of the dead bait's flesh because of the power of the cast. The dead bait was fished on the trace and trebles, with a hook tied below, like a helicopter rig. The hook was covered in silicone tubing and a loop of nylon was tied around the tail of the dead bait, which was

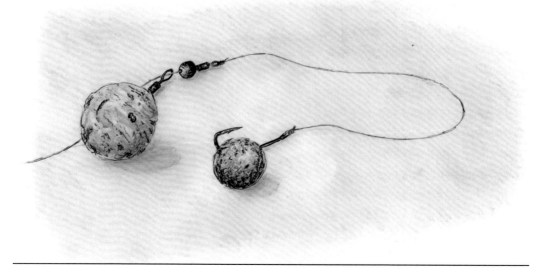

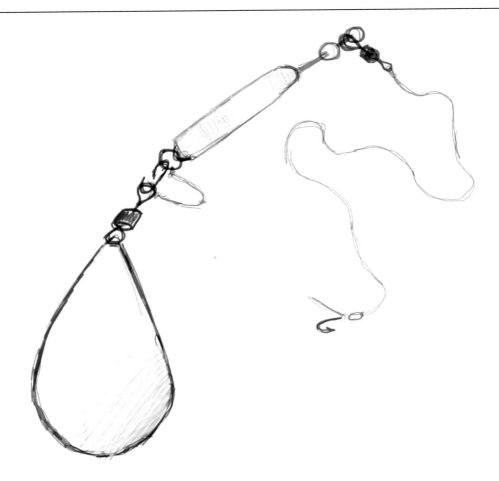

then located over the hook. When casting, the hook and mono took the weight of the dead bait, preventing the trebles from tearing out so that when you cast, the impact of the dead bait hitting the lake's surface would eject the loop of nylon off the hook, leaving it to fish properly with the angler directly in contact to dead bait and trebles. Immediately, I realised that I was on to something. I knew the issue was the weight of the lead; not, as Dougal thought, of it catching in the flints and swan mussels – although of course there would have been times when that was the case. Rather, it was the amazing effect that a comparatively tiny piece of lead has on keeping the carp hugging the bottom while you are playing them.

In the 70s I had fished semi-buoyant legers into holes in weed and I'd come up with this idea because it was virtually impossible to retrieve your tackle from the dense weed beds in the park lake that I was fishing. So, I got some one-ounce Arlesey bombs, stuck rod-handle cork around them and sanded them down to the shape of round balls so they sank slowly. The effect was better than I could have imagined. As soon as I went to wind one in, because of the water resistance, they would shoot to the surface. This made it easy for me to retrieve my end tackle. The amazing thing was, though, when you hooked a carp, because there was no weight to hold it down (the 'weight' was semi-buoyant), they immediately surfaced and all the fight was in the upper layers.

When I think back, it was the same when we free-lined. If a carp was hooked, it would quickly be up around the surface, and it was only when we started to attach the leads on our line that carp hugged the bottom while we played them. In the case of the park lake, this was a massive boon. With the pressure of the rod, they would come up to the surface layers and away from the thick roots of the weed beds. The enormity hit me. If I could get rid of the lead on the take, then the carp would rise to the upper layers immediately, or even the surface, bringing leaders and main line safely away from the top of the bars.

Quickly, I wound one of my rods in. We were fishing with the helicopter rig and this ended in a link clip to which the lead was attached. I whipped the lead off, got my wire cutters out and cut the link clip back so that I just had a hook, to which I tied a piece of 1½lb line, and the other end to my 4-ounce lead. I placed the lead swivel over the hook, and with Essex watching me somewhat bemusedly, I hit the cast as hard as I could and my rig sailed out to well over 120 yards. The rig hit the surface and then I felt the lead bump on the bottom and as I wound in, I felt a momentary resistance of the lead, and all went slack. Eureka! It had worked!

On casting, the lead had stayed on the hook, which had taken the force of the cast off the weak link, but as soon as it hit the surface, it bounced off the hook so now I was fishing the weak link of 1½ lb line, which had snapped as I went to retrieve the lead. Bingo! The same, I was sure, would happen when a carp picked up the rig; it would snap the weak link and then rise up to the surface layers where it could be played safely over the bars.

Jon saw what had happened and was soon winding his rods in and playing around with his rigs as well. The first time he did it, the lead didn't eject from the hook, so we realised that a little experimentation was required to cut the hook back by the correct amount to ensure ejection; but then, we overcut the hook, and it wouldn't stay on for the cast. Later, I realised that if anything, it was better to have the hook slightly longer so at times the lead might not eject when it hit the water, but it would always eject from a taking carp.

In my early experiments, if you didn't get a take it meant losing a lead because the weak links made it virtually impossible to retrieve the lead without the link breaking. As well as that, I dropped some fish because they weren't pricked deeply enough, and this was due to the weak link snapping before the full weight of the lead could come into play to prick the carp properly. I'd worked out a ratio of weak link to lead weight, and it's one that I still employ today for the occasions when I return to my break-off helicopter rigs.

Basically, the equation is: a pound of line to an ounce of lead - i.e. for a 2-ounce lead, use 2lb line; for 3-ounce, use 3lb, 4-ounce, use 4lb, and so on. If you keep to this equation you won't go far wrong, and you'll ensure that you properly prick the carp. Alternatively, if the bottom is particularly snag-ridden, then leave the hook slightly over-length. As I mentioned earlier, if you get it right, even though the lead remains on the hook, when you get a take it will bump off. However, if you don't get a take, because the lead is still on the hook you can retrieve it and save yourself the cost of a new lead.

Sadly, this was to be my last session at Harefield that winter, as work took over and then the winter freeze-up put a halt to the fishing. Events with regard to Harefield overtook me, but not so with Jon. He got on break-off lead rigs with devastating effect the next season, catching over 70 carp; a record number for Harefield in a season and I have no doubt that was achieved in between the partying.

He rang me one day, to tell me about when he'd first really got on the carp with the break-off rig. He'd had six takes one afternoon, and landed the lot. When he was hooking them, they were coming to the surface and roaring up the lake, leaving anglers standing there in amazement, unable to believe their eyes and wondering what the hell Essex was doing! What Essex was doing was a little bit of lateral thinking, and that's a lesson I have never forgotten. Sometimes, when you have a problem that you can't crack, try to get out of the box and look at it from a completely different direction. As I said, anglers tried everything from 100lb nylon leaders, to steel trace wire in order to avoid being cut off and losing at least 90% of the carp they hooked, but all it took was a fixed-spool sea reel and a piece of 4lb line to snap.

This new concept of lead discharge got me thinking in an entirely different direction. Until then, a rig was termed 'safe' if the main line travelled through the lead attachment, thereby ensuring a carp wasn't tethered to line and lead. This was okay in theory, but a couple of times I'd wound in rods at Harefield with swan mussels firmly clamped to the main line above the lead. Had the line been cut or snapped above the swan mussel, I would have left a carp towing a lead and a swan mussel as well. Indeed, I could think of several times in the past on other lakes, when I found branches tangled up in my line above the lead; there was also that supermarket trolley at the Snake Pit. So, if I could design a commercial system that would eject the lead, this would be a big step forward in carp safety – and not only the safety angle, but as Harefield had proved, the ability to land the carp.

This idea put the odds in my favour when landing carp. I've been a fan of

ABOVE
Nice one Dougal!

lead ejection for over 20 years, and I've written about it for that long too, and yet I still see so many anglers who don't get it, resulting in needlessly lost carp. The whole point of a rig that has ejected a lead is the ease of playing a carp that it gives you. As I mentioned, the fish come up to the mid- to surface layers, giving you a direct contact with them, they are easier to control and playing time is reduced. This is especially relevant with weedy lakes, where you can stop the carp burying in the weed through the application of direct pressure, getting them up and away from weed. Even if they do get you in the weed, you have a significantly greater chance of getting them moving again, as there is no lead on the line to jam up and snag you.

From Dougal's clever thinking - and thus my eureka moment - I think it's fair to say that terminal tackle, and lead arrangement in particular, changed forever. I designed the Safety Bolt Bead which, with its numerous copies, has sold in its millions and is without doubt the most popular form of lead attachment that carp anglers use today. Nice one Dougal!

Chapter Twenty-Two

Advanced Lead Discharge

S ince those pioneering days at Harefield with break-off leads, I have learned much about lead discharge. It still features heavily in my fishing to this day, so I think it worthwhile reiterating what I have already written, to a degree, and exploring the subject in greater depth.

In the early 80s, when we first realised the advantage of the bolt rig and fixing the lead, we had to devise a method to fix it on the line and one way was via a link clip off your hooklink swivel. We quickly realised the danger to the wellbeing of carp, of such 'tether rigs', though. Should your main line snap, you would leave a carp towing a hooklink and a lead around and obviously, that lead could catch in a snag and cause the carp to become tethered. The first step to deal with this situation was to fix the lead on the line but to enable the line to pull through the lead and fixture should the main line break above the lead. Various beads and stops were experimented with, but none were entirely satisfactory.

I bought out the first commercial version called the bolt bead, which was basically a moulded run bead with a spigot. The bead was mounted on the line, a piece of tube located over the spigot, and the other end sleeved the hooklink swivel to hold it in place, while the lead was attached by a link clip to a secondary hole in the bead. This way you could fish a bolt rig, and if a carp ran into a snag, the piece of tube would pull off the bolt bead and a broken main line could then pull through the bead, so releasing the carp from the snagged lead. It was this principal that anglers adopted throughout their rig designs, and manufacturers followed.

Until Harefield, the only other type of rig that we used with a fixed lead was the pendulum style, commonly known as a helicopter rig. Again, if the main line was severed it would pass through the hooklink swivel leaving the lead behind. As I mentioned in the Harefield chapter, there is a potential issue with rigs that only allow for the fish to rid itself of a tethered lead by way of a severed main line passing through the lead attachment or hooklink swivel. i.e. the line can only pass through the lead attachment if the main line above it is free to pass through it. Line tangles, or the main line being caught up in branches, or as I experienced at Harefield, swan mussels clamped on the line, are all examples that can prevent the main line from passing through and out of your lead attachment.

The Safety Bolt Bead was radical in that it didn't require the main line to pass through the bead, as it discharged the lead, but my first design attempted to reconcile both issues. Not only could the lead pull off the bead, but also the hooklink swivel which was plugged into the front of the bead could pull out, so that a severed main line could pass through the bead cleanly.

At the time, this design was necessary because the bead was going against the established angling practice of main line discharge, rather than lead discharge, and certainly

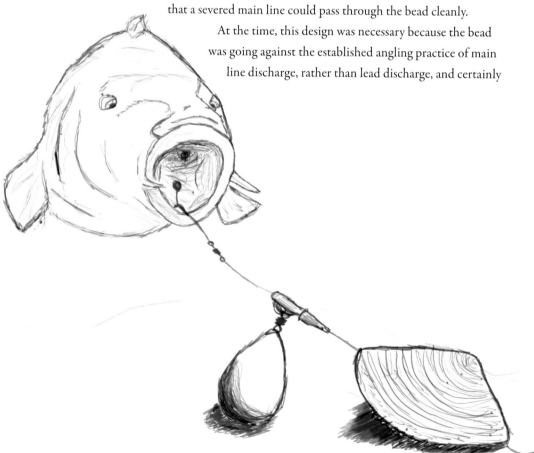

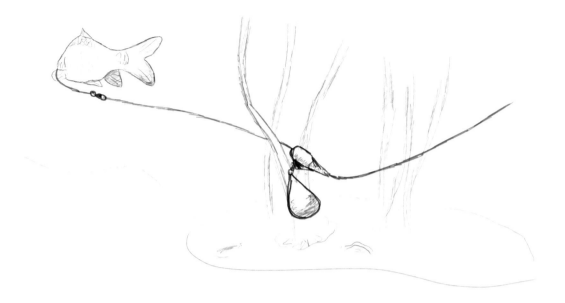

it took a long time for anglers to get their heads around it. The most difficult element to get across was actual lead discharge, and even today many anglers just do not want to lose a lead every time they get a take. On waters without snags I can see where they are going, after all, if you can safely land the carp with the lead attached, why waste a lead every time you catch one?

I can give you one reason; rigs that discharge leads on the take can be a massive edge in dealing with riggy carp. Carp that are pricked up on a rig with a fixed lead attached have learned to sit tight on the spot, to manipulate their mouths, as well as swing their heads violently, and use the weight of the lead to bounce the hook out, more often than not without the angler having any idea that there was a carp hooked up at all. At best you may get a bleep or two, which most would put down to liners or wind etc.

Some years back, I fished a lake with a youngster from work and after teaching him my thoughts on rigs, and especially lead discharge, his results went through the roof and he was so convinced that he wouldn't fish any other way, even when we joined a club lake that didn't contain any snags or weed, but the carp were particularly riggy. I felt that there was no need to eject the lead, and I fixed my tail rubbers onto my bolt beads so tightly that they wouldn't discharge without some force. Then I began to question why I was getting my arse kicked by my young apprentice, and eventually worked out that it was all down to the fact that his leads discharged easily, leaving the carp without a lead to work the hook against to rid themselves of it. So, I make the point; lead removal can be a major edge to putting carp on the bank on riggy waters where they would

ABOVE
My current safety bolt bead design, with locking pin.

otherwise sit tight until they rid themselves of the hook.

Several instances made me rethink the original safety bolt bead, and the hooklink discharge element. One case in particular, was when an aged friend called for my help when he had a fish snagged at range. I went out in a boat and got over the snag, and the carp was some 40 yards away, but after a lot of pulling and heaving I had the fish underneath me. The carp had snagged the bolt bead and lead in a lily root and because there was less force required to pull the hooklink out than there was to discharge the lead from the bead, (he'd pushed a tail rubber on as tightly as he could), the carp was tethered to the lily root, but on a running line. All I could do was pull the fish back to the lily root, but I couldn't get the bead, lead and the carp out of the snag. Eventually, the carp did get off the hook, which was a gutter because it was a monster common!

I realised it was important to put all of the energy into discharging the lead, which is why I came up with the idea of pinning the hooklink swivel into the bead. This way, you can always guarantee that the lead discharges, and cannot snag, and equally to the point, line discharge through the bead is now illustrated to be detrimental, as I have explained. If there is a snag obstructing the main line behind the bead, then your main line cannot pass through the bead, and if a fish can pull your hooklink out of a snagged bead and lead, then you have that nightmare situation whereby all you can do is pull the fish back to the snag, but can't necessarily release the lead.

The key to proper lead discharge off your bead depends upon how tight the rubber is located over the clip. Some of the most popular copies of my safety bolt bead are, in my humble opinion, a step backward in carp safety and they can be possible death traps. I am referring to the types of bead where the hooklink swivel can pull out, and there are ridges on the spigot, to enhance the grip of the tail rubber. The angler is tempted to jam the tail rubber on as tightly as he can, so there is never sufficient energy to discharge the lead before the hooklink swivel is pulled out of the bead.

I have gone as far as I can with my present bolt bead designs in producing carp-safe rigs. There are two versions; one is a compromise, for the anglers who really don't want to lose a lead, and so we have done our best to keep it in the clip unless the lead becomes entangled in a severe snag. This standard Safety Bolt Bead ensures that the lead will take heavy casting pressure, as well as not eject on the take, but because it is pinned, should a carp swim into a snag it has the opportunity to pull against the snagged bead and discharge the lead. This clip should only be used in snag free waters, or those with what I would describe as 'hard snags', such as roots, trees, large rocks, flints and swan mussels.

The other bead that I have designed is the Weed Safety Bolt Bead. As its name implies, it's designed for fishing weedy lakes and there is a balance going on with this design. I want the lead to eject immediately on the take, but to ensure that when the carp straightens the hooklink, bringing the lead into play, there is sufficient force to prick the carp properly. The tail rubber pushed fully onto the spigot provides that necessary resistance to guarantee that a carp is properly pricked, but not so much resistance that the lead cannot eject on the take.

As an aside here, I have seen rig articles in which anglers have cut back various makes of lead clip and are fishing without any tail rubber. I've tried all of that, and I experienced dropped takes because there wasn't the necessary amount of resistance that the tail rubber provides to ensure that the hook is pulled in.

If there is one situation where lead discharge is absolutely essential, then it is in weed. I am amazed at how many anglers do not understand or accept that it is crucial on weedy lakes that you can eject the lead. If the lead remains on the line then you will certainly lose carp. If they reach weed, and bury into it, the lead is a massive snagging point, and once it is snagged carp find it particularly easy to rid themselves of the hook. In my opinion, on weedy lakes it is essential that the lead ejects immediately upon the take, instead of the lead remaining on the bead until the carp hits a weed bed.

My reason for this conviction is that weed is not a solid, unyielding snag. It has a dampening effect, taking the energy out of the bead, and its ability to discharge the lead cleanly. The problem with the Weed Safety Bolt Bead is that contrasting mechanics are at play. You want the lead attached to your bead with the minimum amount of resistance, to ensure that it comes into play to prick the carp properly, but then can eject easily on the take. However, that amount of resistance may not be sufficient to stop the lead blowing off on the cast – particularly when using PVA bags etc. Indeed, I have had anglers complain to me about this. You can't go against physics, but the solution is simple; just wrap some PVA tape around the bead to prevent the lead from detaching on the cast, and/or impact with the surface of the water.

There is still a place in my armoury for break-off leads, using a weak link of monofilament, especially when fishing weedy and/or snaggy lakes with a chod rig. A few years back, I fished a lake with the choddie where there was no dense weed, but I did know the bottom was layered with blanket weed, and despite my total awareness of the advantages of break-off leads, on this particular lake I got what I would describe as lazy. I talked myself out of going to the extra trouble of tying up a weak link for my choddie, and fishing it hook-discharge-style in the same way as I'd discovered at Harefield. Instead, I took the easy route of clipping

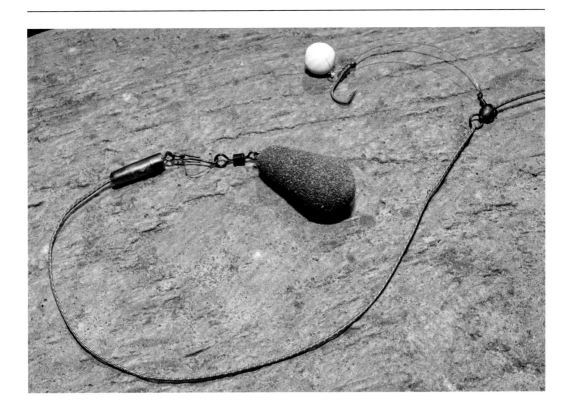

ABOVE
*I won't chance a bead
slipping, so I splice
in a rig ring...*

the lead on, only to lose the biggest common I have hooked in my life when it bored into blanket weed on the bottom, until I had such a weight of weed on the line the fish was unmoveable and lost. I have no doubt that if I hadn't been lazy, and the lead had snapped off when that carp took my chod rig, I would have immediately got it up in the water, and away from any danger. In this case, it wasn't the bars at Harefield, but I kicked myself for not taking a leaf out of my own book.

While on the subject of chod disasters, I also lost a massive carp when using a chod rig in open water with the lead attached by a link clip. I made my set-up with a bead glued 12-inches above the lead on my leadcore as a stop for the hooklink. In this instance, the carp was so powerful that it broke the seal of glue, and the bead and hooklink slid down to the lead. It was up on the surface attempting to get into a reed bed and as it violently thrashed its head, the lead, being so near the hooklink, catapulted the hook out in the same way as when I lost the Silver End big girl on a short bolt rig.

Nowadays, I won't chance a bead slipping, so I splice in a rig ring with a bead behind it for the hooklink to butt up against. Then I splice 12-inches of leadcore below the ring for my lead attachment, and I do the same on waters where leaders are banned, when fishing a naked chod. Conversely, if I am fishing

ABOVE
...I modify the link clip, cutting it back to form a casting hook ...

OPPOSITE PAGE
A lucky escape from the gardes de pêche, but a carp captured!

break-off-lead-style I modify the link clip, cutting it back to form a casting hook, to which I tie my weak line and then my lead. As the lead snaps off on the take there is no chance that the carp can use the lead to rid itself of the hook.

I have one other experience to relate to you regarding break-off leads which may help you to put an extra bonus fish or two on the bank. In the early 90s Nigel Botherway and I fished a massive French reservoir and we took a swim off Dave Plummer, who was guiding a party of carp anglers. Dave told us that the swim had proven very productive. A lot of fish had been hooked, but many had been lost too, because the going area was next to a submerged forest of tree stumps.

As we stood talking to Dave, while watching his crew pack up, one of them had a take and within seconds, the carp had gained the sanctuary of the tree stumps and was lost. Immediately, I saw the answer; my Harefield break-off lead rig. I showed the concept to Nigel, and that's how we fished, landing every fish we hooked.

This was at a time when night fishing wasn't legal in France, but you know how it is, it's difficult to wind a rig in at dusk when dirty great carp are rolling over it. Anyway, to cut a long story short, we found ourselves hiding in a reed bed, with just our noses sticking above the surface of the water so that we could breathe, while two gardes de pêche in a Zodiac inflatable were searching for us by torchlight only yards away!

To my horror I had a take on one of my rods, which were hidden up in the reeds just 20 yards away. The bite alarm emitted a few bleeps and then stopped. Luckily, the gardes de pêche couldn't hear it because of the rumble of their outboard motor engine. At the time, I assumed that it was a dropped take, but

while we were waiting for the gardes de pêche to move on, I kept having the odd bleep. My impression was that the carp was actually still on, and had gained the sanctuary of the trees. Eventually the gardes de pêche gave up their search, and left us in peace, so we emerged from the reeds and I walked down to my rod expecting to be snagged, only to be surprised to find myself attached to a carp in open water, which I successfully landed.

We experienced similar takes after this event, and I'm sure that the carp were breaking the weak link of monofilament, and with only the momentary feel of resistance they didn't notice they were hooked up, and in danger! The odd bleeps were the carp moving around, continuing to feed.

I took this lesson to Star Lane while fishing the Snag Bush, which was suicide because if you were lucky, there was a slim chance of landing one carp in four, but I decided to have a go with the break-off leads, fished on a slack line. I got a quick, sharp take, and then there was a window, unlike the normal occurrence in this swim when in a millisecond of a take the carp would destroy you as it sought the sanctuary of the roots of the bush. This carp didn't panic, and gave me enough time to get on the rod and heave, so pulling it safely away from the roots. I had a further three takes that day, and only one panicked and got into the roots, so it could be worth trying when fishing snaggy swims. The method puts the carp off guard somewhat by not raising their sense of alarm, and giving you vital moments to get on them and pull them to safety.

Chapter Twenty-Three

Snake Pit: Off My Trolley

P hil Harper didn't stay at Harefield all season like Zen and me, but went back to the Snake Pit, and one night while fishing from the Hole in the Wall, he caught the magnificent common. From recollection, he was up with Rob Maylin and the famous five and they'd all gone to the pub for a drink and got somewhat blasted. On his return, Phil had

made a 'pub cast' and in the early hours of the morning he had a take, resulting in the amazing Snake Pit common at a new weight of 41¼lbs. Phil is a formidable angler, but like all of us he's had his sagas, so it's sweet when it comes good, and sometimes it's when you least expect it. Top angling, mate!

Damien Clarke moved on and one of his friends also caught the esteemed fish in a somewhat bizarre way. He told me the story of how his mate had visited him one night and fancied fishing, so he borrowed a rod from Damien, went round to the Hole in the Wall and cast to the right, into a

snag-lined channel which was the entranceway to the snags. Apparently, he had cast around and found a clear, smooth, rock-hard patch.

Now, when Damien told me that, I was amazed because I'd spent hours mapping the contours of the Hole in the Wall and had never found this clear spot. Anyway, Damien's mate had a take in the night and he thought it was a coot so he gave the offending bird a load of stick, only to slip the net under the Snake Pit common. He never did report the capture to the press, because he considered that it didn't count. Well, jammy, it may have been, but in my book, it surely counted! His thinking was that Damien had been fishing the Snake hard, and he'd just popped over and caught the fish. He hadn't put the time and effort into it and so it wasn't deserved.

Even more incredible, though, was the solution to the mystery of the clear spot. It had really bugged me that I had missed this so-called clear spot, and I had to find the answer. I went out in my inflatable boat and searched the channel for that gravel spot, and there definitely was no such thing. The whole area was solid with four feet of weed, but then I drifted through a bottleneck in the snags to a small pool beyond, that I'd never checked out before because I considered it too dangerous to fish. Among the four-feet-long weed I found an area of precisely 6'6"x 2'6" - an old door! I guess that the carp gods were smiling on Damien's mate, that night. Amazingly, he'd cast his bait up the snaggy channel, and that was a gamble in terms of managing to land anything that might be hooked, to say the least, and onto the one possible spot where a carp could find it; an old door lying nestled in the thick, dense weed.

Damien had the march on me because he'd been baiting the lake heavily for some months and by the time I arrived in the early autumn, he'd already caught Brian Ash's common and lost a fish or two in the Snags swim. These snags, which sat between the swim that Damien was fishing and the Hole in the Wall, took up the whole corner of the lake and were the main residence of the Snake Pit carp when they were not feeding, (so that's most of the year, then) and they would lie up for weeks at a time. It was interesting to watch the carp in there, though.

There was a pool right in the corner of the deepest snags, and although a few attempted to, no sane or ethical carper would ever have fished it, it was suicide, but it became the spot to watch. You could climb up a tree and see all the residents lying among the submerged branches in this tiny pool. You could go back the next day, and they'd be in more or less the same positions, hardly moving at all, and even when they did their movements were sluggish and laboured. Then one day, and it might be weeks later, it would be as if a switch had been tripped. The carp would be really active, as if they'd been energised, then that night you might hear them crashing in the main lake and this was when a take was on the cards. It was only after carp had been seen active in the snags that they were ever caught. It was demoralising really. I'd travel all the way to the Pit for a weekend, get set up and then if conditions allowed, I'd look into the snags only to see a load of moribund carp and I just knew I was wasting my time.

By the time I arrived at the Pit in the autumn, I was 'Billy No-Mates'. Phil had pulled off having got the common, and Zen had moved on to the Lea Valley. In my absence, Phil had told me about the weed and how much of a problem it was, but the weed growth by now was unbelievable. In fact, there were virtually no clear spots in the whole lake, and most swims were only fishable in the margins. Further out, you'd have to use a boat to locate little patches of gravel that weren't choked with weed.

My confidence was further dented by a strong odour emitted by this weed. I was using fishmeals and when I wound them in, all I could smell was stinking silt and Canadian pondweed. No matter what I did to the flavour level and combinations, nothing solved the problem. Phil had kept at it after the common and tried to catch the other residents but by autumn, he'd given up because the lake was, in essence, just one solid weed bed. Despite Damien's good start, he was faring no better, and no carp were caught that autumn.

April the next year found me drifting around the lake in my boat. The weed had died right back over the winter and so I felt confident for the start. I'd had a lot going on in my life during the close season, so I hadn't spent much time checking the lake and baiting. However, I felt that I'd come up with a pretty instant bait, that didn't require heavy application because I'd thought a great deal about my bait and how to get over the odour issue.

The previous autumn, when I'd moved back on to the Snake Pit, I'd had massive bait concerns because of the increased weed growth and the silty bottom. Like I said, I'd wind in my baits, sniff them and smell only pondweed and silt. It's said that if you put a bait on the right spot, a carp will always find and eat it, but in the case of the Snake Pit, how often would I be on the button, finding the exact spot that only a few carp in ten acres were feeding on? I'd reasoned that I needed a bait with such strong attractors that the carp would home in on them.

I experimented with all kinds of flavour combinations, but none of them made any difference. However much my baits were loaded, the next morning when I wound in, they would reek of Snake Pit. I hadn't cracked the problem by the close season either, so I kept working on it, leaving various baits in marginal places to be fished out in the morning and sniffed. Then one day, I cracked it by dropping the fishmeal. I wasn't sure about it at first because it was at the time of the fishmeal boom and everyone felt that without a decent amount of fishmeal in your bait, things were against you.

Fishmeals really do suck in lake bed odour, though, and while it could be argued that it doesn't matter because carp will detect a food signal if you put a bait on a feeding spot, it mattered a lot to me. I put attractors in bait to attract and I can't fish confidently if I can't smell the attractors when I'm winding in and the bait smells the same as the lake bed. How's any carp supposed to find that?

The philosophy has stayed with me until this day and maybe it is just a confidence thing, but I do believe that I catch a lot more fish when the bait comes back smelling of roses – or whatever I'm using. If I'm on a lake where the bed affects the smell of my bait, I'll change the recipe until I get it right.

In the end, to crack the odour problem, I drew on the old lessons that Fred Wilton had taught and made a high-protein birdfood bait. I switched to Amber Bird Food and made up a recipe of attractors that was to prove devastating in future years. In fact, I can tell you that a similar recipe is still used by some of the very top carp anglers today, even though at least two of them are sponsored by other bait companies, so you'll never hear mentioned the true reason for their success.

The Amber Bird Food recipe is based around what I believe to be one of the best carp attractors ever – Strawberry Supersense Oil Palatant. I used 5ml in a 4-egg mix, together with 15ml of olive oil, because on particularly stinking lake beds, the oil helps to lock in the flavour. I also wanted the flavour to seep out and pull the carp in, so this was achieved with 3ml of Big Strawberry, and 1ml of Intense Sweetener rounded the flavour off. It was so good that you could quite literally drink it and in fact, I got quite addicted to taking the odd slug or two, but I stopped when it kept repeating on me and I burped strawberries.

There were loads of things going on here. The Big Strawberry flavour, I hoped, would leak out over a long

Snake Pit Strawberry recipe:

3ml Big Strawberry
1ml Intense Sweetener
5ml Strawberry Supersense Oil
Palatant
15ml extra-virgin olive oil
4 medium eggs

Mix all of the above thoroughly and then add Amber Attractor base mix until you have a sticky paste.

Note: It is important to make the paste on the wet side because birdfoods absorb moisture rapidly and could become too stiff and start to crack as you are rolling the boilies.

distance, whereas the Strawberry Supasense oil would be locked in, but with the oil in the birdfood base it wouldn't be washed out like it was with the fishmeals. The olive oil was an added guarantee to lock the flavours in and when I scooped my first trial of the Strawberry Birdfood out of the Snake Pit, I was over the moon, it smelt pukkah.

Incidentally, that recipe of flavours on Nashbait Amber Attractor is one of the best fish catchers I've ever used and the bait I will always turn back to when silt or weed odours mask my bait.

On June 15th I was bivvied up in the Hole in the Wall in anticipation of the start, while Damien was in the Snags swim. We had the carp covered, as there were two paths they would take in and out of the main snags; the channel to my right in the Hole in the Wall, and in the case of the Snags swim there is a gap in the bushes halfway out in the pool on the left side. It was clear that Damien had spent a lot more time visiting Snake Pit in the closed season than I had, and certainly, he had baited the hell out of it, with Solar's Squid and Octopus Koi Rearer, so I just felt that he was well prepared and on the cards to catch the common.

Opening night was quiet. I had seen the big common in the snags during the day of June 15th and she was still in there early in the morning of the 16th, but then she moved out of the jungle and Damien spotted her mooching along the front of the snags, near the gate, so he moved around to the Dance Floor swim. He had the take that night. I heard him scream for help and it was a blood-curdling sound in the darkness that made the hairs rise on the back of my neck.

When I got round to him, the rod was in the rest. He explained that he'd hooked a carp and it had swum through a bush and snagged him, so he decided the best course of action would be to slacken off and see if it would swim out. I remember thinking, 'well, that's that, then; the times I've tried that trick, and it's never worked for me.' Just then, line started to peel off the reel, Damien picked up the rod, leaned into it and the Snake Pit common popped out of the snags – unbelievable - and a few minutes later I slipped the net under her.

I saw little point in staying, so I packed up soon after the photo session and as there was nowhere else I fancied going, I went back to work. After only a couple of days, though, I was restless so I decided to have the afternoon and night on the Snake. If nothing else, it would help me to keep in touch with the lake and its carp for when the next opportunity might arise.

I arrived about noon on a lovely, sunny day with a light, warm breeze blowing into the gate snags. I spent ten minutes trying to identify a dark shape among the shadows cast by the bushes and surface scum weed; was that a gas bottle, a bag of refuse, or the Snake Pit common? I eventually concluded it wasn't, and that no carp were in the snags despite the perfect conditions, so I went for a walk around. I had only gone 30 yards when I looked down from the high bank and saw the entire population of Snake Pit carp. With the demise of the big mirror, known as Rael's Fish, the day before this had now dwindled to just two; the 40lb common and the smaller common that Brian Ash had originally caught at 22lbs. There were now just two carp in ten acres.

These two carp were making their way down the right-hand bank, five yards out, swimming tight to the marginal weed bed, which stretched all along it. They were moving leisurely and I walked slowly, shadowing them until they came near to the far end. Then they turned round and made their way back up to the spot at the other end where I'd originally picked them up. They repeated their swim back down to the bottom and again, turned in exactly the same spot as previously. I noticed that there was a kind of horseshoe of clear water in the weed at this point. It was a great turning point for the carp and, I figured, an ambush point for me.

I followed them up to the other end, looking for other spots but then they faded from sight and I didn't see them at all for the rest of the afternoon. I could only hope they were still around, or would be back. In any event, I'd made up my mind that I'd fish the night in the horseshoe-shaped clearing in the weed. It was an area of the lake that I'd never fished and I'd never seen anyone else fish it, either. Part of the reason for that may have been that the bank at this point was steep and, I would guess, 15 feet or more above water level. In the close season, though, a club member must have fancied his chances because a small area had been cleared next to the water's edge, about big enough to fit a guy sitting on a box. I figured that if I pushed my umbrella into the brambles to hold them back, I could just get my bedchair in along the water's edge and use the cleared spot to step onto from my bedchair.

I struggled down the bank, cutting myself to ribbons on the brambles, opened up the legs of the bedchair and placed it in the small area designed for a matchman's box. I couldn't open it out completely because of the brambles so I got my umbrella out with the intention of forcing it into the vegetation so I could make a clearing under which to put my bedchair.

Mobile phones had just come out and I had the coolest, latest model, which was about the size of a house brick, but half the thickness – real cutting edge and at £1000, it needed to be! It was a good investment for me, though, because it meant I could fish without stressing or worrying about work, and important messages could be relayed to me, too. It was so big that it was half hanging out of my pocket so, mindful of the value and the necessity to look after my brand new phone that had arrived that day, I placed it on the bedchair while I opened the brolly, caught the phone on it and watched as it threw itself into the lake. On retrieval, it fizzed a bit, burped and then died. Bang went a thousand quid; not a good start!

With the umbrella pushed into the bank, there was just enough area of reasonably flat bank to perch my bedchair on, leaving the 'matchman's box area', about two-feet square of dry ground, to put my feet on when I got off the bedchair. The weed stretched from the margin out for about eight to ten yards on my left, but where I was fishing, the weed growth stopped just five yards out, forming a horseshoe-shaped clearing. As I mentioned, it was in this clearing that the fish turned on their patrol route. Turning points on a patrol route are perfect spots to ambush carp, and these have proven very productive to me in the past on other waters because the carp linger momentarily and so are more likely to notice food and to investigate.

As I swung my two hook baits over the marginal weed, I did have a feeling of unusual confidence for the Snake Pit, even though I sat on the high bank as the evening light faded and saw no sign at all of the carp. Nonetheless, I went to bed with a feeling.

At 4.15am, I sat bolt upright as the buzzer emitted a single bleep, and then just a few seconds later, there was a second bleep. My eyes immediately went from the now motionless line off the rod tip, to the spot, just as a single bubble surfaced and burst. It couldn't have been more than two or three millimetres across. 'A gill bubble', I thought. 'They're here'. I sat there, frozen, waiting for the take which didn't come but I just knew, or rather I felt a presence. The carp were here and if I kept absolutely quiet, I might get the pick up.

My problem at this point was that while I'd been up on the top bank the evening before, one of the locals had come over and seen me, gone up to the off-licence and come back with a few tinnies. Those few tinnies were now telling me that they wanted to escape and I was bursting for a pee but totally paranoid and aware of my predicament. Just five or six yards away there could be the biggest common carp in England; one vibration through the bank and she'd be gone. Slowly, I lay back on my bedchair and closed my eyes, hoping the pain would ease and I'd doze off and forget that I needed a pee, but it wasn't going to happen. The pressure in my bladder was mounting and I just had to go. I moved to get off my bedchair but it made a loud creaking noise and I froze to the spot. If the carp hadn't heard me by now, they surely would if I tried again - but the pain was relentless, and so I tried anyway. It was obvious that there was no way I could get off the bedchair without scaring every carp within miles, or so I thought, and after all, this was one of the original Fox bedchairs. Those of you who have one will know what I mean.

Things were getting serious as the pain increased. Then, I spotted my lemonade bottle and formed a plan. I'd already thought of just peeing over the side of my bedchair, but the problem with that was I only had a small area of two feet square dry bank, and I didn't want pee-soggy socks when I slipped out of my sleeping bag. Gently and stealthily, I went through a number of small manoeuvres until I was lying on my side, and then took the top off the nearly empty lemonade bottle. I would hardly claim to have a big knob but nonetheless it was like going for the bull on a dartboard as I tried to line up with what now seemed to be the pin-head-sized opening. I'm quite proud to say that I achieved my goal without splashing one drop on my precious two foot square bit of earth, although my fingers were a little messy. I can still feel the relief of the moment when intense pain eased from my bladder, as a steaming stream emptied into the lemonade bottle.

I lay back in a euphoria of relief, and must have fallen asleep because the next thing I knew it was 5am and I had a screamer! I was up, out of the bag and standing on my two foot square of precious dry bank, holding the rod which had hooped over dramatically with what could only be a Snake Pit carp. The fish moved off steadily, ticking line off the spool toward the centre of the lake when I felt a different sensation through the rod. We've all been there. We've all had that sickening feeling when you feel the line rubbing against something and you just know it ain't going to be good.

Sure enough, it all went solid and I swore inside. After all this time, all the effort, why were the carp gods being so cruel? Then, I felt that something seemed to ease a little. I wasn't certain, though; had I imagined it? When you're solidly and hopelessly snagged, it's so easy to think that something has eased and a fish

is coming out. You visualize it, in your desperation. Was this the case, now? I felt sure that I was gaining distance and I can't say it was line, because I certainly wasn't gaining any tangible element that could be measured, but it just felt that in the rod, something was slowly shortening the distance between me and the carp. I increased the pressure as much as I dared and now I knew that the snag was on the move and although I couldn't feel anything alive, just a dead weight so slowly moving toward me, I just prayed that the carp was somewhere in the middle of it.

I was now gaining line gradually, and I could have sworn that I saw a reddish tinge in the depths. I kept peering at that spot and sure enough, there was something distinctively red down there. Little by little, it came into view until I could read the word 'Sainsbury's'. My carp had swum straight through a bottomless supermarket trolley and my heart sank. I was gutted. I felt sure that the carp was long gone and now I had the right hump, so I heaved with all my might and the trolley broke surface, along with a big flank of gold about four yards further out. It was one of those moments that really focus the mind, and never had my mind been more focused than at that moment! How the hell I was going to get myself out of this shit? I really didn't have a clue. Try to put yourself there: Where do you start? What do you do first? Do you try to net a supermarket trolley? How do you net the carp that's on the other side of the trolley? Do you try to get the trolley out, past your rod and line, through the bottom of it, to enable you to then play and land as normal? Should I just dive in, swim through the bottom of the trolley, and grab the carp in a bear hug? Answers on a postcard.

I couldn't imagine how I was going to clamber through the trolley or pass the rod and reel through it and still keep the rod bent and in contact with the carp. In a way, the article about the guy who had murdered his mum that I'd written for Carp Fisher, came to my rescue. On publication, a committee member of the club had seen it and like all on the committee, he didn't possess the slightest sense of humour or understand poetic licence. He thought every word I'd written was serious and because it had appeared in print, it must be true.

That committee member was the reason that, on this one and only occasion, I was only using two rods, because he'd decided to make me his personal crusade and had started to fish the Snake Pit in order to keep an eye on me. Luckily, he had moved on the previous evening for the night, had seen me into a fish and come round to investigate. Between us, we manhandled the trolley out and while he held it up, I passed the rod through it while keeping the tension on, and after a lot of messing about I finally slipped the net under the common.

It wasn't *the* common, but it was a Snake Pit common, and a fish that I would put among my top catches. It was the carp that Brian Ash had originally caught,

which had kept growing, and now this chunky, deep fish looked as if it could possibly go 30lbs. I sacked her and because I didn't have a mobile phone any more, I shot up to the phone box to ring Gary Bayes, which is a challenge in itself early in the morning. As soon as he heard what I'd caught, though, he was suddenly wide awake and said he'd be up right away.

OPPOSITE PAGE
The Snake Pit's other common: 31lb 12oz.

I couldn't believe it. He arrived half an hour later on a journey that should have taken at least an hour – there were no speed cameras then! Because there was no bank, as such, at the water's edge, we decided that it would be best to bring the fish up on to the top, so I lifted the sack out of the water while Gary held on to me and pulled me up the steep, treacherous slope. There we weighed her at 31lbs 12oz. What a result! Once the photographs were done, Gary held on to my arm while I gingerly made my way back down the bank and he followed me to take a couple of shots as I returned her and watched as she waddled away into the clear depths. I had an immense feeling of achievement and well-being.

As the last vestiges of her golden flanks disappeared into the depths, I turned around and froze, my mouth half open. I wanted to shout a warning, but no sound would come out as I watched Gary thirstily gulping down the last dregs from my lemonade bottle!

With renewed confidence, I was on it, fishing the Snake Pit two or three nights mid-week, and weekends, pulling off in time for the long drive back to an even longer day at work. As every day went by, the situation at the Snake Pit became harder and harder. I have never seen weed growth like it and within another week or so, the Snake Pit was top to bottom solid with weed. It could take me two or three hours to find a new clear spot from my boat and the only way to identify readily the small clear spots that I had found was to use markers, something I wasn't that keen on because I always worried that the Snake Pit carp might spook off them. In the end, I cut my markers down and came up with an adjustable system so that only an inch or two stuck out of the water, and this looked like an old stick so that other anglers wouldn't see where I was fishing, or nick my markers. I left them in the lake throughout the year so the carp would treat them like a natural feature.

Two months after the capture of the smaller Snake Pit common, I was set up one weekend in the first swim down from the gate, the Dance Floor, and woke up on the Saturday morning to the normal sight of three motionless indicators. I sat there brewing a cuppa while watching the sunrise, when to my left, some 15 yards up the margin, where the snags started, I thought I saw a carp's tail momentarily break surface, but it could have been a tench.

The morning passed quietly, well, relatively. Clearly the builder had another big demolishing job on the go because there was a constant stream of lorries dumping, followed by another steady stream of locals trundling along behind my swim with their supermarket trolleys. One guy, who didn't have a trolley, stopped above the swim and shouted down to attract my attention; he couldn't see me underneath my brolly. Somewhat reluctantly, I got out wondering what nutter I was being confronted with this time, only to find a guy with a clipboard asking me if I would sign a petition.

"What petition, mate?" I said.

"The builder who owns the pit has put in planning permission to back-fill it and then to restyle it into a golf course and the locals are outraged," he told me.

I was somewhat bemused by this because it seemed that most of the locals who frequented the pit were equally intent on back filling it with their own various forms of rubbish. Clipboard Man went on to explain that they considered the lake to be a place of natural beauty and took great pleasure in taking evening strolls as they enjoyed the scenery, wildlife, convoys of supermarket trolleys and packs of raging pit-bulls.

I considered what difference a petition would make, signed by a few locals when up against the might of a respected local builder, who presumably had some influential friends.

"Never mind your petition, mate. Get the place listed as an SSSI," I suggested.

My new friend didn't know what I meant so I had to explain that if the Snake Pit was a site of special scientific interest, because of its rare fauna and/or flora, then it was likely to be safe.

"How do we do that?" he asked.

The week before, I'd been reading in the Sunday paper about crashing numbers and concerns of extinction of one creature that would serve the purpose.

"Just say there are great crested newts in here," I said. "That ought to do it."

He seemed very interested in what I had to say and left after I finally agreed to sign his petition.

Other than that distraction, the rest of the day passed uneventfully until around 5pm when, on exactly the same spot 15 yards to my left, a fish rolled. It didn't make much disturbance but I could have sworn I saw a flash of golden flank – carp, not tench I was sure! I got into my boat, paddled out and using a glass-bottomed bucket, I peered through it into the weed-choked depths. I could see that the weed was thinner in one place, an area of about four feet at the bottom of a bank of deep weed, and the water was cloudy and murky. Something had been feeding here. Carp or tench? What did I have to lose?

As I paddled back, Robbo turned up. He was a bit of a local face and larger than life in more ways than a few, but compared to the rest of the locals he was reasonably sane. He seemed to be attracted to me like a magnet and often, when I was over, he would just turn up. I had no option really but to humour him the best I could and I will admit that he did amuse me and I got used to his company.

On this occasion, his timing was perfect because he could help me position my rod. I had a fourth rod that I used for plumbing, with a Triton Sea-Spin baitrunner; the first baitrunner available in the UK. It was old by this time but still reliable so I rigged it up and paddled out with the bait, while Robbo held the rod and let line out from the bank. While it was only 15 yards away, positioning the rod was not easy because of the way the snags lay. I couldn't cast in a straight line to the spot, so I had to paddle out and 'bend' the line around a couple of protruding branches, before I could lower my rig on to the spot.

As I peered over the edge, I noticed that the water had cleared. I could see my rig and bait sitting in the bottom of the gully on what was actually silt, not even weed, but I did think that I'd blown my chances. If it had been a carp, it had moved on.

I got back to the bank, took the rod off Robbo and propped it up on the one remaining front bank stick that I had, with the butt resting on the ground, and clipped the line tight into the line clip. There was no room for a slack line here. If I had a take, I had to be on it quickly.

Nothing happened that afternoon, or evening. Darkness had fallen and I was sitting there drinking tea when suddenly, there was a crack as the line of my fourth rod was pulled out of the clip. At that instant the butt flew into the air, almost straight into my hand. The rod arced over with the power of something mighty, and then sprang back; the line was slack and the fish had gone. I'd never felt such power and I knew in my heart that I'd just lost the other Snake Pit common. Not the small common – but the big girl. When I'd hooked the smaller common she just plodded off - this was the larger turbo-charged version. Gutted, or what.

I can still relive the pain that I felt that evening. Only a long-term carp angler, who has committed so much of his life to hunting one carp only to lose it, will know how I felt. The events went through my mind; the take had been so positive and was full-blown, to say the least, with the rod tip being so dramatically pulled over that the butt of the rod left the ground and flew up in the air, and yet the hook had fallen out.

I tested my baitrunner and my heart sank when I realised what had happened. The baitrunner tension was as slack as could be, so when the line was pulled from the clip, there would have been an 'overrun' effect, with loose line being ripped off the spool and the line going from super-tight to suddenly slack would bounce the hook out. I never fish with slack baitrunners. I have the tension as tight as I dare, to aid the hook being pulled in and to ensure that it stays in.

Robbo had loosened off the baitrunner to give me line as I rowed out and I could only blame myself because I had failed to check the tension when I'd taken the rod off him and set it up in the rest. I wasn't to get another chance that season. The weed made finding a clear spot virtually impossible and it seemed that finding a carp was equally so.

The following spring, I checked around using the boat and found that the weed had died back over the winter, but I reasoned it wouldn't stay that way so I made a plan. I'd start again in the Dance Floor swim where I'd lost the big common. This swim was proving to have a bit of a track record. Zenon had caught the big common from there, albeit out in the middle, but more interest was Damien's capture, to the left out to the front of the snags, and my loss of the previous year also to the left, along the bank from the gate snags. I reasoned that sooner or later, on a warm day and with the right wind, the big common would be in the gate snags, and on its way in or out, I hoped it would find my bait and start visiting that spot regularly.

I spent a lot of time out in the boat, probing in the thick, dense, smelly silt, and eventually, I found an area 10' square of thinner silt, that didn't stink like the stagnant stuff, so I drove up there three times a week, baiting with boilies. It was early April, so my midweek trips were in darkness, but at weekends I took out my glass-bottomed bucket and looked over the side, scanning the bottom for signs of boilies left uneaten. Well, there weren't any, but that didn't mean anything because the Pit was alive with coots, and as I peered through the inch-thick lens of my bucket, I could see that the weed growth was of more concern than the birds. It was growing daily in front of my very eyes. In a week, I wouldn't have been able to spot a boilie, anyway. The weed looked to be about a foot high, and I was in trouble; my spot was going to disappear. If it was carp that were taking my boilies, they were picking them up off the top with no reason to dig into the weed.

I came up with an idea. The next time I went up to bait, I took a bucket each of hemp and trout pellet to try to get the carp clearing the weed, but there was the odd roach, allegedly, in the Pit, and certainly a handful of tench, and while there had never been a sighting, I felt sure there must be eels. I hoped that if I could attract everything else in the Pit to feed in my area, they would help to clear the spot and keep it open. I couldn't have anticipated how well this plan would work as I poured in my hemp and pellet, then looked through the bucket and saw the bait lying in and on top of the weed, over an area of about four square feet.

The next weekend, when I looked through the bucket, I was amazed to see an area of at least 10' square, completely cleaned of any weed. In fact, by the start of the season, the area was more like 20' square, surrounded by weed, which was now up to 6'high.

It was obvious that my bait was being eaten, and the boilies were going as well, but was it carp? I knew that the coots were eating my bait, but how much? I needed to find out, so one morning I baited with boilies and then sat on the bank to watch. There was a coot's nest in the snags, some 30 yards from my baited area and the first thing I noted was that they considered my baited area to be their territory and didn't allow any other coots near it. So, I counted the number of times they dived down and took baits over the next four hours, multiplied this by 12 hours and so calculated a rough figure of excess boilies to feed in for the coots.

I also started baiting with tiger nuts. I figured that there wasn't much in the Snake Pit that could eat them, so if they were getting mopped up, it was odds on that the culprit was one of the two carp, if not both.

The week after I'd baited with tigers, I looked through the bucket with a tingle of excitement. There wasn't a tiger nut in sight but, equally exciting, there were lines of reddish stuff along the bottom. I had altered my bait after the loss of the big common, changing the flavour and adding Robin Red to it. What I was looking at was, without a doubt, red carp poo.

My confidence was sky-high as I made my way up the A12 in the early hours of June 15th to ensure that I procured my swim and despite the fact that I arrived at 4am, I was still relieved to see that no one else was bivvied up. That afternoon, Robbo came over with his wife and we chatted for a while, then we watched in awe as a huge common head-and-shouldered directly over my baited area. On seeing this carp, Robbo decided that he was going to do the night, too, so he was back early that evening and chose to fish the Snag swim. This was his first time over at the Snake Pit since the previous season and he hadn't even thought about fishing, let alone about bait so he asked me if he could have some of mine. I have to say, I was reluctant after all the effort that I'd put in with my baiting campaign, but soft as I am, I gave him a handful of boilies - I just made sure it was a small handful.

Darkness was falling and I confess that I got my baits out before the midnight hour because the only way was by boat, and after seeing the common there was no way I was going out after dark, rowing around in circles in an attempt to spot the half-inch of marker sticking out from the surface. In fact, I hadn't even told Robbo that the spot where we'd watched the big common roll was marked because I'd been baiting it and feeding this area for eight weeks.

It was exactly one minute past midnight when a buzzer screamed out of nowhere and at full bore. It went quiet, then "Oh my God! No... No... Noooo!..." It was Robbo and I heard all this from the other side of the lake. He was soon round and I had no doubt, from his description of how when he'd hooked into the fish, it had totally destroyed him on its way to seeking sanctuary in the dense snags, that he'd lost the big common. I sat in my swim for the next six days and nights with no sign of her as she sulked in the snags.

Within a further two weeks, my cleared area had gone and it was obvious that the carp were locked up in the snags because whenever I went round, I saw them in there. I don't believe they went out into the main lake at all, and certainly hadn't been to my baited area, otherwise the weed wouldn't have taken over.

I assessed the situation and decided that I needed and wanted to catch some carp. Friends were telling me about their frustrations on other waters, but their takes had dropped off dramatically and on questioning, I felt sure there was a rig problem. I couldn't keep in touch with the carp and what they were learning so that I could hold my own on a circuit water, while I was stuck on the Snake, especially blanking. More to the point, the Snake Pit was never going to be about the rig edge. Success was quite simply, down to finding the spot where a carp would feed, and making sure that you had a hook bait there when it was feeding. I needed a break, so I chose to stop hitting my head against a brick wall, when the only winner was going to be the summer's weed growth. Instead, I'd go to Star Lane.

Chapter Twenty-Four

Star Lane: The Rig Revolution

It was difficult for me to drag myself away from the Snake. Whenever I get my teeth into wanting to catch a particular big carp, I can't let go, and for me not to be on the water shows a lack of effort, laziness, or just plain giving up. In this instance it was none of that, though; there comes a point when you have to ditch your pride, stubbornness or whatever, and realise that you are just wasting your time.

I managed to talk myself round, and see sense. The fact was that the aquatic plants in the Snake Pit were in battle mode. When I first arrived, the lake was covered in a kind of pond plant that I didn't recognise. It had a long stem, and leaves that started about halfway up its length and continued up to the surface where the leaves and flowers floated on the top. However, this plant died off to be replaced by Canadian pondweed that rapidly took hold until it completely choked the lake from around July/August.

It was hard to quit, but I decided to go after another magnificent fish. More to the point, I was getting really excited about conducting some rig experiments. I had a rig theory to test out that was so massive, it was like having a secret that you're bursting to tell all your mates about, but can't. It was huge and I thought the potential could be enormous, but I didn't have a carp to try it on while I banged my head on the Snake.

When I'd been on Waterways in Cambridgeshire, something happened that changed my whole thinking. I'd put a couple of rods out; one in the margin and one out in the middle of the lake, over weed. This was a courageous move in those days. We didn't go after the carp in the weed because we were scared to, and never found a way to tackle them.

On a previous visit to Waterways, I knew that I had carp in front of me but couldn't figure out why I wasn't catching, and so I climbed up a tree to watch. I was fishing over an area of clear gravel and it wasn't long before I saw a carp approaching. Its dorsal went up as if it was agitated, and it swam quickly over the gravel and my baited spot, then went over the weed, tipped up and dug around, presumably finding something to eat before moving off.

Not long after, another fish came along and on arriving at the gravel area this carp changed direction, avoided the clear spot, moved over the weed and started to feed, no doubt on the odd boilie that I had put out which had missed the spot. It was obvious that the fish were spooking off the clear areas that anglers always fished to, so they were conditioned to the danger. I set to figuring out how to catch them over the weed, and that's how I came up with the sliding/adjustable helicopter rig that was to prove so effective.

On this particular session, I was back up the tree watching the carps' reaction to my rig in the weed when one mooched up the margin to where my nearside bait was. It was a good fish in the low-20s, and upon arriving at my baited area it immediately tipped up and started feeding. I watched it suck in my hook bait and then heard the bite alarm bleep so I began to climb down from the tree, and then because the alarm had ceased, I stopped my urgent descent. I looked down and could see that the carp was still over my bait, but I was amazed to see the hook link entering its mouth.

It just sat there, seemingly huffing and puffing and I could see its gills opening and shutting vigorously. Then, it blew the rig, hook bait and all, out of its mouth and waddled off. It seemed to be completely unconcerned. I was absolutely gob-smacked. I'd just seen a pricked up carp get rid of the rig, but I was more astonished because this carp hadn't panicked on feeling the lead and being pricked by the hook. I would have expected it to roar off, but it didn't, it just sat there cool and calm until it rid itself of the hook. It was clear that it knew what it was doing, and it did it without panic, as if being hooked up had become an occupational hazard.

The relevance to me was the clear proof of what we had already suspected in the past, i.e., when the takes slowed down and became just bleeps, or silence, that did not necessarily mean that you weren't getting bites any more, rather that the carp had sussed you. Now I had actually seen what they were doing for myself! It was a revelation.

As an engineer, I became fascinated with how that carp had ejected my hook. I couldn't understand it at first. In essence, a hook is a tiny, heavy element with no particular surface area that would allow the carp to blow the hook out easily. Then, I had my first eureka moment. I figured it wasn't the hook but the boilie; the large mass of the boilie helped the carp to blow out the hook. Imagine attaching a balloon to a small basket. If you blew at the basket only, you'd never get it to lift off the ground, but blow against the balloon hard enough and it would lift, taking the basket with it.

It was my second eureka moment, though, that changed everything. I visualised that pricked-up carp blowing against the bait, which would try to exit the mouth, but the hook anchored in the mouth would prevent this, so the only way the carp could eject the bait and the hook was firstly, to remove the hook point from its mouth. I realised how they did that was by sucking, and that was why the Waterways carp appeared to be huffing and puffing so much. Carp manipulate the muscles in their mouths and suck against the boilie until the hook point is loosened and sucked out, then the carp blows and the boilie exits the mouth followed harmlessly by the hook, bend first. We used to think of carp blowing baits out, but we never thought of them sucking to pull the hook point out.

My mind buzzing was with all this so there began an obsessive time of rig experiments, and it was painful, to say the least. I was becoming a self-harmer, digging hook points into my hand, mimicking sucking and blowing carp and assessing the effects. Quickly, it became apparent that one element that aided the carp to rid themselves of the hook was fixing the hair to the shank. I realised that I needed to be able to present the boilie properly by way of retaining an anchor point for the hair up the shank, but then, if I hooked a carp, I needed a mechanism to change the anchor point and get the boilie out of the way, and this is how the ring blow out rig was born.

At this time, the hair was pinned by tubing dead in line with the point. A carp sucking and blowing could, I believed, eventually loosen the grip of the hook and then easily blow it out. Now it made sense to me why the carp had soon wised up to the original hair tied to the bend, because at this position, the hair being on the centre line of the hook, made it easy for the carp to suck the point out. Moving the anchor round to the shank took the straight line advantage away from the carp as the hook would pivot instead of being directly dragged out by a suck. In time,

ABOVE
I tied the hair to a ring directly opposite the point.

though, with a little messing about and experimenting and learning to suck as well as blow, which would eventually loosen and detach the point of the hook, the carp had learned how to deal with a shank-pinned hair.

A rig I experimented with and wrote about in the Angling Times in the late 80s came to mind. I called this the Revolving Hair Rig. It was made up of a ring mounted on the shank of the hook, trapped between two pieces of tubing opposite the point of the hook, and a hair was tied to the ring. It was just an idea that I tried, giving the hair more movement, albeit still attached to the shank via the ring. It may have caught me a bonus fish or two, I'm not sure, but now my mind went back to the ring.

I tied the hair to a ring directly opposite the point. If a carp was pricked and sat tight, when it tried to blow the bait out the ring would slide down the shank and over the eye, making it very difficult for the carp to use the mass of the boilie to rid itself of the hook. If it sucked, the ring, which was now below the eye of the hook on the hooklink, was prevented from sliding back up the hook shank to the anchor position, opposite the point of the hook where the carp had learned, with a bit of jiggery-pokery, to rid itself of the hook. When it sucked, the hook would pivot on the point, thus preventing the carp from achieving the correct angle to suck the point of the hook out.

RIGHT

The original hair, tied to the bend on the centre line of the hook, so if a carp sucks, everything is in line and the hook point is easily drawn out

BELOW

Moving the anchor point to the shank meant the hook would pivot slightly so that the point of the hook is harder to suck out

BOTTOM

With the anchor point taken away from the hook, when a carp sucks, the hook pivots and the point stays in. When they blow they are blowing against the volume of the boilie, ensuring the hook point stays in.

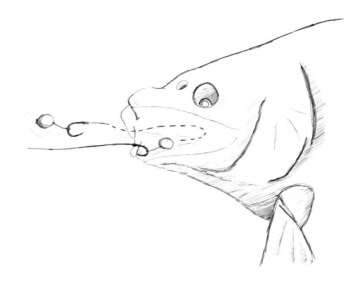

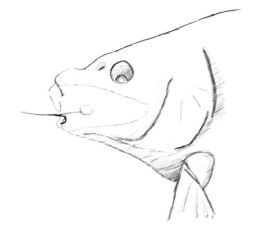

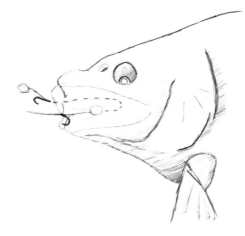

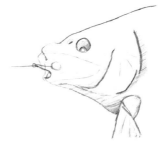

Star Lane seemed to be the perfect water on which to test my ring blow out rig. I'd known the lake for nearly 20 years and knew when the carp were responding well and so conversely, I knew when I had an issue. I had dropped back on to the Lane a few times while writing Nashy and Hutch. I couldn't keep writing about blanking at the Snake, so I did a few sessions on the Lane to make my writing a bit more interesting for the reader. I found the lake very different from when I'd fished it in the 70s and while I did catch a few, I struggled, and could find no way of catching regularly. So, now was the time to test my rig.

Apart from the Lane being ideal for my rig experiments, a big fish had come through and a cracker at that, of around mid-30s. It was a wary fish as well, only coming out, at most, once a year, so I really looked forward to the break from the Snake to have a reasonable number of carp to go at, rather than just two, with the added incentive of a very seriously desirable mid-30 mirror.

My first session was a Tuesday night mid-weeker. I got down to the Lane about 4pm and planned to do the night, pack up and be in work by 7am. I chose to fish the top end, which is known as the brickfield end, because behind it was the old brick works. There is a dominating swim on a point (Brickfield Point) where you can look straight down the length of the lake and see what's going on. To the left of the point is a bay that the carp loved to visit, depending on conditions. It was the first swim in this bay, which I rather obviously named The Bay, where I enjoyed much of my success in the early years. In front of this swim was a large bed of reed

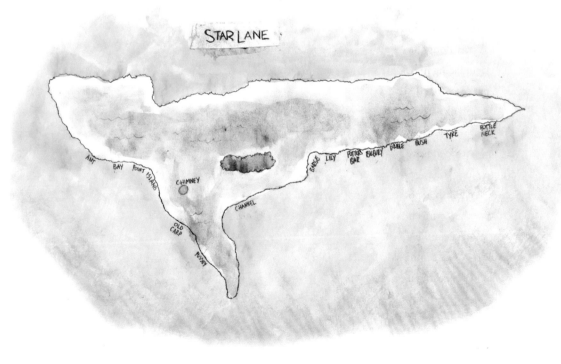

mace with a small gap in the middle of maybe two feet across. The carp would enter this gap and swim through a tunnel in the reed mace, which opened up to a pool. It was completely hidden and inaccessible to anglers so it was true sanctuary for the carp, but by casting baits tight and accurately into the entrance to the tunnel, I'd enjoyed some immense hits.

However, over the years since I'd last fished it, the swim had changed. I heard later that the farmer, whose fields were adjacent to the far bank and out of bounds, used to dump potatoes into this bay, but something had changed and it was clear that it was not favoured by the carp like it had been.

My old friend, Dave Potter, who was manager of Penge Angling, Rayleigh, was fishing on Brickfield Point when I arrived. He'd been there for a couple of days but without success. I cast my rods out in the bay, walked the ten yards to his adjacent swim for a catch up and a cuppa and we chatted into the evening.

His swim was not only a great vantage point to see right down the lake, and for that matter enable a cast halfway down it, but it had other options too. The main water in front of Dave was flanked on the right by an island which stopped some 30 yards in front of him, forming a bay to his right. There was a swim on the far bank right-hand corner of this bay, which I named The Chimney, where anglers could not only cast into the bay but also along the edge of the island. The Chimney was alongside a channel that went around the back of the island into a reedy bay. It was a great ambush point to watch for carp mooching down the channel. If this swim was vacant, as it was, it gave the angler on the point a lot of options. So Dave had one rod cast down the left bank which was out of bounds to anglers, his middle rod was along the left margin of the island, and a third 30 yards or so, to the island margin facing him, which would ambush any carp on their way to the island channel, or so he hoped.

As we drank our cuppas that evening, it was that island margin we had our eyes on, and two or three times carp rolled but unfortunately, Dave didn't get as much as a bleep; if I had been Dave I would have gone round to The Chimney. The Lane had taught me a long time ago the importance of line angles. It really was so stark over there. You could fish a spot from one swim and angle and totally blank, only to move round to another swim and hit it from another angle, and you'd have it off.

I packed up in the morning to get to the office and left lucky Dave to enjoy the blissfully sunny summer day, but I was back about the same time that afternoon when Dave was packing up because he'd blanked and had enough. As we spoke, a fish rolled along the front of the island and I remarked on it but Dave said, like the evening before, that he'd seen several fish through the day roll along the margin but they weren't having it.

As Dave got into his car and drove off, I got into mine and went to the car park nearest The Chimney. I figured carp had been showing down at the island for at least 24 hours, so a different line angle was called for. I soon had my rods out and the right-hand rod directly in front of me and cast just a few feet off the island margin had my new ring blow out rig on it. It was the only rod with the rig on it; after all, this was a somewhat far out theory that had to be proven, and I can't say at this time that I was totally sold on it, so to lessen the odds of a potential blank the other two banker rods had 'normal' line aligner rigs on them. I was on the line aligner by this time. At Harefield, Chris Ladds had shown me his edge of filing the hook eye to a flat, to grip the hook knot and make it kick off at an angle.

A guy called Dave Benham started writing a series in David Hall's magazine, Coarse Fishing, about his trials and tribulations of trying to grasp how to catch carp as a beginner. I found his articles fascinating because he just wasn't getting it at all. He had everything upside down and it was so frustrating when reading of his consistent failures, that I found myself wanting to help him so I dropped him a line and it started a string of correspondence.

I tried to explain the mechanics of the hair rig and how it worked, but he just wasn't getting it, and so in the end I tied him up a rig with the eye filed flat and the knot kicking off, and sent it to him in the post so that he could read my text as well as have a physical example of the rig in his hand as reference. I'd tied the rig up at work, and didn't have my tackle box with me or any Superglue, so the knot wasn't glued down firmly, retaining the kicker, and it must have moved in the post.

The next week I received a letter back from Dave, with a rig. He had messed around and came up with an idea and wanted my opinion. In order to make the necessary kicker angle permanent, instead of going through the fiddly process of filing the hook eye flat and gluing it, he slid a piece of tube up his hook link and over the eye of the hook and then, taking a needle, and placing it just inside the end of the tube, he pushed it through the underside wall and passed the hook link through. Dave had just invented the line aligner!

BELOW
The line aligner rig.

I immediately saw the relevance, and upon dragging it across my hand, saw how quickly the hook turned and pricked. I thought it was awesome and from then on I dropped Chris Ladds' way of kicking off the hook link and adopted Dave's. It was a great edge which I kept totally secret, except for telling a lad who worked in my office, Andy Khakou, who was fishing with me at the Snake Pit at the time.

One day, six months later, I picked up a fishing mag in the office which had just arrived in the post that morning, and opened it up to an article by Jim Gibbinson. I screamed, "Noooooo!" and Andy came running over. There was Jim describing the line aligner. I'm not sure if Jim came up with it by his own thought processes, or if he also had correspondence with Dave Benham, but whatever, the line aligner was a big step forward in rig development because it greatly aided the hook's ability to turn and prick. This was before the knotless knot had evolved, whereby you can pass the line through the top of the hook eye, exiting through the underside and creating the necessary angle.

Anyway, back at Star Lane, it couldn't have been more than 30 minutes after casting out the right-hand rod along the island margin before I started having what I can only describe as a weird occurrence. The alarm bleeped spasmodically as the bobbin effectively trembled, then it lifted an inch, dropped an inch, lifted half an inch, and then stopped. I waited a moment for a run to develop, but it didn't, so I chose to hit this tenchy-looking occurrence anyway; no tench ever put a curve in my rod like this, though. Clearly, I was into a heavy fish which roared off from the island, hell bent on taking me around Brickfield Point and into the bay, and if it had succeeded it would have been all over. I piled on the pressure, only for it to turn around and rocket toward me and one of the most dangerous snags in the lake. The reason for the swim's name, the Chimney, was an old metal chimney that had been dumped in the lake when one of the brick kilns was rebuilt; if the carp made the sanctuary of the chimney, I could forget it.

I kept the rod at maximum compression but was recovering line at the same time, to reduce the angle. The carp swirled just four feet off the chimney and then I had her around it and safely in front of me. Carpet Steve, one of the old members of Star Lane who I'd known from years before, netted her for me.

"Kev," he said. "You jammy bastard. You've been on here one day and you've caught the big 'un!"

Jammy maybe, but I could make a case to the carp gods that I had earned this result. I had committed myself to moving swims to change the line angle and most relevantly, I'd caught one of the largest carp in Essex - and one of the most rarely caught - on my new ring blow out rig.

The strangeness of the take, the trembles and twitches, were clear signs of a carp that was used to picking up rigs and sitting tight on the spot until it rid itself. This time, though, a clever fish had been caught out on the carp world's first-ever capture on a blow out rig.

ABOVE
Jammy? You decide!

You can imagine how I was buzzing, and my head was filled with the potential of my discovery. For the remainder of the year's carping I drifted, if you like, from water to water and then back to the Lane again for a week or two. It was a journey of experimentation and trialling, to find out as much as I could about the blow out rig. It was with some reluctance that I faced up to the fact that I should go back to the Snake Pit this next season. I really was torn. I was so enjoying the rig thing and knew that if I took my blow out rigs to any top circuit water, I could do serious damage. I had an edge and one that was ahead of the game, but it would have to wait as I also desperately wanted to end my saga at the Snake Pit and land that immense common.

Chapter Twenty-Five

Snake Pit: The Dead Zone

I could see nothing wrong with repeating my plan of the year before. I didn't think that the plan had failed, rather circumstances had got in the way – the main one being, me rather generously, or stupidly, giving Robbo a handful of my baits. That had resulted in him losing the big common, which then stayed in the snags, sulking. In the meantime, the weed growth made the lake unfishable.

So I elected to fish the Dance Floor again, the only change being to move my spot a little nearer to the bank on my left. Putting a bait there was more awkward but I felt that the new area was preferable to rebaiting an old spot. It was a repeat of the previous close season. The more I baited, the more the area was cleared of weed and if I'd had doubts that the swim clearers were not carp, they were dispelled one Saturday afternoon at the beginning of June when I rowed out to my spot, put the glass bucket over the side and peered through the lens. Directly beneath me, seemingly unconcerned, was the Snake Pit's big common, rooting around the bottom, presumably in search of any leftover baits that it had missed since I had last baited, three days before. Was I on a high!

I had seen a couple of other anglers over the Snake looking around, more than once, so I made a decision to guarantee that I got my swim for the start. The way the weekend fell meant that, to be safe in my mind, I had to get up there three days before the start – keen or what? Wouldn't you be if you were about to catch the UK's best common? What weight would it be? Maybe 47…48lbs?

You'd have thought that I'd be bored sitting in my swim for three days until the start, but it was to the contrary. I couldn't believe how fast time flew and that by bedtime I had struggled to do all the things I wanted to fit into the day.

There was one bizarre incident on the night of June 14th. It was around midnight when I was awoken by a very frantic Khan, my Doberman, who used to sleep behind my bedchair in the back of my brolly. He was up, over me and my bed, and out of the bivvy like an express train with a roaring bark as he disappeared into the reeds. Clearly, there was an intruder in our swim. When you consider the kind of people who frequented the Snake, I have to say, that I was tense. Then, there was a lot of shouting and high-pitched shrieking coming from the reeds, with Khan barking incessantly. He really could give it the big 'un when he wanted to. Khan was as soft as a brush and would never hurt a fly but he'd learned at an early age that he was a Doberman. Humans thought Dobermans were big and bad, and that they could be mauled to death, so Khan learned that if he stood on tiptoe to make himself look bigger, puffed his hackles up and woofed loudly, he could have great fun frightening people.

On this particular night he was in his element, scaring the shit out of the most bizarre-looking little man I have ever beheld on a carp lake. I pulled the man out of the rushes and tried to settle the situation down, giving Khan a kick

so he'd pay attention to my commands and stop being a bully, and so rescue the man from the edge of cardiac arrest. This guy looked to be in his 40s. He was a little over five feet tall, dressed in a safari suit of beige-coloured trousers and jacket, and he wore a pith helmet and round glasses with lenses that seemed all of an inch thick. In short, he could have walked out of an African jungle with Livingstone, so you can understand why I was wondering what the hell this bloke was doing in Essex, at the Snake Pit, in the middle of the night, and in a reed bed, to boot.

I'd got used to the nutters and thought I knew them all, but this one appeared to be from a different planet until he explained that he was some sort of scientist who had been contracted by the local builder. He told me that the builder had applied to the council for planning permission to fill in the lake and turn it into a golf course, but there had been a huge amount of resistance to this plan and it had caused disruption in the neighbourhood. Emotions were running high and the local community had marched through Colchester to the Town Hall with a petition. I heard that some of the marchers got quite heated and the police were called to calm the situation down and prevent a riot.

The 'scientist' went on to tell me that the builder's biggest concern was the suggestion that the lake was a habitat for the great crested newt. Should this be proven to be the case, his client would lose his planning application as well a huge amount of money. It must be noted that there is quite literally millions to be made in filling in holes in the ground with our nation's waste, let alone the opportunities for reinstating that land for commercial or residential use.

'Shit', I thought. 'I hope the builder never sees that petition with my name on it or finds out that it was me who'd tipped off that guy about the SSSI and the great crested newt idea'. At the time, I never dreamed that I'd be the reason for near rioting in Colchester.

I did worry for a moment, because I was renting the lake off the builder and it was only a verbal arrangement. The angling club that controlled the Snake Pit had given up on it, so it had been left and I'd heard rumours from anglers talking about going over there to catch the Snake Pit common and then moving it. I wasn't having any of that, so I approached the builder. He'd said that I could rent it off him but he wasn't prepared to give me a long lease because if/when his planning permission was granted I could obstruct his plans.

It was a bit of a predicament for me because without the lease, I felt I couldn't develop the lake, and apart from that I wasn't sure how it could be a viable fishery for most, who after all, do like a bit of action along the way from time to time. If I had restocked the lake then I could be putting the two

commons at risk with the new introduction, maybe bringing in a virus that they were not immune to. To endanger the UKs most magnificent common was not worth any risk, so in the end I opted for Nash Tackle to pay the money on the verbal agreement, and if anyone fancied fishing it and they could convince me that they knew what they were doing, I let them fish it free.

The one remaining question to be asked about the little man in front of me was: What the hell was he doing in a reed bed on the Snake Pit, with a butterfly net (forgot to mention that) at midnight? It's amazing the knowledge you can pick up in the most obscure places and times of day. It transpired that late in the night, and midnight was the perfect time, great crested newts will move under the cover of darkness into the margins of ponds and lakes where, if you have a powerful torch and should they exist, (cough), they should be fairly easy to locate. Well, I didn't know that!

He hadn't managed to locate any when Khan found him and he seemed put off searching any more that night. I don't know whether or not he ever did find a great crested newt, but while I doubt it, it is a fact that the Snake Pit is still there to this day.

It was set to be an interesting start. Apart from my Out of Africa experience, I had both of the commons rolling and head and shouldering over the baited area - just a matter of time, Kevin. With relief and anticipation as June 15th had come round, the baits were rowed out before it got dark and I sat on the ground with my back leaning against my bedchair, my favourite position to this day, as I waited. It wasn't even worth getting into bed; surely it was only a matter of minutes before I got the take?

The next thing I knew, I had woken from a nightmare, shivering and feeling numb. The vision of the Demon Eye had returned and as I tried to shake off the eerie feeling that overwhelmed me, I realised that it was daylight. As I came to my senses, my eyes settled on my unmoving monkey climbers and I had a sickening realisation. I attempted to shake it off with positive thinking. Okay, they hadn't fed in the night, so the action would come some time soon, during the day. It didn't. Nor did it come the next night, the next day, or for that matter for the next five days and nights. I was absolutely gutted and totally mystified that I'd blanked. How and why had the carp suddenly stopped using the feeding area? I just couldn't figure it out. I knew I hadn't scared them and it certainly wasn't my lines going through the swim, because I'd dropped my hook baits tight to the edge of the weed, making sure that the line was concealed in it. There was no logical reason that I could think of.

I couldn't remember such despair. I'd been after this carp for so long, and

I'd served my dues and really put the effort in to make it happen. Normally, the carp gods pay you back when you've worked hard and deserve it. I couldn't understand why they'd deserted me, and why the nightmare of the Demon eye was back. Could it all be over a sodding great crested newt?

My opening week's session came to an end and it was the weekend of the EFFTEX show. This is Europe's biggest tackle show that was held in Amsterdam in those days, and I had to attend it, but I fished up to the last minute, packed up just after dawn and pulled off. As it happened, it proved to be one of those weeks. Not only had I suffered the immense disappointment of blanking on the Snake, but also I was eventually told, after a four-hour delay at the airport, that my flight was cancelled. As it was a two-day tackle show, there seemed little point in travelling the next day, only to arrive at the end of the show.

By the time I'd packed up at the Snake Pit, it had been around 4.30am I was told later that the police had arrived at 6.30am. Maybe, in a way, that was the only bit of luck I'd had, missing them. God alone knows how long I could have been detained otherwise.

They started on the top bank, going left around the lake as they dragged it. Seven days later, after a complete circumnavigation of the lake, they arrived in the Dance Floor swim and dragged it. It was there that the frogmen found the body. Apparently, on the night of June 15th, a guy had left a party up the road. He'd been in a fight and so was somewhat the worse for wear, as well as being as drunk as a lord. He'd begun the walk home and on reaching the Snake Pit gate, chose to take a short cut. I never heard a thing, presumably because I was so tired that I was out of it. Somehow, he had fallen into the lake and drowned. It was no wonder I'd blanked when I'd spent the opening week fishing over a dead body.

Chapter Twenty-Six

Snake Pit: Requiem

Failing to catch the Snake Pit common because some bloke had inconveniently decided to drown himself on my baited area did make me feel that someone was trying to tell me something. Really, I'd near enough had a gutful and you have to wonder at the curse on the Snake Pit; the original captor who then committed suicide, the murderer I had to deal with who killed his mum, and the guy that fell into my swim and drowned. I felt equally cursed as my prize had been cruelly snatched from me on at least three occasions that I knew of; my own loss, Robbo's loss, and the dead body saga. Apart from all that, I had to tolerate all the various unsavoury characters in the area, and be on my guard to ensure that I protected my kit and my car; and on the subject of cars, that's when I cracked.

I let the lake settle down for a couple of weeks because a shoal of police frogmen had been rampaging around so the carp would be shaping up and well entrenched in the back of the snags. Deciding normality (if that's a word that can be considered for the Snake Pit) would have resumed, I popped over for a weekend to have a suss around and try to come up with a new plan. I left my marker rod in my motor for five minutes while I made my way to the Dance Floor swim and during those few minutes my windscreen was caved in, and the rod taken. I figured that I needed a break from this place and I didn't have time to start from scratch again. The weed had covered my baited area, and it would only be a few more weeks before it reached the surface, and became so bad that the

whole lake would be unfishable. At least that's how I convinced myself at the time, but in truth, I had a need to catch some carp and pursue my blow out rig theories.

I have a saying based on experience through decades of carping; when you find a lake, get on it and milk it because it never lasts for ever. Regardless of the impossibility of the Snake Pit, I should have noted my own saying. The next season I was to receive some devastating news. There were events leading up to this news. A guy had contacted me who had caught a large carp that famously lived in a small river on the outskirts of Ipswich. The fish was named Dippy and ended up being moved to the Snake Pit later on. This guy had caught Dippy on Nashbait and he rang me to ask if he could become a fieldtester so that in return for promoting our bait, he would get a good deal. I met him and he seemed okay.

He kept in touch and seemed unusually interested in my exploits at the Snake Pit, and one day, when he was down picking up some bait, I told him the story of the guy with the petition and the great crested newt ploy. It wasn't long after this conversation that I had a phone call from the owner of the Snake Pit. It was a short, brisk call; one of those when you just know the guy on the other end of the phone is seriously pissed off. The builder told me that I'd lost the lease and I was off the venue. He'd been informed of the trouble I'd stirred up in an effort to thwart him from filling in the pit, and in particular, he knew that I had signed the petition and was the one behind the great crested newt population suggestion. Clearly, my treacherous fieldtester had stitched me up.

Shortly after this, the water was taken over by an angling club, with which the field-testing snitch was significantly involved. In fact, I understood that he was in charge of running the Snake Pit. Then I heard that Dippy had arrived, with a number of other carp; an event that filled me with horror and concern for the two commons. My concerns were to prove very real, when one evening I had a phone call from Dougal, who told me that he'd just got back from the Snake Pit, after going up there with Micky Kavanagh, who was at that time on the committee of the Carp Society. They had been following up reports that the Snake Pit common was in severe distress, covered in fungus and clearly in trouble and so they went up there to try to net both carp with the hope that they could be saved. Their visit was in vain, though. Neither Snake Pit common was ever seen again.

At the time, I saw the betrayal of the field tester, whose name I have so obviously not revealed, as the harbinger of my misfortune. I felt sorry for myself, betrayed, and thus cheated out of catching the magnificent Snake Pit common, a unique fish and one of the greatest carp ever to grace an English lake. It could be looked upon another way, though; maybe the carp gods were teaching me character building. There are times when you have to deal with failure, and in life you can't always enjoy success. We all need to experience disappointment in order to redress the balance and to build strength of character. Clearly, the carp gods had decided I should be thwarted from catching the Snake Pit common and instead, they released me and sent me on my way to seek new adventures and my ultimate destiny.

BELOW
...to seek new adventures...

Epilogue

As I put the final words of this book to paper I felt released from a burden, followed by an overwhelming feeling of elation. It was so similar to the feeling you experience as a long-term carp angler when you've endeavoured to catch carp for many years, finally setting your sights on a monster and you pursue that monster for a very long time until a day comes when she graces your net. Only a true, big carp hunter can know the feeling of being released from a self-inflicted trial of endeavour, challenge, pain and suffering, and despair at times. Relief overwhelms you, quickly turning to joy and you need to shout your achievement from the rooftops. You pick up the phone and ring those dear to you, those close to you who will understand.

I rang Jeff Pink, affectionately known by his carp fishing friends as Pinky, a kindred spirit who has shared many adventures with me over the years; trials and tribulations, loss and glory. We shrieked down the phone at each other, two brothers experiencing joy. I haven't seen Jeff for some two years, but to my mind he was the obvious one to call.

The carp are just a means to a comradeship and love between men that lasts all our lives, until the day we die and that's the true essence of carp fishing.